HOW
BIG-TECH
BARONS
SMASH
INNOVATION—
AND HOW TO
STRIKE BACK

HOW BIG-TECH BARONS SMASH INNOVATION—

AND HOW TO STRIKE BACK

ARIEL EZRACHI AND
MAURICE E. STUCKE

HARPER
BUSINESS

An Imprint of HarperCollinsPublishers

HarperCollins books may be purchased for educational, business, or sales
promotional use. For information, please email the Special Markets Department
at SPsales@harpercollins.com.

FIRST EDITION

Library of Congress Cataloging-in-Publication Data has been applied for.

ISBN 978-0-06-303088-6

22 23 24 25 26   LSC   10 9 8 7 6 5 4 3 2 1

To Miriam and Elizabeth

Contents

HOW
BIG-TECH
BARONS
SMASH
INNOVATION—
AND HOW TO
STRIKE BACK

Introduction

ANY NAVIGATOR KNOWS A basic rule. A small degree error, insignificant in a short voyage, will increase the longer one travels. It's known as the "one in sixty rule of thumb." A one-degree error in navigation will lead a pilot one mile away from her destination for every sixty miles of travel. Many airplane crashes, sailing accidents, and maritime mishaps have arisen from a seemingly insignificant drift off course.

What does the one in sixty rule have to do with innovation in the digital economy? In many ways, it helps illustrate how seemingly insignificant flaws in past assumptions and policies have led us off course. It helps us appreciate the impact and actual costs of past economic and industrial policies that failed to adapt to the changing dynamics of competition and innovation in the digital age.

A slow-moving tanker ship has ample opportunities to correct the navigation error. But as speed increases, it is harder to fix quickly. Suppose you are on the X-43 jet traveling at 6,598 miles per hour, and you are off course by just 1 degree. In that case, you will stray over one hundred miles away from your destination in the first hour alone . . . and in the digital economy, we are traveling at supersonic speed, with more significant degrees of error.

In late 2017, the European Commission asked us to research innovation in the digital economy. Our earlier work, including *Virtual Competition*, raised the concern of policymakers around the world as we uncovered several significant risks of the digital economy that affect price, quality, and consumer well-being. But on innovation, we, like many others, were optimistic. At first, we didn't think we were off course. But, as we dug into the data over the next few years, we found multiple fallacies about innovation in the digital economy. Our counterintuitive findings were unsettling.

After submitting our report to European policymakers, we wondered if our report was collecting dust on some desk. But we began getting calls from other policymakers who had seen our report, and they too had similar concerns. That led to more unsettling truths.

We intuitively know something is amiss. Lots of us, as surveys reveal, are concerned about corporate power in many markets, including in the digital economy. But, seemingly, people still believe, as we initially did, that innovation has been unaffected. It remains synonymous with the online economy. Indeed, as the COVID-19 pandemic showed, we can do more online, from social interactions to work, from shopping to learning. But as we increasingly go online to socialize or shop, we instinctively understand that many of these innovations have a dark side—whether to our privacy, well-being, or autonomy. The heady tech utopia of the 1990s now seems a dystopia, where many devices, apps, and services come from digital ecosystems controlled by a few powerful firms (whom we call the "Tech Barons"). Think, for example, of Alphabet (Google), Apple, Meta (Facebook), Amazon, and Microsoft (GAFAM for short).

These Tech Barons not only govern the competition within their tightly controlled ecosystems, but they also determine the nature of innovation that makes it to the market. And to protect their interest, they make sure to only advance and allow innovation that does not disrupt their business models and profits.

This puts companies, consumers, and innovators in a tough spot. *Why?*

Because the digital economy is central in our modern world. We now spend a lot more time online, and for many companies, that means if they don't have a significant online presence, they might as well not exist. Competing means more than being online. It means having a compelling presence, scale, customer base, and innovative products. It means companies re-engineering themselves into AI-centric firms, where the underlying data pipeline helps train and improve the algorithms, which drive many of the companies' critical functions—everything from setting prices to personalizing services to predicting behavior.[1] Not surprisingly, *Harvard Business Review* heralded AI as the "most important general-purpose technology of our era."[2]

The shift to digital seemingly offers new opportunities. We have already seen how popular platforms, like Airbnb, Uber, and Lyft, have disrupted the hotel and taxi industries. Amazon already disrupted retail, and, along with Netflix, Apple, and Google, is disrupting the cable and entertainment industries. With the metaverse on the horizon, where we'll access the internet through virtual reality, no company can afford to sit on the sidelines.

It is not only market dynamics that are rapidly changing, but also the expectations for growth. In 2019, General Motors sold globally around 7.7 million cars—an impressive twenty times as many cars as Tesla sold in that year (about 370,000 vehicles). And while Ford sold more than six times as many cars, Tesla by early 2020 was worth more than Ford and GM combined.[3] And Tesla is staking its future on smart, self-driving cars.

Given the nature of the digital economy, with network effects and economies of scale, the nimble and adaptive first movers will thrive, while the laggards will rarely catch up. (Consider Microsoft, which had the technology for smartphones years before Apple, but was too late in introducing its Windows phone.)

So, the prevailing message is that companies need to quickly identify and exploit opportunities in the digital economy. Being a fast follower won't cut it. If a company isn't among the initial rivals in these "winner-take-all" online markets, it will quickly be displaced by those who are.

Innovation and creativity, we are told, are the key to success. And the underlying assumption is that the digital economy is open terrain for any disruptor willing to experiment and quickly learn from its customers' behavior. If you are good at what you do, you will make it! The digital economy appears contestable, with millions of advertisers, apps, merchants, and websites competing for revenue and our attention.

"OK," we hear you say, "but where is the catch?"

While these assumptions might have been valid in the 1990s, that is not the case today. A few Tech Barons—most notably, GAFAM—are now the critical gatekeepers in most of the world, and the contestability in their ecosystems is carefully orchestrated. Most importantly, the viability of new products and services within their ecosystems relies on data and interoperability, often controlled by them. As the digital economy expands to new industries and the metaverse, so will the Tech Barons' power.

Based on our research and discussions with market participants, four things become clear: *first*, the Tech Barons design their ecosystems to favor their own interests (at the cost of crushing beneficial innovations); *second*, the Tech Barons' value chain dictates the type and scope of innovation that you will find, and in looking at the value chains, we can predict that innovations will become scarier (envision virtual reality headsets that can decode your emotions and private thoughts); *third*, even if you can avoid some or all of the Tech Barons' ecosystems, you cannot avoid the toxicity of some of their innovations; and *finally*, while the Tech Barons are in the news for their mounting antitrust attacks, the likely relief, if any, will not fix the underlying problems.

As we continue along the current path, we will soon feel the full magnitude of the one in sixty rule, as valuable innovations are stifled and toxic innovations (which primarily extract or destroy value) flourish. The digital platforms are often analogized to a coral reef, where various app developers and technologies ultimately contribute to the platform's structural complexities. Instead, we'll see putrid red algae that attack these coral reefs—where the Tech Barons kill off healthy innovators by depriving them of the "oxygen" needed to survive.

Should we care?

Yes—whether you are a company seeking to exploit an opportunity online, a parent concerned about the effect these technologies have on you and your children's mental health, or a policymaker seeking to restore competition online and make these markets more contestable.

Companies that seek to innovate in the digital economy are directly affected by these dynamics and need to know what drives the Tech Barons' strategies and how they will perceive and react to different innovation efforts. This knowledge offers insight to what opportunities exist for disruption as the Tech Barons' ecosystems expand.

While the Tech Barons may change over time, the underlying forces of the digital economy will not. So, companies need to understand how their innovations affect the prevailing Tech Barons' value chain.

Consumers need to understand what innovations to expect and how they'll likely affect their well-being, privacy, and autonomy. While no one can predict the exact form of these innovations, we can get a glimpse by better understanding the Tech Barons' incentives. Indeed, based on the patents we've reviewed, we'll likely see some truly toxic innovations.

Policymakers should be concerned since innovation is necessary for economic growth and overcoming the challenges of population growth. Entrusting the Tech Barons to determine the scope and trajectory of digital innovation will undoubtedly leave us worse off.

Of course, the Tech Barons prefer that we stick with the current antitrust policies, which were designed many years ago and are ill-suited to deter their power over the supply and demand of innovation across their vast ecosystems. Although nearly all the Tech Barons are being sued across several jurisdictions, they have little to fear. Even if the competition authorities prevail, the relief will likely be too little and too late. Even if all the recent policy proposals are enacted, they will unlikely prevent the toxic innovations.

The current Tech Barons and their successors will continue to distort the path of digital innovation absent corrective policies. The costs of going off course are huge—to our well-being, autonomy, and democracy. To address our pressing needs, like global warming, wealth inequality, social unrest, growing population, and the present threats to democracy, we need disruptive innovations, and we need them sooner rather than later.

These insights are not only relevant to the current big tech firms. They apply to digital markets generally, where network effects, economies of scale, and new weapons are altering the rules of competition. Our broader principles will apply to future ecosystems and innovation therein.

In what follows we'll consider how the Tech Barons differ from powerful platforms and apps. If apps are worth millions, and platforms are worth billions, then Tech Barons, in controlling the ecosystems, are worth more than billions. They are quasi-sovereigns. We'll next meet the pirates— namely, companies with disruptive technologies that add significant value. While the Tech Barons tolerate innovations that do not threaten their ecosystems, they will smash these pirates.

Figure 1 illustrates the Tech Barons' ability to use multiple weapons to kill or marginalize innovation pirates and influence the scope and nature of innovation that reaches the market. Tech Barons can distort the supply and demand of innovation within their ecosystems, as well as the paths of innovation outside their ecosystems. As a result, the market delivers fewer disruptive innovations that add significant value, more innovations that sustain the Tech Barons' power, and more innovations that extract or destroy value.

After seeing the inflow of toxic innovations, your reaction might be to avoid the Tech Barons' ecosystems. Some of you might already have deleted your Facebook account, switched to DuckDuckGo's search engine, and canceled Amazon Prime. But the ripple effects of these toxic innovations extend far beyond the Tech Barons' ecosystems and digital economy.

We'll see how these innovations are harming our children, ripping apart our social fabric, and undermining political stability and democracy. And the Tech Barons know this. This is problematic, especially as the Tech Barons' ecosystems expand.

Figure 1

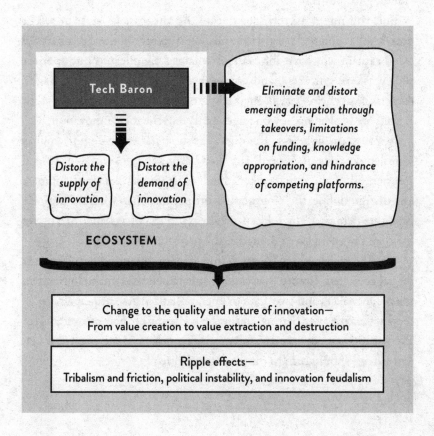

Some of you might still hesitate. Consider some of the policymakers who responded along these lines: *Granted these companies wield a lot of power, but we don't want to chill innovation.* Why is it that some policymakers are adamant that we should simply keep calm and carry on? The answer is found in the ideological buffet served up by the Tech Barons and interest groups on their payroll. The ideology is so alluring precisely because we have heard it so often, and it often contains kernels of truth. Later in this book we will consider the allure of this "ideological buffet."

But, you might ask, what about all the antitrust lawsuits in recent years? What about the legislative proposals to rein in the Tech Barons? We'll explain why toxic innovation remains a significant blind spot for policymakers, enforcers, and courts. Even if all the legislation passes, even if the agencies win all their lawsuits, and even if some of the Tech Barons are broken up, it won't necessarily end the toxic innovation.

It may seem hopeless. The digital economy is careening off course. Our democracies are in peril. The Tech Barons always seem to be several steps ahead of the policymakers. And while companies must compete and disrupt online, their journey is more perilous than what the business literature depicts. Our children already stand less of a chance of a better life than ours. Are they doomed to the precariat worker class?

No. The upside is that we can restore contestability and fairness in the digital economy. Toward that end, we offer three fundamental principles for policymakers and two ways to operationalize these principles. You'll see, by the end, why betting on the Tech Barons or their ecosystems for the disruptive innovations to solve today's problems is such a terrible bet. Instead, we should turn to the pirates and cities.

CHAPTER 1

The Rise of the Big-Tech Barons

YOU MAY REMEMBER THE Hunger Games book and film trilogy. In this dystopian universe, the Gamemakers orchestrated the ultimate survival-of-the-fittest game. The Gamemakers did more than design the competitive process; they oversaw it. At times, they nourished and supported a tribute to increase his or her chances of winning. With a flick of a switch, they could deprive the disfavored tribute of resources. No matter which tribute prevailed, the Hunger Games served to entrench the power of the Capitol elite.

The Gamemakers offer an apt analogy of the architects and controllers of competition in today's digital economy—the Big Tech Barons. We already know the Tech Barons are powerful, but do they promote or hinder innovation? The answer, to the surprise of some, is complicated.

Tech Barons Are Different

It has been said that apps are worth millions, and platforms are worth billions. But on top of the food chain are the Tech Barons' ecosystems. As Google's CEO told investors in 2019, his company builds ecosystems, not products: "If you look at an ecosystem like Android, this is what we do. And so that's going to be a focus for us."[1]

In the management literature, an ecosystem commonly "refers to a network of interconnected organizations that are linked to or operate around an organization or a technology platform and that produce valuable goods and services."[2] Of course, not all online ecosystems are alike—some are more open, horizontal, and democratic than others.[3]

So, what distinguishes a Tech Baron's ecosystem from popular apps, platforms, and other ecosystems?

First, the Tech Baron's ecosystem spans beyond one particular platform or market and is characterized by multiple popular interlocking platforms, each attracting many developers, products, and services.[4] For example, 60 percent of iPhone users also use an iPad (tablet), and Apple seeks to decrease switching costs from iPhones and iPads to "lock customers into [its] ecosystem."[5] Thus, the ecosystem is more powerful than the sum of its parts—the platforms, services, the data collected, and the analytics undertaken. Why? Because one might avoid a platform, but not the Tech Baron's expanding and tightly controlled ecosystem. We'll see shortly the difficulties a *New York Times* reporter faced when trying to avoid these ecosystems.

Second, in designing the ecosystem and supporting infrastructure, the Tech Baron ensures itself unparalleled access to data and other critical inputs of the digital economy. The Tech Baron can pull the personal and commercial data and place it in its reservoir. That data can then be used to improve the Tech Baron's products, services, technology, and algorithms and give it a significant advantage over others. As we'll see later, the data also alerts them of competitive threats and changes in market dynamics. Uber as a platform might have a god's view of where people are traveling. But the Tech Barons have a broader god's view of the digital economy.

Third, interconnections are also vital in the digital economy. And who controls them? You guessed right—the Tech Barons control the bridges (interoperability) and the information flows (basically what information the companies or individuals receive). Thus, in contrast to open ecosystems, the Tech Barons determine the configuration patterns within the ecosystem and external relationships outside the ecosystem.

Fourth is governance. As a gatekeeper, the Tech Baron creates and enforces the rules of the ecosystem. So, Google sets the rules for not only its search advertising and YouTube display ads; it, along with Facebook, effectively determines and enforces the rules for display advertising on millions of apps and websites. And just like the Gamemaker in the Hunger Games, the Tech Baron makes sure that the rules (and dynamics of competition) within its ecosystem ultimately benefit them. The Tech Baron's terms are not subject to negotiation. Nor is there a right to due process when access is denied.

Fifth, while the Tech Baron is not immune from competitive pressure, its gatekeeper position enables it to block innovations that might jeopardize its ecosystem. It takes the destruction out of innovation's potential creative destruction, and its influence extends beyond its ecosystem.

Later in this book, we will expand on many of these points and illustrate how the Tech Barons shape the innovation paths.

Their Rise and Reach

Often, a Tech Baron begins its life as an online platform, interface, or business that many customers, business users, and advertisers value. Several characteristics of the digital economy enable a leading platform/interface to enjoy exponential growth and a tipping effect, where the winner takes all or most of the market.[6] Key here are network effects (think of Facebook), extreme scale economies (consider search engines), control over the user and seller interface (think of Amazon's shopping platform), the platforms' advantage in attaining and sustaining our attention (think YouTube), control over personal data, and advanced analytics to monitor and analyze market dynamics and users (using AI for personalized services, identifying patterns, and accelerating innovation).

Consequently, a positive feedback loop emerges in that digital market that helps the strong become stronger as the weak get weaker.[7] Once the market tips in its favor, the platform successfully leverages its power to other high-growth industries, platforms, products, and services to extract more value. It is now on its way to becoming a Tech Baron.

To identify some of today's Tech Barons, let us look at market valuations. Five companies in 2021 accounted for approximately 25 percent of the S&P 500's market capitalization.[8] They were Google, Apple, Facebook, Amazon, and Microsoft. We will use these digital giants to illustrate the Tech Barons' powers, including their ability to affect innovation paths. GAFAM are certainly not alone. In China, for example, significant Tech Barons include Alibaba, Baidu, and Tencent. The strategies, principles, and effects discussed in this book apply to existing and future Tech Barons, regardless of their country of operation and origin.

To appreciate the breadth of their ecosystems, consider a *New York Times* tech reporter who tried to block Google, Amazon, Facebook, Apple, and Microsoft for over six weeks.[9] It was really hard.

Cutting Amazon meant not only losing access to the largest shopping platform and retail seller (outside China),[10] Prime video and music services, Alexa devices, Whole Foods shopping, and hardware, including Kindle and Ring devices, but also losing access to any website hosted by Amazon Web Services, the internet's largest cloud provider. As the reporter noted, "[m]any apps and a large portion of the internet use Amazon's servers to host their digital content, and much of the digital world became inaccessible when I said goodbye to Amazon, including the Amazon Prime Video competitor Netflix."

When she tried to block Google, the entire internet "slowed down" because almost every site she "visited was using Google to supply its fonts, run its ads, track its users, or determine if its users were humans or bots." So, she couldn't sign in to the data storage service Dropbox because the site thought she wasn't a natural person. Uber and Lyft also stopped working for her because "they were both dependent on Google Maps for navigating the world."

While Facebook was "less debilitating" for her to block, she "missed Instagram (which Facebook owns) terribly" and stopped getting news from her social circle, like the birth of a good friend's child. "I just assume that if I post something on Facebook, everyone will know about it," her friend later told her.

Apple was hard for the journalist to leave, since she relied on the company's hardware. Moreover, you will be relegated to a flip phone or landline if you avoid Apple's iPhone or any phone using Google's Android operating system. As the Supreme Court recognized, this is not a feasible alternative to participate in today's economy, democracy, and society, especially when "nearly three-quarters of smart phone users report being within five feet of their phones most of the time, with 12% admitting that they even use their phones in the shower."[11]

Like Amazon, Microsoft has a cloud service, and so a few sites went dark for the reporter, as did two Microsoft-owned services she frequently used, LinkedIn and Skype. (Moreover, writing her story likely caused her to rely on some operating system—probably Microsoft's or Apple's—and some word processing application, likely Microsoft Word.)

As the tech reporter concluded, some of these giants provided "the very infrastructure of the internet, so embedded in the architecture of the digital world that even their competitors had to rely on their services." So, it isn't just avoiding their products, but the "thicket of more obscure products and services that are hard to untangle from tools we rely on for everything we do, from work to getting from point A to point B."

The Tech Baron's products and services not only work seamlessly within their ecosystem, but their interlocking platforms support many other products and services upon which we also rely.

Just consider Facebook's mass outage in 2021 that left billions of users without access to Facebook, Instagram, WhatsApp, and Messenger. It also affected over two hundred million businesses that rely on Facebook's tools. In speaking with ten online creators and small business owners who use Meta's services, CNBC found that each business lost between "a few hundred dollars to over $5,000 from sales, affiliate links, sponsored posts and product launches" as a result of the six-hour outage.[12] Imagine the cost to the business if Facebook shut them down for a week or month.

The Tech Barons' control over these key ecosystems translates to significant market capitalization and profits.[13] Not surprisingly, the Tech Barons continuously expand their ecosystems, bringing together more products and services. Many investors bet on their expansion. The Australian competition authority, for example, found, "50–67%" of the 2019 share price for Facebook and "46–64%" of Google's 2019 share price "can be attributed to expectations for future growth."[14] The market is betting that the Tech Barons' ongoing expansion will fortify their power and increase profitability.

Tech Barons' Investment in Innovation

At this stage, you may rightly ponder that these are big corporations, but surely they also promote innovation?

Here is where things get interesting. Tech Barons certainly promote innovation but also stifle plenty. In this chapter, we'll focus on the narrative that highlights their positive impact on innovation. We'll spend the next chapters unraveling the darker side of the innovation story.

The CEOs of Google, Apple, Facebook, and Amazon skillfully presented the positive narrative when they testified before the U.S. Congress in 2020. And although economists have long debated whether monopoly or competition best promotes innovation, all four CEOs deftly covered all the bases to appeal to the different economic schools of thought.

The CEOs harkened to the *Schumpeterian hypothesis*, which, in the words of Austrian economist Joseph Schumpeter, considers competition to be a "gale of creative destruction."[15] Under this school of thought, competition is "for the field," rather than "within the field."[16] The U.S. Court of Appeals in the *Microsoft* monopolization case, for example, cited Schumpeter that in technologically dynamic markets, "entrenchment may be temporary, because innovation may alter the field altogether."[17] So, the tech platforms compete through innovation for temporary market dominance, "from which they may be displaced by the next wave of product advancements."[18]

To impress upon his company employees the gales of creative destruction that could topple his company at any moment, Facebook's CEO Mark Zuckerberg told Congress about the company sign: when Facebook moved into the campus of the former tech firm Sun Microsystems, Zuckerberg said he "kept their sign out front, on the back of ours, to remind us that things change fast in tech. I've long believed that the nature of our industry is that someday a product will replace Facebook. I want us to be the ones that build it, because if we don't, someone else will."[19]

Amazon's CEO harkened to another Schumpeterian insight. While we may romanticize innovators as start-ups toiling away in their garages (like Amazon), there are many innovations that only big, well-financed companies can deliver. As Jeff Bezos testified:

> I love garage entrepreneurs—I was one. But, just like the world needs small companies, it also needs large ones. There are things small companies simply can't do. I don't care how good an entrepreneur you are, you're not going to build an all-fiber Boeing 787 in your garage.[20]

While all four companies disclaimed significant market power, their CEOs harkened to Schumpeter's hypothesis that companies with market power are better positioned to induce technological change. After all, the tech giants' platforms are the coral reefs stimulating innovation. Smaller firms lack the resources and incentives to underwrite these platforms.[21]

But the CEOs did not want to align too closely with the Schumpeter camp, as it links innovation to monopolies and the pursuit of monopoly profits.[22] So, the CEOs also aligned themselves with the economist Kenneth Arrow and his followers, who posit that competition best promotes innovation.[23] The CEOs repeatedly testified how innovation spurs competition, which drives more innovation. Competition "makes space for the next great idea," Apple's CEO said.[24] Facing this competitive pressure, Facebook "consistently added new products for people that enhance their ability to connect and share what matters most to them."[25]

Any power (which the Tech Barons disclaim having) is fleeting. Companies must continually innovate, otherwise they will decline.[26] Google, according to its CEO, "operates in highly competitive and dynamic global markets, in which prices are free or falling, and products are constantly improving."

Because of the intense competitive pressure, their companies, according to the CEOs, don't live the quiet life of monopolies that underinvest in new technologies (or only invest when they generate additional profits): instead, they must spend billions of dollars annually in research and development (R&D). Facebook invests around $10 billion annually in R&D.[27] Google's CEO noted how every year, the company is among the world's biggest investors in research and development: "At the end of 2019, our R&D spend had increased almost 10 times over 10 years, from $2.8 billion to $26 billion. We've invested over $90 billion over the last 5 years."[28] If it doesn't, the company will fall behind.

Indeed, these companies certainly invest heavily.[29] In looking through their financial statements over the past decade, Google, Apple, Facebook, and Microsoft spent billions of dollars annually on research and development. (Amazon does not break out R&D separately in its annual reports, combining it with content.)

As Table 1.1 reflects, these four companies collectively spent over $451.6 billion on R&D over eleven years. To put that number in perspective, their combined R&D expenditures over eleven years exceeded the gross domestic product of over 160 countries in 2020.[30] The four companies' R&D expenditures would exceed the total market value of all final goods and services produced in Nigeria in 2020. (Nigeria's GDP is ranked 27th of 194 countries.)

The numbers represent a relatively higher investment/revenue percentage (19 percent on average for Facebook, 15 percent for Google, 13 percent for Microsoft, and 4 percent for Apple) compared to other industries (health care averaged 10.2 percent, communication services averaged 5.2 percent, and industrials averaged 7 percent of revenues).[31]

Table 1.1

	FACEBOOK		GOOGLE		APPLE		MICROSOFT		OVERALL TOTAL
	R&D Expenses (in millions)	Percentage of Revenues	R&D Expenses (in millions)	Percentage of Revenues	R&D Expenses (in millions)	Percentage of Revenues	R&D Expenses (in millions)	Percentage of Revenues	
2010	$144	7%	$3,762	12.8%	$1,782	3%	$8,700	14%	$14,388
2011	$388	10%	$5,162	13.6%	$2,429	2%	$9,000	13%	$16,979
2012	$1,399	27%	$6,793	13.5%	$3,381	2%	$9,800	13%	$21,373
2013	$1,415	18%	$7,137	12.9%	$4,475	3%	$10,400	13%	$23,427
2014	$2,666	21%	$9,832	14.9%	$6,041	3%	$11,400	13%	$29,939
2015	$4,816	27%	$12,282	16.3%	$8,067	3%	$12,000	13%	$37,165
2016	$5,919	21%	$13,948	15.5%	$10,045	5%	$12,000	14%	$41,912
2017	$7,754	19%	$16,625	15%	$11,581	5%	$13,037	13%	$48,997
2018	$10,273	18%	$21,419	15.7%	$14,236	5%	$14,726	13%	$60,654
2019	$13,600	19%	$26,081	16.1%	$16,217	6%	$16,876	13%	$72,774
2020	$18,447	21%	$27,573	15.1%	$18,752	7%	$19,269	13%	$84,041
Total	$66,821		$150,614		$97,006		$137,208		$451,649

Source: Form 10-Ks for Google, Apple, Microsoft, and Facebook

With these impressive numbers, GAFAM could self-proclaim themselves as the crucial engine for modern innovation. Of course, with their hoard of cash, the Tech Barons could double or triple their R&D expenses if they wanted. But still, in absolute numbers, their investment is evident and rather impressive. That investment, they repeatedly note, enables them to deliver innovative services and products, greater efficiencies, better communications, and more of what we want.

In between the buzzwords that peppered their discussion, a sense of benevolence emerged. Not only are the Tech Barons investing in R&D, but they do this to address our needs, our desires, and with a look toward a brighter future, to benefit our lives. As Facebook's CEO testified, "In a competitive economy, innovation leads to improvements that benefit consumers."[32] Later Zuckerberg added, "We create technology to enable social good."[33]

Google also contributes to the greater good "by building products that are helpful to American users in moments big and small, whether they are looking for a faster route home, learning how to cook a new dish on YouTube, or growing a small business."[34] Google's CEO added how "[s]urvey research found that free services like Search, Gmail, Maps, and Photos provide thousands of dollars a year in value to the average American."[35]

Apple's CEO noted his company's promise to "build things that make us proud."[36]

One can also find the Tech Barons' innovation narrative in their financial reports. As Bezos wrote to investors in 2021, "[c]ustomers complete 28% of purchases on Amazon in three minutes or less, and half of all purchases are finished in less than 15 minutes. Compare that to the typical shopping trip to a physical store—driving, parking, searching store aisles, waiting in the checkout line, finding your car, and driving home. Research suggests the typical physical store trip takes about an hour. If you assume that a typical Amazon purchase takes 15 minutes and that it saves you a couple of trips to a physical store a week, that's more than 75 hours a year saved."[37] So, as Bezos calculated, if you multiply these 75 hours with a conservative value of our time ($10 per hour), that's $750 in value each year. If you subtract the cost of Prime, that gives you Amazon's value creation for each Prime member of about $630 per year, or $126 billion for Amazon's two hundred million Prime members! (And that doesn't even include the cost of gas to drive to the store.)

Coral Reefs for Third-Party Innovations

No doubt the Tech Barons can tally how they save us money. But their contribution to innovation doesn't end there. Besides their investment in innovation, Tech Barons often attract other innovators.

Under their narrative, the Tech Barons lower the barriers to innovate in their ecosystems. And at one level, their portrayal has some appeal. The ecosystems, and the platforms they control, provide the infrastructure that enables future innovation, fostering growth, efficiencies, and dynamism.[38] They often act as intermediaries that seamlessly connect and allow for efficient information flows among individuals, app developers, websites, sellers, and advertisers. Their platforms and services (such as cloud computing) can significantly lower costs that have traditionally inhibited innovation, including the costs for an innovator to enter the market (entry costs), the costs to develop infrastructure, the costs for the intended users to find these innovations (search costs), and, once users find them, the costs for users to experiment with these innovations (transaction costs). The Tech Barons also offer a valuable "one-stop-shop" solution.[39] By promoting interoperability and functionality, other products and services can attach to their platforms and operate from them, using the cost savings to invest in research and development. So, as these traditional costs and barriers decline, innovation levels should increase, and we should be better off.

Consequently, their ecosystems' platforms are often analogized to a coral reef. Just as the reefs "provide a home for at least 25% of all marine species, including fish, mollusks, worms, crustaceans, echinoderms, sponges, tunicates and other cnidarians,"[40] the Tech Barons' innovation platforms can attract complementary technologies. The more apps, technologies, and services their platforms attract, the larger they grow, and the more diverse the ecosystem's services become, which, in turn, lowers the economic costs to innovate for everyone within their ecosystem. As Facebook's CEO testified before Congress:

In 2007, we launched the Facebook Platform, a set of tools for developers and businesses to build complementary services on Facebook. Our vision for Platform has always been to foster an ecosystem of apps that build on top of Facebook and create a richer and more interesting experience for people. At the same time, we have developed rules to make Platform work better for everyone and to protect the significant investments we made in capital and talent to develop it.[41]

Amazon as well has "invested tens of billions of dollars in infrastructure and technical services . . . [and] has innovated and invested heavily to help third-party sellers succeed."[42]

Google likewise "deliberately build[s] platforms that support the innovation of others."[43] Google's CEO cited the mobile operating system Android, upon which thousands of device makers and mobile operators can build and sell devices for free, thereby enabling cutting-edge smartphones, "some for less than $50."[44] Google notes that its "continuing investments spur innovation that improves our own products and services. They also support and accelerate innovation by others."[45]

Think of Google's and Apple's mobile phone operating systems and the millions of apps that work seamlessly with your smartphone, tablet, and other devices. Think of the many apps, games, and social plugins that let you interact with your friends on and off Facebook. And think of all the apps and skills currently being developed for Amazon's and Google's digital personal assistants, which enable you to do everything from ordering a pizza, to having a book read to you, to playing an adventure game. Or consider the role Microsoft plays in attracting innovation. By 2021, "leaders in every industry—including 95 percent of the Fortune 500—run on [Microsoft's cloud computing service] Azure."[46] Using Microsoft's Azure Cognitive Services, start-ups can "build applications that see, hear, speak, search, understand, and accelerate decision-making."[47]

So, the Tech Barons view themselves as the modern Atlas in shouldering the coral reefs' operation.

Reflections

Looking at the Tech Barons' infrastructure and investment in innovation, some are optimistic. After all, we're on the frontier of even more exciting developments, ranging from artificial intelligence to the Internet of Things (with digital personal assistants) and driverless cars. It is, therefore, of little surprise that as a society, we often bet on the Tech Barons, particularly GAFAM, to help lead us to more discoveries and sustainable growth.

It is a beautiful, aspirational narrative. But it hides a darker reality. A reality in which Tech Barons quash disruption, stifle third-party innovation efforts, and limit innovation diversity within their ecosystems. With power comes the ability to reorient innovation efforts away from market demand. The result? R&D efforts that focus on exploiting users and extracting value. To see why and understand the true power of the Tech Barons, we first need to talk about the innovation pirates.

CHAPTER 2

The Tech Pirates

INNOVATORS ARE OFTEN REFERRED to as *pirates*. You may have heard the quote, "You don't change the world by joining the navy, you change it by becoming a pirate." A fine metaphor. Indeed, Apple's CEO Steve Jobs used it in his inspirational 1983 speech to Apple developers. The team was working on the Apple Macintosh computer, and Jobs set the tone for a creative, ambitious, unhindered, fast-moving operation.[1]

The message resonated well. As one software engineer on that Macintosh team recounted, "Being a pirate meant moving fast, unencumbered by bureaucracy and politics. . . . It meant being audacious and courageous, willing to take considerable risks for greater rewards." At some point, the team's headquarters flew a black pirate flag featuring a skull and eyepatch, designed as the Apple logo.[2] That's the pirates' spirit!

Innovation pirates develop tomorrow's technology. Our society relies heavily on their creativity and motivation. Their organization, business models, and cost structures are geared toward uncharted waters. And they often persist, against the odds, regardless of the uncertainty and risk. Think of them as rebels and explorers, driven by more than immediate profits.[3] In our story, these pirates are the heroes.

To distinguish innovation pirates from other companies that invest heavily in R&D, we should first consider two categories of innovation—sustaining and disruptive. Then we'll consider the value of innovation.

Disruptive vs. Sustaining Innovation

Apple considered itself a pirate innovator. Those who recall its famous "1984" commercial, where a few controlled all the technologies in this Orwellian future, might agree.[4] The Macintosh personal computer sought to disrupt the IBM/Microsoft hegemony, and both the commercial and Macintosh computers disrupted their respective industries.

While the term *disruptive innovation* (and notions such as *radical innovation*) dominate the business literature and debate, they are often used to describe varying phenomena. As one 2020 business survey noted, "it is not always clear what disruptive innovation exactly means, what will be disrupted, and by whom."[5]

Central to the concept of disruption has been the work of the late Harvard Business School professor Clayton M. Christensen. In his seminal book *The Innovator's Dilemma*, Christensen shed light on the unique characteristics that often separate well-established, well-managed firms from disruptive innovators.[6] The former, being successful and competent in servicing their clientele, will seek to innovate and deliver value to their customers. Their innovations tend to be *sustaining* and focus on satisfying present and future customer needs while securing profits and growth.[7] They will strive to innovate and improve products and services by giving their existing customers something more and better in what they want.[8] Indeed, it is rational for the established firms to continue offering sustaining innovations that their customers want and refrain from introducing innovations that their customers don't demand (and whose only appeal would be in lower-end segments or new markets where the margins and profits are lower).

In contrast, Christensen's disruptive innovators offer "a very different value proposition than had been available previously."[9] Being free from the need to service a large existing customer base and free from the short-term growth requirements of the leading organizations and their high-cost structures, the disruptive innovator can experiment and offer novel value propositions. Typically, the revenues, margins, and profits are initially much lower in these low-end or emerging markets compared to the established markets. Under Christensen's theory, the established customers don't necessarily want or can't use these disruptive innovations when introduced (for example, the established mainframe computer manufacturers did not want smaller disk drives).[10] But over time, if successful, the disruptive innovation will cannibalize and challenge the existing industries.

Christensen's ideas help us appreciate how different corporate structures, values, and cultures can affect whether the company focuses and pursues sustaining or disruptive innovation. His theory, however, has been criticized for its "conceptual ambiguity, insufficient supporting evidence, and for lack of predictive power."[11] One notable criticism is that Christensen's theory captures only a narrow dimension of disruptive innovation: the innovator only enters a low-margin market or new markets with different customers. Since disruption comes in many forms and in different market settings, his theory has limited applicability.[12]

With these limitations in mind, over the past decade many leading thinkers have developed and refined the definition of *disruptive innovation* to capture the different dimensions of disruption.[13] Consequently, the term now includes multiple taxonomies, business models, and processes.[14]

For our purposes, when we refer to disruptive innovation, we discuss a process in which the innovation pirate's business model, products, or services (whether low- or high-margin) disrupt (or are perceived to disrupt) the existing value chain.[15] Pirates' disruption comes in the form of a new value proposition that threatens the current or future value chain (which is the prevailing business model, the range of activities needed to create a product or service, the profits generated from them, and how the profits are allocated among the firms).[16]

To illustrate, let's look at the value chain of the app ecosystem on your smartphone. Most of the apps within Apple's and Google's app stores are free.[17] So, the dominant business model for most apps is behavioral advertising where user data is collected for personalized ads and targeted marketing (consider the ads that follow you across the internet after you search for that product or visit the manufacturer's website). Some apps rely on a paid or freemium model (where "the initial download is 'free,' but revenue comes from in-app purchases or payments for upgrades").[18] To analyze the value chain, we can look at the steps and information flow used to generate value and consider who captures what portion of that value within this app ecosystem. In the app ecosystem where behavioral advertising predominates, the value chain analysis would consider, among other things, how the value is created (namely the ability to predict and manipulate human behavior and target ads accordingly) and how the profits are distributed. In analyzing the freemium business model, the value chain analysis considers, among other things, the steps to create the app and deliver its services,[19] which app users generate the most revenues,[20] and for every dollar spent downloading an app (or buying things in the app), how much the app developer gets versus others, such as Google and Apple, who control the app stores and in-app payment systems.[21]

A sustaining technology would promote this app store ecosystem without disrupting the value chain. As Steve Jobs recognized, the "purpose in the App Store is to add value to the iPhone" and ultimately "sell more iPhones."[22] By contrast, a pirate's disruptive innovation could disrupt any component of the value chain, such as introducing privacy measures that hinder the app ecosystem's behavioral advertising business model.

The Pirate's Journey

The pirates' disruption may be triggered by a myriad of innovations, some *radical* and *discontinuous* (in the literature, these terms often refer to highly novel innovations), others offering *breakthrough* and *disruptive* innovation (in the literature, these terms tend to refer to innovations that have a high impact).[23] And while we tend to imagine the lone innovator introducing a radically new innovation, disruption does not necessarily depend on a "big bang" technological breakthrough. Many disruptive innovations result from combinations of existing value offerings and can involve preexisting (and at times off the shelf) technologies.[24] As Steven Johnson noted, all of the key elements of Johannes Gutenberg's printing press preexisted. Thus, Gutenberg's genius wasn't "conceiving an entirely new technology from scratch, but instead from *borrowing* a mature technology from an entirely different field, and putting it to work to solve an unrelated problem."[25]

Often, the pirates, like everyone else, will not know how their innovation will fare, how someone will use their products, or the exact market and demand characteristics.[26] They engage in trial and error, with the hope of identifying new entry points to a market and new potential demand to innovative propositions. They engage in a high-risk (and potentially high-return) business. As Square's cofounder notes, they may not even set out to disrupt: "The entrepreneurs that succeed, and rise to the top of their industries set out to build, not destroy. If disruption occurs, it is merely a side effect."[27]

Since their initial strategies for entering these markets will not always succeed, the pirates gear their organizations toward ongoing discovery. First they must learn how the customers will actually use their products. The adroit pirates next must update their offerings and the underlying value chain. The pirates simultaneously must seek new connections to help build out their platforms (and budding ecosystem) to achieve scale. So, they must conserve enough resources for this trial-and-error process.[28]

With a diversity of innovations, new combinations emerge, disrupting earlier combinations. The decision-making authority within the pirate's ecosystem is less concentrated, left more to the network than any one entity. So, the pirates' platform gravitates closer to the fertile innovative zone, which is between too much order (i.e., the Tech Barons' highly controlled ecosystems) and anarchy (such as the dark web).[29]

In their journey, the pirates will face many obstacles. Some are *internal* and relate to corporate culture, management, strategy, organization, skilled staff, and resources. These impediments are affected by the degree of difficulty and disruption pursued and the ability to commit and effectively engage in exploration innovation. They go to the core of the innovator's capacity to deliver disruption in uncharted water. Other obstacles are *external*. These relate to the legal, regulatory, economic, and market conditions; users' adoption rate (such as the extent to which customers are locked in to existing products or hesitant to switch); their products' interoperability with, and integration of, other technologies; and scalability. The list goes on.[30] The pirate's obstacles vary by industry and technology and its corporate structure and size. But the rhythm of innovation is to overcome these barriers. So, the pirate must access the market and scale by testing its innovation, learning from customer usage and feedback, and revising and redeploying the technology.[31]

In the digital economy, however, another significant external threat may undermine their survival—the risk of being quashed by the Tech Barons. After all, built into the pirates' disruptive strategy is its threat to the Tech Barons' ecosystem and profit model. That tension is at the heart of the digital innovation story.

Thus, pirates would often (but not always) seek to avoid the Tech Barons' elephant trail. To establish themselves, they will seek out emerging or insignificant smaller markets or create new markets by targeting these new customers with a different value proposition.[32] To succeed, they often redefine the buying criteria for the category.[33] Over time, as they test their technologies, and gain scale and success, they will journey into the mainstream.

In contestable, undistorted markets, one would expect an evolutionary pattern of disruption. Successful pirates innovate and establish new markets that grow in size and consumer base. These pirates eventually shift their focus to sustaining innovations (catering to their existing customers' needs). Although they want to remain disruptive, their need to protect the current value chains will increasingly constrain them.

Over time, the next wave of disruptors will challenge the entrenched innovation pirates.

Indeed, empirical observations support this distinction: large firms engage in relatively more *exploitation* R&D (to improve the existing product lines that they are currently serving). In contrast, entrepreneurs and small firms have a comparative advantage in *exploration* innovation (to acquire new product lines and explore novel technologies).[34] That cycle of innovation helps expand the boundaries of what is possible.

How Disruptive Are the Tech Barons?

Do Tech Barons engage in disruption like pirates? At times, they do, and at times they don't. It often comes down to their value chain.

Within their ecosystem, the Tech Barons will tend to engage in *sustaining* innovation that seeks to preserve and improve the existing value chains. Innovation efforts will naturally focus on improvements (such as the additional services offered to Facebook users). The Tech Barons will allow others (apps and websites) to introduce innovation into the ecosystem, but only to the extent it does not alter profits and power. The key to any advancement would be its fitting within the existing value chain and the barons' vision of how their ecosystem will evolve. After all, the Tech Barons invested heavily in establishing and expanding their ecosystem, creating a valuable customer/user base, instilling usage habits, and, of course, monetizing the business strategy. Accordingly, the Tech Barons protect the value chains that deliver them substantial profits.

Think of Apple's walled garden as an example. Apple heavily invests in innovation within its walled garden to improve its offering. It also invites other app developers to innovate and lets them into its app store, as long as they comply with its set rules—all activities within the ecosystem support Apple's viability and profit stream. Apple's former head of app review, Phillip Shoemaker, has described the App Store as "antiquated," with "no radical innovation, only evolution" for the last ten years.[35] Disruptors, as we will see in the following chapters, are not welcomed.

Outside their ecosystem, many Tech Barons take a different stance. They will use their vast resources to develop disruptive innovation outside their core businesses and challenge other value chains. Consider how Google describes X, which is its "Moonshot Factory":

> X is a diverse group of inventors and entrepreneurs who build and launch technologies that aim to improve the lives of millions, even billions, of people. Our goal: 10x impact on the world's most intractable problems, not just 10% improvement. We approach projects that have the aspiration and riskiness of research with the speed and ambition of a startup.[36]

The Tech Barons will disrupt outside their ecosystem to the extent that it does not undermine their existing value chains. In fact, after disrupting other industries, the Tech Barons will often seek to link the new technology or innovation into their current ecosystem and benefit from scale, network effects, and other synergies.[37] The Tech Barons stake out their disruptive platforms in this land grab while ensuring that the innovation paths will not undermine their existing ecosystem's value chains.[38]

Tech Barons may adopt new value chains for new services. The business model for Google's, Microsoft's, and Amazon's cloud computing services, for example, differs from their behavioral advertising business model for their free (or discounted) products and services. But the Tech Barons cannot easily afford to change the value chains for existing platforms and services. (Why switch to a subscription model or contextual advertising, for example, when the Tech Barons capture most of the value from behavioral advertising?)

This has three important implications.

First, the Tech Baron will not allow any change that might disrupt the prevailing value chain of its preexisting networks and platforms. Rather than allowing pirates to build an adjoining ecosystem, the Tech Baron will direct innovation to improve and fortify its own ecosystem. App developers can complement (or compete) with other apps within Google's and Apple's app stores. But the developer cannot introduce within these ecosystems a superior app store.

Second, as the Tech Baron expands its ecosystem, any new value chain cannot disrupt the preexisting value chains. So, while verbal search ("Hey Google . . .") will likely disrupt written search on your PC or phone, it cannot disrupt the underlying search advertising value chain (where Google makes most of its revenues).

Finally, as the Tech Baron's ecosystem expands, there will be fewer lucrative industries to disrupt. Thus, the Tech Baron's innovation efforts will likely concentrate on the defensive, sustaining innovations that fortify the market power of its existing platforms, products, and services and its ability to capture more profits within its ecosystem.

So, while Google's investment in Android might appear disruptive, it enabled Google to maintain its dominance in search and capture most of the value from its preexisting search advertising value chain. While Google promoted Android as an "open" platform, it isn't. An open platform would have both scale and plasticity (in allowing new configurations and innovation forks), but that plasticity would threaten Google's existing value chain. As a direct consequence, the innovation on Android has been either sustaining or defensive, thereby enabling Google to capture more profits as it captured more of our data and attention. Likewise, the next iteration of disruptive innovations by the Tech Barons will paradoxically insulate the Tech Barons from outside disruption.

The Value of the Innovation

Now that we better understand the distinction between sustaining and disruptive innovation and the potential tension between the Tech Barons and disruptive pirates, we can add another dimension, namely the "value" of innovation.

But isn't all innovation valuable? After all, the term *innovation* implies a positive outcome.[39] The OECD, for example, defines it as a "new and significant improved product (good or service)."[40] Ordinarily, investing in innovation is associated with improved outcomes for most. The assumption is that market forces and consumer demand force companies to invest in research and development, and society benefits from the increase in efficiencies, productivity, and standard of living. Just consider the quotes in the last chapter that associate greater investment in R&D with greater societal benefits.

But in reality, the process of innovation—the introduction of a new idea, technology, method, or product—may not necessarily increase overall welfare.[41] Innovation, once implemented, can be a mixed bag. The term *innovation* is similar to *competition*, which we usually associate as a good thing. But just as competition can, at times, be toxic, so too can innovation.[42] So start-ups, policymakers, and consumers need to understand the dynamics that change the nature and value of innovation.

Of course, value is a tricky concept. To begin with, what some celebrate as value enhancement, others may despise and consider value destruction. Exploring value from different perspectives (such as consumers, businesses, or markets) and using different metrics to assess it would likely result in conflicting views. Furthermore, it is often the implementation and use of innovation that affects its value (rather than the technology or innovation itself). Indeed, value creation is commonly explored as an outcome of business activity.[43]

Still, with all of this in mind, when we focus on the innovation itself, we can consider its effect from a societal perspective—whether it creates, destroys, or extracts value. This perspective is crucial because not all disruptive innovation is necessarily beneficial. Some disruptive innovations can be implemented in ways that either create value or extract and destroy value.

Policymakers rarely discuss the value of innovation. One reason is that policymakers have been heavily influenced by neoclassical economists, who have largely discarded the more abstract dimensions of value. If a product has a positive price or is in demand, then, for these economists, it has value.

But if one doesn't use price as a surrogate for value, how does one assess an innovation's value? While subjective, value is neither amorphous nor linked solely to price. Other definitions of value—besides the monetary worth of something—exist, including the innovation's relative utility or importance.[44] Innovation can increase value by increasing overall utility, which for the founder of utilitarianism Jeremy Bentham was well-being.[45] Some might argue that well-being is as fickle to quantification as value, but the reality is otherwise. Many economists and the OECD are currently defining and measuring the critical dimensions of different types of well-being.[46]

Sometimes innovation will increase overall well-being. Sometimes it may generate mixed effects, whereby it creates some value but largely redistributes wealth. Finally, at times, innovation may be truly toxic— focused on primarily extracting and destroying value.

Doubtful? Ask yourself this: Do we need more technologies that will primarily promote cyber-bullying, cyber-hacking, or the spread of disinformation? Few, if any, would say yes, even though some might demand these innovations and would be willing to pay a significant price for them. We can categorize these innovations as harmful because they destroy value and well-being for most of society. Ditto if the innovations foster addiction to the digital services, are associated with adverse mental health effects, and further encroach upon our privacy without any significant countervailing benefit. They decrease overall well-being.

Society ought to cherish those innovations that can unlock the greatest value and benefit us the most. These innovations can be sustaining or disruptive, within or outside the value chain. Accordingly, value-enhancing innovations could be delivered, in principle, by both Tech Barons and pirates. However, in the digital economy, dominated by a few powerhouses, the pirates have greater potential to deliver the greatest value. Why is this?

First, pirates offer a wider diversity of innovations, both within and outside the Tech Barons' ecosystems and value chains.

Second, from a market perspective, diversity counterbalances the increased concentration of power. In their tightly controlled ecosystems, the Tech Barons reap most of the profits (think of digital advertising). So, the pirates, if successful, can disperse profits throughout and outside the ecosystem.

Third (as we will illustrate in chapter 6), market power and the Tech Barons' control over the ecosystem affect the innovation's nature and quality. Power supports the toxicity of innovation. That is, innovation will likely serve the Tech Barons' interests, not ours.

As Graph 2.1 illustrates, a hierarchy emerges:

Graph 2.1

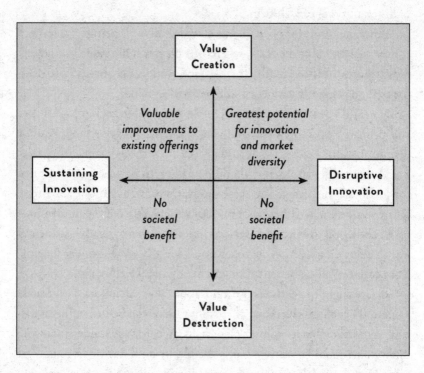

The innovations that our policies should prioritize in the digital economy are disruptive, value-creating innovations not constrained by existing business models or value chains. This is so because pirates, operating outside the value chain, increase diversity and add multiple paths for other value-creating innovations.

Next are sustaining innovations that create value. These innovations are also beneficial as they help improve existing services and products and cater to the changing needs of users.

On the flip side are sustaining or disruptive innovations that should be treated with suspicion. Extractive innovations (at the intersection of the axis) do not necessarily increase overall well-being by simply shifting wealth from one group to another. Likewise, our policies should not promote innovations that destroy overall value—whether they are sustaining or disruptive.

Of course, it isn't always obvious when innovations can create or destroy value; that depends on the context. Suppose an electrode connected to your brain can decode your thoughts. Does that innovation provide value? Yes, for people who cannot speak due to stroke, traumatic brain injury, and neurodegenerative diseases. But no, if the technology is used to exploit the person.

The nature of implementation and the overall context are of great significance. As we saw with the Tech Barons, that context is often driven by the value chain and market power. If the prevailing ecosystems' business model relies on behavioral advertising, and if users have few, if any, viable alternatives to that dominant ecosystem, the new technology will likely be used to manipulate users (as we will explore later).

This leaves us with a helpful insight on the *likelihood* of value-creating innovation: it will decrease as an ecosystem's power increases, as users have fewer viable outside options (they cannot easily switch), and as value chains and profitability are linked to value extraction. Put differently, market power supports value extraction.

The Ultimate Innovation Pirates

Ecosystems can offer fertile ground for disruptive innovation. They facilitate complex interactions, business alliances, and collaborations.[47] But when one firm controls an essential ecosystem, that market power enables value extraction; the ecosystem's value chain evolves to implement that strategy, and the ecosystem no longer acts like a coral reef. Instead, it offers a narrower value proposition driven by the Tech Baron.

This is where pirates can play a central role. In exploring disruption both within and outside the entrenched companies' value chains, the pirates can potentially offer significant heterogeneity, choice, and value, both within and outside of consumer-facing industries. When the pirates' disruptive innovation creates value and serves broader societal interests, the pirates provide the ultimate contribution. From here on, we will refer to these value-creating innovators as the Tech Pirates.

Think of these Tech Pirates as innovators that throw wild parties that bring together creative types from all fields. Ideas collide with other ideas. Their parties aren't so explosive as to risk burning down the entire house, thereby destroying all the innovation.

Consider Airbnb, which did the unthinkable—a platform where strangers live at other strangers' homes—thereby disrupting the hotel industry. But providing cheaper accommodations in many locales was not the platform's core value. Instead, the start-up describes its business as "a community based on connection and belonging" where its hosts "are everyday people who share their worlds to provide guests with the feeling of connection and being at home."[48] Nor are people "users." They are "guests," who often share "a curiosity about the world and open-mindedness to other people and cultures." So, it is not about scaling and network effects per se—the sheer number of hosts (four million) or guests (hundreds of millions) or the platform's geographic reach (about one hundred thousand cities across the world). Instead, it is each host's and guest's individuality "that makes Airbnb unique." The platform scales not from accommodations but in connecting people who can share their interests and talents from "exploring graffiti art in New York City to finding hidden jazz clubs in London" and offering "authentic activities." A cynic might respond that all of this is a marketing ploy. But when "connection," "belonging," "curiosity," and "diversity" drive that ecosystem's value chain it presents far more opportunities for expansion than facilitating cheaper lodging opportunities.

Thus, the pirates' parties are far less hierarchical than the Tech Barons' parties, where the carefully screened guests are busily scrubbing the floors, painting the interiors, and polishing the Tech Barons' silverware.

Because of this relative freedom, the Tech Pirates are disproportionately responsible for disruptive innovation and its diversity. Whereas the Tech Barons might disrupt large, well-established sectors with a significant potential pay-off (such as automobiles and health care), Tech Pirates are not necessarily constrained by the need to avoid cannibalizing existing value chains. Tech Pirates seek innovation anywhere the opportunities arise—small markets, emerging markets, or existing large markets. They don't have to ask how this innovation might affect the sales and profits of their current products and services. Nor are they burdened by Wall Street's expectations, as their market valuations (if they are public) expect growth in the millions rather than billions of dollars.[49] So, they can afford to pursue smaller profit margin opportunities in smaller emerging markets.

When successful, their innovation efforts lead to new market spaces and technologies that separate them from the competition.[50] By offering us new products, services, processes, or technologies outside the Tech Barons' value chains, Tech Pirates can improve our privacy, autonomy, and well-being and unleash the most value.

Whereas the Tech Barons seek to monopolize the process of innovation, the Tech Pirates can foster heterogeneity of innovation and support the diffusion of knowledge outside the prevailing ecosystems. Their creations can create opportunities for new players to enter and disrupt other markets.

Reflections

Ideally, we would have significant investment in sustaining and disruptive innovation by the Tech Barons as well as the plurality introduced by innovative Tech Pirates. In practice, however, the Tech Barons operate to limit external disruption to their value chain. The friction at the heart of the digital innovation story now becomes apparent. Tech Barons don't mind innovations that disrupt outside their ecosystems. But they are concerned about any disruption that challenges (or potentially challenges) their ecosystem and value chains.

And while the business literature notes the difficulty in predicting the disruptiveness of innovation and the challenge for the incumbents to avoid being disrupted, the digital economy offers game-changing technologies that reverse the odds. As we'll see in chapter 3, the Tech Barons have tools that earlier monopolies lacked. Being in control of the ecosystem, they can use advanced technologies to identify, hunt, and marginalize the Tech Pirates that pose a potential threat. The Tech Barons do not have to worry about false positives (killing companies that may not turn out to be a Tech Pirate). Their concern is false negatives (not identifying potential threats to their value chain). With deep pockets, the rational strategy is to be as aggressive as one can be—namely to acquire, kill, or marginalize any possible threat (with limited pushback from government agencies). It brings to mind the last words of the Spanish general and conservative prime minister Ramón María Narváez, who supported Queen Isabella II. A priest asked Narváez on his deathbed if he would forgive his enemies. Narváez replied, "I do not have to forgive my enemies. I have had them all shot."

The Tech Barons benefit as they entrench their power and ringfence their value chains, while we pay the price in the loss of innovation plurality.

This is not an abstract proposition but a reality in the digital ecosystem economy. Consider WhatsApp. An outsider would not deem the texting app as a threat to Facebook's social network. Nor did WhatsApp's founders originally foresee their app disrupting the world's largest social network. Indeed, one of the app's cofounders shared an earlier version of the texting app with friends, "but none of them liked it." Moreover, "issues like battery draining, crashing of the app, etc. made [the cofounder] so disappointed that he lost all the hope and started to look for a new job."[51]

After WhatsApp's launch in 2009, it began rapidly acquiring users, and its functionalities, such as adding pictures, changed in response to how users were using the texting app.

But as WhatsApp was evolving, Facebook used advanced technology to monitor and assess the threat to see whether "an app offering mobile messaging services would enter the personal social networking market, either by adding personal social networking features or by launching a spinoff personal social networking app."[52] In an April 2012 email, for example, Mr. Zuckerberg identified the threat posed by the "messaging apps . . . using messages as a springboard to build more general mobile social networks."[53] And by October 2012, three years after its launch, Facebook executives and employees saw WhatsApp as a serious strategic threat. As a Facebook business growth director predicted internally, "[t]his might be the biggest threat we've ever faced as a company."[54] As Facebook's director of product management wrote to colleagues: "[T]his is the biggest threat to our product that I've ever seen in my 5 years here at Facebook; it's bigger than G+, and we're all terrified. These guys actually have a credible strategy: start with the most intimate social graph (I.e. [sic] the ones you message on mobile), and build from there."[55] At a February 2013 Facebook board presentation, the directors were warned that mobile messaging services were "a threat to our core businesses: both [with respect to] graph and content sharing. [T]hey are building gaming platforms, profiles, and news feeds. [T]hese competitors have all the ingredients for building a mobile-first social network."[56]

Through trial and error, WhatsApp was evolving beyond a texting app, and was adding features that threatened Facebook's social network. Indeed, WhatsApp was not tied to a particular platform (as was Apple's iMessage), nor was WhatsApp concentrated to specific regions (unlike LINE, Kakao, or WeChat). Being a Tech Pirate, WhatsApp offered innovations (both functional and privacy) that provided users greater value. Its innovations also challenged Facebook's value chain and offered a different value proposition. Plus, WhatsApp was scaling quickly, having, by February 2014, over 450 million monthly active users worldwide and gaining users at a rate of 1 million per day, placing it "on a path to connect 1 billion people."[57]

To eliminate the threat, in 2014 Facebook purchased the company for $19 billion. Facebook internally described the acquisition as a "land grab" that "[p]revents probably the only company which could have grown into the next [Facebook] purely on mobile."[58] Once under the Tech Baron's control, WhatsApp's business models and innovations were modified and aligned with Facebook's value chain. Facebook "cabined" WhatsApp to mobile messaging services,[59] and users were left with less innovation heterogeneity and fewer options outside the Tech Baron's value chain.

WhatsApp's fate is not unique. In subsequent chapters, we will explore other Tech Pirates that posed a threat and were targeted by the Tech Barons. For example, we will consider the fate of the privacy app Disconnect (which Google kicked out of its ecosystem), the search engine DuckDuckGo (which promotes privacy, but many have never heard of because of Apple's revenue-sharing agreement with Google); Aptoide (which was subject to Google's dark patterns); and Sonos (which was forced to limit its innovations of speakers with multiple digital assistants).

The next few chapters will elaborate on how the Tech Barons can distort the supply of, and demand for, innovation and undermine the risk of disruption. The Tech Baron, like the casino, does not always win. But it doesn't have to. It just needs to exclude those that threaten its value chains and profits (just as casinos use facial recognition software to exclude card counters and anyone else who has devised a way to improve the odds in their favor). The disruptive Tech Pirates may unwittingly find themselves at the center of the Tech Barons' dartboard. The potential threat they pose to the barons' hegemony may result in their being hunted and eliminated.

CHAPTER 3

Disrupting Disruptive Innovation

I N THE ANCIENT CHINESE military treatise *The Art of War*, Sun Tzu wrote:

The good fighter is able to secure himself against defeat. . . . Thus it is that in war the victorious strategist only seeks battle after the victory has been won, whereas he who is destined to defeat first fights and afterwards looks for victory.

The Tech Barons can secure themselves against defeat and tip the odds heavily in their favor by designing and controlling their ecosystems. They can plan and execute strategies that determine the flow of innovation and the level of access granted to third parties. Through their shaping strategies and attrition warfare, the Tech Barons can thin the ranks of disruptive Tech Pirates and manipulate the supply of innovation to protect their value chains. Using a range of exclusionary strategies, they won the battle before it began.

Those familiar with markets and business environments know that exclusion can be observed in many industries. Often, this strategy involves a company that leverages its market power to weaken rivals. Sometimes, the monopoly restricts access to a critical input; at other times, the dominant firm forecloses its rivals' access to distributors or customers. But in the Tech Barons' world, exclusion takes a distinctive dimension, exhibiting the scale, impact, and precision that earlier monopolies only dreamed of.

To appreciate the potency of the Tech Barons' exclusionary power, we will first look at the technologies they deploy to scan the ecosystem and identify and target potential disruptors. We will then explore some of the Tech Barons' myriad exclusionary tactics to decrease the odds of dynamic disruption. As their grip over the ecosystem increases, innovation diversity diminishes.

How Tech Barons Spot Tech Pirates

Few Tech Pirates announce themselves as disruptive innovators. Indeed, Tech Pirates are often unaware of how disruptive their innovations will be.

Past monopolies did not often know where or when the next nascent competitive threat might emerge. For the lazy monopolists, that shortcoming presaged their demise. For the neurotic monopolists it led to tyrannical behavior, with them indiscriminately lashing out at potential rivals. But they generally never saw the lethal threat.

This left monopolies open to the risk of disruption from innovation that emerged outside their network of existing suppliers and customers. The business and strategic literature underscores the challenge in identifying disruption.

But Tech Barons have the edge over traditional industries. So what makes them different from past monopolies, like Kodak, in their ability to identify potential disruptors at an early stage? How does big data analytics act as a game-changer?[1]

The Tech Barons, unlike past monopolies, don't just benefit from market power; they control expanding ecosystems, where others operate. From this position of power and collection of data, which is further enhanced by the use of search inquiries; monitoring of social network postings and tweets; and surveilling service providers, sellers, or users, the Tech Barons can identify market patterns and discern trends (and threats) well before others.[2] They deploy advanced analytics that transform the near-perfect market surveillance into a detailed picture of ongoing market activities, trends, and emerging threats. We refer to this technology as *nowcasting radars*.

Using their nowcasting radar, these Tech Barons can monitor in real-time competitive portals where start-ups may emerge—within and outside their ecosystem—and identify and neutralize nascent threats. They can track the nascent competitive threats shortly after they take off and intercept or shoot them down long before they become visible to competition authorities and others. At times, the Tech Barons may better understand the technology's disruptive potential than the Tech Pirates themselves, as they see the whole ecosystem and can identify trends, opportunities, and threats.

Data advantage turns the nowcasting technology into a game-changer. Facebook, for example, acquired the data-security app Onavo to track users' smartphone activity.[3] That technology was central in Facebook's identifying WhatsApp as a potential threat. As several US states alleged in their complaint against Facebook:

> Zuckerberg and his top executives closely monitored the Early Birds Reports and other analyses derived from Onavo data to watch for emerging competitive threats. For example, Onavo data and analytics played a significant role in Facebook's targeting and ultimate acquisition of WhatsApp. According to one Facebook executive, Zuckerberg was "focused on Onavo data" identifying new market entrants with "extreme growth." Sheryl Sandberg, according to Guy Rosen, applauded the Onavo acquisition and described it as the "gift that keeps on giving."[4]

Facebook, of course, is not alone in its ability to monitor its ecosystem and beyond.[5] Amazon, for example, accessed third-party sellers' data "to identify and replicate popular and profitable products from among the hundreds of millions of listings on its marketplace."[6] Superior surveillance, access to data, and advanced monitoring enable the Tech Barons to identify user trends and potential threats.

For Tech Pirates operating inside or adjacent to the Tech Barons' ecosystems, the exposure is evident. Being subjected to ongoing monitoring and targeting, Tech Pirates have fewer places to hide. They operate in a landscape that is often transparent to the Tech Baron, who has access to non-public information and insights on market trends. So, the nowcasting radar itself can chill disruptive innovation. Would you set sail if your moves could be precisely monitored? Perhaps. But would you do so if you could be torpedoed at any time?

Tech Barons' Torpedoes

Besides its nowcasting radar, the Tech Baron can resort to an arsenal of additional weapons to distort the supply of innovation, all of which are designed to diminish the Tech Pirate's viability and ability to scale up.

We'll look at three strategies: (1) excluding the Tech Pirate from the ecosystem or reducing its visibility; (2) reducing interoperability with the Tech Pirate's innovation; and (3) copying the Tech Pirate's innovation. Tech Pirates must either sail to another ecosystem or adjust the innovation to comport with the existing value chain to survive.

As we'll see, the critical point is that the Tech Baron, with its torpedoes, can blast the Tech Pirate out of the market, platform, and ecosystem. The more powerful the Tech Baron, the more lethal and exclusionary its torpedo, and the fewer times it needs to resort to its arsenal. The knowledge and threat of a torpedo and the floating bodies of pirates will likely chill future disruptors.

Exclusion Torpedo

Apple and Google control the two dominant mobile phone operating systems and app stores. They design the interface, set the rules of engagement, and determine which apps enter their app stores. Let's consider a simple example of exclusion—Google or Apple kicks an innovative app out of its app store. The impact is not simply being removed from a particular platform but being banished from their entire ecosystem.

Tech Pirates that wish to develop apps with new services or technologies must rely on Google's and Apple's software development kits (SDKs). They need to create an app record, beta test the app, submit the app and metadata to Google and Apple for review, and await the Tech Barons' decisions.[7] In controlling the entry gate, the Tech Barons can kill disruptive innovation before we are even aware of it. Alternatively, the Tech Barons can demand changes to the app to align with their strategies and value chains.

The simplest, most lethal form of exclusion is to reject an app whose innovation threatens that ecosystem or kick it out when the threat becomes apparent.

Apple, for example, rejected almost one million apps submitted for the first time and rejected nearly one million app updates in 2020.[8] These are high numbers, but of course not all those excluded are Tech Pirates. Many apps were likely banned for the opposite reason—because they undermined our interests.

For example, Apple removed 48,000 apps for using "hidden or undocumented features," often software tools that Apple uses internally for its own apps; 150,000 apps because they were spam or copied another app; 215,000 apps because they collected too much user data or other privacy violations; and 95,000 apps because they changed after Apple's review to become a different kind of app, including gambling apps or pornography. But that leaves hundreds of thousands of apps kicked off for other unspecified reasons. The bottom line is that between 2017 and 2019, Apple reviewed roughly five million apps per year, including updates, and rejected between 33 and 36 percent of them annually.[9]

Needless to say, an exclusion initiated by Apple to protect our privacy and interests is welcomed. But the point here is the Tech Barons' absolute power over access. There is no guaranteed right of due process. No assured recourse to the courts or antitrust agencies. Because of Google's and Apple's scale and control over the mobile operating systems, there is no alternative. If you offer a new ride-sharing app, and Google and Apple reject your app for whatever reason, your app is dead. If the Tech Baron does not want you in its ecosystem, your chances of survival are slim to nil. And if you happen to be a disruptive Tech Pirate with value-creating innovation, your loss is also ours.

Once excluded from the app store, the app is hobbled and cannot achieve the necessary scale. The app is not only banished from the app store but the entire ecosystem. One cannot currently install an app on one's iPhone unless it's included in Apple's App Store. That means no access to the estimated 118.1 million iPhone users in the US[10] and over 1 billion iPhone users worldwide. Apple users typically buy other Apple products precisely because they synch, so the app is now invisible on the smartwatch and iPad. Although customers may technically download the Tech Pirate's software on their MacBooks or iMacs, why bother when they can't use it on their other Apple devices.

Thus, banishment from the app store means banishment from that ecosystem. Immediately the app loses a crucial audience segment and scale, as Apple users cannot download Android apps and vice versa.

Even wildly popular apps like the gaming app Fortnite are not immune. Despite being available on multiple platforms, Epic Games saw a 60 percent decline in the number of iOS users playing the game after Apple kicked Fortnite out of its app store.[11]

If Google kicks an app out of its Play Store, it is possible to sideload the app. Still, as we'll see in the next chapter, it will likely remain invisible to the estimated two billion Android users worldwide.[12]

To understand the crippling effect of exclusion and how it may deprive us of value-creating innovation, let's consider the mobile application Disconnect. One of Disconnect's cofounders, Brian Kennish, was an engineer at Google. In 2010, he read how the most popular apps on Facebook "were transmitting users' identifying information to dozens of advertising and internet tracking companies, without disclosure or permission."[13] So, Kennish went home and wrote an "extension" for Google's Chrome browser, which blocked connections between third-party sites and Facebook servers without interfering with the user's connection to Facebook. Within two weeks, his extension was downloaded fifty thousand times. After realizing that his employer was among the more significant collectors of the personal data that his extension was intended to protect, Kennish left Google in November 2010 to focus on online privacy.

Disconnect offers four privacy functions: the ability of users to see otherwise undisclosed web tracking and privacy policies, virtual private networking (VPN) technology, private search, and private browsing.

Unlike many other apps within the Google ecosystem, Disconnect does not secretly collect users' geolocation information. Nor does it track users' activities across the web. Unlike Google and the many apps in Google Play, Disconnect does not rely on advertising revenues. It does not sell its users' data to advertisers, ad networks, or data brokers. Disconnect makes its money "by selling its products to users."[14] The basic version of its mobile app is free; users pay for the "Pro" and "Premium" versions.

After launching its mobile app in 2014, Disconnect received an e-mail from the Google Play team. Google had removed the app from its Play Store because the app "interferes with or accesses another service or product in an unauthorized manner."[15] As Google warned the app maker:

All violations are tracked. Serious or repeated violations of any nature will result in the termination of your developer account, and investigation and possible termination of related Google accounts. If your account is terminated, payments will cease and Google may recover the proceeds of any past sales and/or the cost of any associated fees (such as charge-backs and transaction fees) from you.[16]

Disconnect was popular. As the *Wall Street Journal* reported, "In the six days it was available in Google's store, it was downloaded more than five thousand times."[17] Google readmitted Disconnect, only to kick it out again.

Disconnect tried to make its app compliant with Google's rules. But Google's policies were "so vague that Google could, in essence, ban any app in its store."[18] As Disconnect's cofounder said, "It's like a Kafka novel—you're getting kicked out or arrested for reasons you don't even know."[19]

Disconnect was not alone. According to the *Wall Street Journal*, Google had removed other ad-blocking apps, such as Adblock Plus, from its Play Store. While kicking out some apps that safeguarded users' privacy by preventing tracking, Google did not kick out all apps promising to protect users' privacy.

Disconnect eventually complained to the European Commission, contending that Google had abused its dominant position. In its ninety-five-page complaint, Disconnect questioned why Google does not protect Android users from the risks associated with tracking. For example, Google's Chrome browser does not provide details on which websites and web services respect "Do Not Track" requests or how they interpret them. As Google reports, "most Web services, including Google's, do not alter their behavior or change their services upon receiving Do Not Track requests."[20]

Disconnect also explained how Google's privacy features in 2015 were weak. Google told users they could opt out of targeted advertising. But app developers could circumvent Google's targeted advertising opt-out feature in Android. Moreover, Google's opt-out feature only stopped Google from showing you "interest-based" ads. Opting out did not stop ads altogether, including ads based on your recent searches or general location. Opting out would not disable other companies' interest-based ads. Nor did the opt-out automatically apply whenever you used other browsers on that device or other devices. Thus, you would have to opt out for each browser you used on each PC, tablet, and smartphone. Nor would opting out keep you opted out after you cleared your browser's cookies. Nor would it opt you out of interest-based ads in services where cookie technology may not be available. Nor did the opt-out feature prevent Google or any other company from tracking you; it only prevented a targeted ad under certain circumstances.

Google, for its part, rejected the complaint as baseless; Disconnect was removed from the ecosystem because its blocking services prevented other applications from legitimately earning money. That interference infringed Google Play's apps policy. Google noted that over two hundred privacy apps that did not violate its policies were available in Google Play (but none of these apps ever disrupted Google's business model).

After Google removed Disconnect from its Play Store, Android users could no longer search for or find the privacy app in the Play Store, and its downloads and sales for a premium version of the app declined.

Disconnect developed the technology to empower users and allow them to circumvent the ongoing harvesting of their data throughout the digital ecosystem. The new disruptive technology threatened to undermine the Tech Baron's value chain—its behavioral advertising model.

So even though Disconnect complained to the European Commission in 2016, no enforcement action, as of early 2022, was taken. The privacy application became invisible within the Android ecosystem. We were curious what impact this banishment had on the Tech Pirate's privacy innovation. So, we spoke with Casey Oppenheim, Disconnect's chief executive officer. He described the challenging reality faced by innovators that promote technology that may destabilize the interest of the Tech Barons:

> You are in a difficult situation, you can invest hundreds of thousands of dollars in new technology, and of course there are also significant opportunity costs, and yet there is no legal recourse if the platform decides to exclude you. This creates a significant chilling effect. The reality is that from both a financial and legal perspective, it is difficult to invest in a product that is disruptive to the platform's interest. With the way the rules are set and imposed on app providers, they can kick you out for any reason once you disrupt their ecosystem. In the mobile ecosystem, two companies—Google and Apple—can decide if you live or die. You simply don't exist unless you are in their app stores.

The chilling effect on disruption is apparent. In blocking Disconnect, Google sent a message to every other app developer that is potentially interested in investing in a privacy app that could undermine Google's behavioral advertising model.

The result? If the ecosystem is your gateway to customers and the market, you'd better align with its strategies. So, Disconnect's existence hinges perilously on Apple's beneficence. If Apple wants to co-opt Disconnect's privacy technology, it can. If Disconnect complains, it has no recourse. And if Apple also kicks out Disconnect, it is dead.

The Interoperability Torpedo

Microsoft, Amazon, and Facebook don't have significant app stores. So, how can they torpedo Tech Pirates? Even when the Tech Barons do not engage in outright exclusion, they may undermine disruption from Tech Pirates through technological foreclosure and reduced interoperability. These powerful gatekeepers can block or weaken the Tech Pirates by denying them synergies.

Interoperability, as an important 2020 congressional antitrust report described, is "fundamental to the open internet."[21] Interoperability opens the supply lanes for innovation by increasing the opportunities for synergies and reducing customers' switching costs. At a basic level, the Tech Pirate's technology must work well with other essential services within the Tech Barons' ecosystems. If it doesn't work, users will blame the Tech Pirate, not the Tech Baron. So, one significant risk is that the Tech Baron will hinder the performance of the Tech Pirate's technology or its ability to communicate seamlessly with the customers.

For example, the Tech Baron can deny the Tech Pirates access to its application programming interfaces (APIs). APIs are "'libraries' of prepackaged computer code that assist different pieces of software in communicating with one another."[22] App developers use APIs "when they want their app to request data from the operating system or from other applications, among other tasks."[23] So, Google Play Services APIs are essential to app developers. Without access to Google Play Services, "any app using location and mapping functionality (e.g., ride-sharing and real estate apps), push notifications (e.g., many apps that create reminders, location-based triggers, or personalized notifications), or Google's Ad-Mob (i.e., apps that monetize through in-app advertising) will not properly function."[24]

But, even if the Tech Pirate's technology works at a basic level, the Tech Barons can improve interoperability for its own (or favored) technologies, which effectively degrades interoperability for the disfavored technologies.

Think about it. How many of us use (or even remember) MapQuest, which was once the dominant mapping application? AOL purchased it in 1999 for $1 billion; Verizon later acquired it when acquiring AOL. In 2019, Verizon sold MapQuest to System1, an ad-tech company, for an undisclosed amount, which was "not material enough for Verizon to file paperwork."[25]

Multiple problems befell MapQuest, including underestimating Google Maps. But a crucial issue was interoperability. Not only did Apple and Google set their competing mapping apps as the default on Android and iOS (which as we'll discuss in the next chapter affects the demand for innovation), but each Tech Baron had its mapping app work seamlessly with its other products and services (such as the browser, search engine, and calendar, which automatically used the Tech Baron's mapping app).

Interoperability is so vital that even the Tech Barons warn their investors about how other Tech Barons might hinder their interoperability. Consider Facebook's warning of this risk:

> We are dependent on the interoperability of Facebook and our other products with popular mobile operating systems, networks, technologies, products, and standards that we do not control, such as the Android and iOS operating systems and mobile browsers.[26]

So how could a Tech Baron reduce interoperability? Facebook identified myriad ways, including:

- Changes, bugs, or technical issues in such systems;

- Changes in its relationships with mobile operating system partners, handset manufacturers, browser developers, or mobile carriers; and

- Changes in terms of service or policies that
  * degrade its products' functionality,
  * reduce or eliminate its ability to update or distribute its products,
  * give preferential treatment to competitive products,
  * limit its ability to deliver, target, or measure the effectiveness of ads, or
  * charge fees related to the distribution of its products or its delivery of ads.

Ironically, while Facebook warns investors about how the other Tech Barons can hinder its apps' functionality, Facebook used this torpedo to kill off Tech Pirates. One example is the Facebook Platform, which the company built early on as an operating system to connect other applications to Facebook's social graph. Zuckerberg touted it when testifying before Congress in 2020.

Seemingly the Facebook Platform is a "triple win."

Facebook users win (in quickly signing on to apps and webpages with their Facebook ID, using Facebook's social plugins, like the Like button, while on other websites or apps, and using other features like finding their Facebook friends on the new app or website).[27]

Third-party developers win (in attracting Facebook users, reading from and writing data to Facebook, and integrating their pages with Facebook's).

Facebook wins (the more app developers that build onto its platforms, the more attractive Facebook becomes relative to rival social networks; Facebook collects more data on its users and non-users when they aren't on Facebook, which the company uses to increase its advantage for behavioral advertising revenues).

As Facebook grew, it recognized that "access to its social graph provided other applications with a tool for significant growth."[28] By 2012, with its dominance secured, Facebook reexamined its position. As one of its senior executives observed:

> When we started Facebook Platform, we were small and wanted to make sure we were an essential part of the fabric of the Internet. We've done that—we're now the biggest service on earth. When we were small, apps helped drive our ubiquity. Now that we are big, (many) apps are looking to siphon off our users to competitive services. We need to be more thoughtful about what integrations we allow and we need to make sure that we have sustainable, long-term value exchanges.[29]

So, under its CEO's direction, Facebook used its nowcasting radar to identify whether the app was a "friend or foe." Facebook, as the antitrust authorities alleged, reduced the interoperability of those social apps that became too popular and a potential threat to Facebook's products.

In doing so, Facebook degraded the experience of its users when they were on these threatening start-ups, including Vine, a video-sharing app that Twitter acquired in 2012. Believing that the app "replicated Facebook's core News Feed functionality,"[30] Facebook cut off Vine's access to its Facebook APIs. Facebook users could no longer readily find their Facebook friends on Vine.[31] Vine died a few years later. So, Facebook created "whitelists," where it gave preferential treatment to friends of the company, including Amazon, which "was spending money on advertising and partnering with Facebook on the launch of its Fire smartphone," while cutting off perceived innovation threats.[32]

In reducing interoperability, the Tech Baron can weaponize network effects, increase the innovator's costs to access users, and reduce the functionality of the innovative product. The interoperability torpedo skews the supply of innovations. Social apps, for example, will be less likely to innovate features that might be better than Facebook's, when doing so cuts them off from Facebook's social graph. Instead, to avoid being cut off, companies will innovate on complementary features that will significantly benefit Facebook, but not necessarily Facebook's users, as we'll see in chapter 6.

Copycat Torpedo

Our third torpedo is unique. Tech Barons may use their control over the ecosystem and their nowcasting radars to cannibalize innovations developed by others. What is so special about copying someone else's innovations? It isn't simply about ripping off innovators to make more profits. By copying key aspects of the Tech Pirate's technologies, the torpedo can deprive the innovator of reaching scale, which is often critical in the digital economy. Without scale, the Tech Pirate cannot appropriate its investment in the innovation.

The law, particularly intellectual property law (IP law), offers only limited protection to innovators who find themselves in this position. This is because many innovative products, services, and ideas are simply not protectable under IP law. Not everything can be patented, not everything forms a protected right, and sometimes the innovators lack the financial resources to cover all bases, even when protection might be possible.

Let's start by looking at the defensive use of the copycat torpedo to deprive Tech Pirates' scale: in copying the innovation and embedding it in its own products and services, the Tech Baron reduces the incentives of its users to switch. Being in control of the ecosystem enables the Tech Baron to move fast and cannibalize the threat. Facebook's CEO outlined this strategy:

> It's possible someone beats Instagram by building something that is better to the point that they get network migration, but this is harder as long as Instagram keeps running as a product . . . one way of looking at this is that what we're really buying is time. Even if some new competitors springs [sic] up, buying Instagram now . . . will give us a year or more to integrate their dynamics before anyone can get close to their scale again. Within that time, if we incorporate the social mechanics

they were using, those new products won't get much traction since we'll already have their mechanics deployed at scale . . .[33]

Mark Zuckerberg's insight, while anticompetitive, is brilliant. By 2021, approximately 3.51 billion people were using at least one of the company's core products (Facebook, WhatsApp, Instagram, or Messenger) each month.[34] That's approximately 44.5 percent of the world's population. Each of its interlocking platforms benefits from multiple network effects. As more people join the platform, the more attractive it becomes for others until the market tips in the leader's favor. But network effects also make it harder for others to leave the platform unless they can convince others to switch to another platform. So, Facebook knows that its users' switching costs are already high (especially when users log in to other accounts using Facebook) and get higher as more people join Facebook's platforms.

But now suppose a new platform, like Snapchat or TikTok, emerges with innovations that may lure us away from the Tech Baron. To reduce our incentive to switch, Facebook copies the innovative features of rivals (Snapchat is a great example) or simply acquires them (we'll examine these acquisitions in chapter 5). Most Facebook users will likely ask why switch to Snap when something similar, maybe not as good, but decent, is available on Instagram?

After identifying Snapchat as a possible threat, Facebook sought to buy the start-up. When its offer was rejected, Facebook shifted into cloning mode, trying to eliminate Snapchat's advantage. After it cloned Snapchat's innovative features, "Snap's potential slice of the advertising market shriveled to a sliver."[35]

The copying not only deprives the rivals of scale but also chills the incentives of other would-be innovators. After all, few pirates have the resources to take on the Tech Barons in lengthy and costly legal battles. Rather than disrupt the Tech Baron's power, would-be Tech Pirates again pursue innovations that complement the Tech Baron's services, especially when the Tech Pirate would need to turn to the Tech Baron for funding. It might be the start-up's last cash infusion. In essence, rather than disrupting, the potential Tech Pirate helps fortify the dominant eco-system value chain by offering complementary features.

Besides the copycat torpedo's defensive use, the Tech Baron can use it offensively to simply extract value from third-party innovations (that do not necessarily threaten the ecosystem's value chain).

Basically, the copying by the Tech Barons chills the incentives of future innovators. Amazon, for example, was accused of using its nowcasting radar to cannibalize products and innovation of third-party sellers. Among other things, Amazon allegedly used its investment fund to identify potential threats even before the Tech Pirates' innovations reached Amazon's ecosystem. You may have heard, for example, of the start-up Nucleus, which specialized in the development of voice-activated digital helpers. Its technology impressed Amazon. So, the start-up received a substantial cash injection of millions of dollars from Amazon's Alexa investment fund. But the start-up's luck turned when Amazon released its voice-controlled device—the Echo Show—that embodies the functions of the Nucleus product.[36] Nucleus CEO Jonathan Frankel was "surprised by the brazenness with which Amazon has gone after one of its own portfolio companies." He reportedly said that:

> They [Amazon] must realize that by trying to trample over us—a premier partner in the Alexa Fund ecosystem—that they are going to really cripple that ecosystem and put a warning out for others. . . . If they're really willing to threaten that, it must be a huge opportunity.[37]

Amazon reacted to the accusation by stating that it "did not get the idea for Echo Show from Nucleus." Commenting on this story, one venture capitalist described Amazon's investment and launch of an almost identical product as a "very, very strange coincidence."[38]

Another example concerns the start-up DefinedCrowd, which benefited from investment by Amazon's venture capital fund. Four years after the investment, after being privy to the developments of the start-up, Amazon launched its artificial-intelligence product A2I, which clones much of what DefinedCrowd does. Daniela Braga,

DefinedCrowd's founder and chief executive, noted how the new product from Amazon competes directly "with one of our bread-and-butter foundational products."[39] Ms. Braga was "one of more than two dozen entrepreneurs, investors and deal advisers interviewed by the *Wall Street Journal* who said Amazon appeared to use the investment and deal-making process to help develop competing products."[40]

Commenting on Amazon strategies, one partner at the venture capital firm Bessemer Venture Partners said, "They are using market forces in a really Machiavellian way. It's like they are not in any way, shape or form the proverbial wolf in sheep's clothing. They are a wolf in wolf's clothing."[41]

Reflections

In its controlled ecosystem, a Tech Baron can punish Tech Pirates by engaging in *multidimensional exclusion*. The impact of such exclusion cannot be overstated, as the Tech Barons are much more powerful than past monopolies, which could often engage in unidimensional exclusion.

To illustrate, suppose a Tech Pirate is kicked out of a town (market). While it loses access to the town's customer network and distribution channels, there remain other opportunities in other cities with other customers. That typically was the scenario in the brick-and-mortar economy.

Now imagine if the innovator is kicked out of a country (platform). The path ahead for the Tech Pirate is no doubt harder because it lacks access to an entire infrastructure. But it is still possible to disrupt.

Having been excluded from a platform, the Tech Pirate might have to create or join another platform. However, the Tech Pirate that hopes to become a rival platform runs into the chicken-and-egg problem posed by network effects (where, for example, independent program developers design their products for the leading platform, as was the case with

Microsoft Windows). Disrupting a platform is more challenging than disrupting a single market. The Tech Pirate needs to attract independent developers to create programs for its platform to attract customers, and it needs to attract many customers to attract these software developers.

Nonetheless, a Tech Pirate can still innovate and disrupt with a new platform outside that value chain. Consider Apple's iPhone. It wasn't developed to disrupt the personal computer (or Microsoft's hegemony). Indeed, many of the functions of the iPhone (including apps) weren't part of the original version, which Apple released in 2007. Instead, the iPhone was released to prevent disruption to Apple's preexisting iPod business, as one Apple executive recounted:

> In June 2017, during a talk at the Computer History Museum, Scott Forstall, who led iOS development at Apple under Steve Jobs, said that Apple had been working on a tablet project, but Jobs realized that mobile phones were becoming a threat to Apple's then massive iPod business which made about half of Apple's sales. Jobs was wondering what device could cannibalize its iPod music sales, and a new phone seemed like a needful thing. Forstall and Jobs were at lunch once, when they noticed that no one looked happy using their phones despite everyone having one. So, Jobs suggested shrinking the tablet touch demo to a pocketable size. When Jobs saw a demo of a new phone, he exclaimed, "OK, put the tablet on hold. Let's build a phone."[42]

Microsoft could not exclude Apple's new mobile phone operating system and later tablets that would eventually disrupt its Windows operating system monopoly. In controlling the leading personal computer operating system platform, Microsoft could exclude technologies that threatened its dominance (like middleware such as the Netscape browser). And Microsoft remains the dominant operating system for personal computers.[43] But at that time, Microsoft did not control an ecosystem.

Now imagine if the Tech Pirate is excluded from an entire empire that expands across continents. For the innovator, it becomes far harder to disrupt. Again, not impossible, as even the greatest empires eventually declined. But it takes way longer.

Being excluded or marginalized from the Tech Baron's ecosystem means being invisible in a constellation of products and services (whether computers, smartphones, tablets, smartwatches, digital assistants, driverless cars, virtual reality, cloud computing) that work seamlessly together. Being marginalized from Google's ecosystem, for example, means being invisible on the leading search engine (where many websites receive their traffic), on the leading map service, leading app store, and one of the few significant cloud computing services. But it also means being invisible (or hard to find and use) on the leading mobile operating system worldwide (with a 73 percent share in mid-2021).[44] The Tech Baron can also require app developers, equipment manufacturers, and others within its ecosystem to shun the Tech Pirates (or otherwise risk being expelled or punished themselves). So, the Tech Barons have others within their ecosystems marginalize the Tech Pirates as well.

As the Tech Barons expand their empire, the remaining Tech Pirates are prevented from obtaining scale, foreclosed from accessing even secondary markets, and face a harder time attracting their target customer groups. Under such conditions, the survival rate of the disruptive innovator plummets. Innovation will continue within the Tech Barons' ecosystem, but the nature of innovation changes. Rather than *disruptive innovations*, the innovations might be largely *incremental* and *complementary* to the dominant platform's technology and services (such as developing apps for a mobile operating system). Innovation simply reinforces the Tech Baron's power and user lock-in. As two economists noted, "once a certain technology becomes dominant, subsequent adoptions will most likely be of the same type enhancing its leading position."[45] Thus, the primary beneficiaries of the innovation might change. The supply of innovation, including the raw materials for innovation (such as personal data, which conceivably could benefit multiple constituencies, including nonprofit and governmental entities), now primarily serves the Tech Barons' interests.

But some Tech Pirates will likely escape the torpedoes. As they do, they might expect consumers to reward them by at least trying their product. But upon arriving on the shore, the Tech Pirates might find few, if any, customers to greet them or try their innovation. That's because, as the next chapter explores, the Tech Barons can also distort the demand for disruptive innovation.

CHAPTER 4

Distorting the Demand for Innovation

BIRDS MIGRATING ACROSS THE world, for many, reflect freedom, the blithe Spirit, as the poet Percy Shelley noted on an evening walk with his wife, Mary. Migration also reflects evolution, as some species survive by changing their habits in search of warmer, more hospitable climes.

The blackcap, for example, used to escape the harsh winter of eastern Europe and migrate to southern Europe and Africa. The arduous journey, which at times required crossing the Mediterranean, was essential for food and survival.

Since the 1960s, however, a new pattern emerged. More blackcaps migrated to the UK, which, while known for many delights, a pleasant winter is not among them. How did that happen? Humans.

Increasingly the British have been putting out bird food during the winter, turning an otherwise dreary season for blackcaps into a Las Vegas food buffet. From the birds' perspective, there is no evolutionary mandate that they travel to warmer climes. They can migrate to where the weather is lousy but the food is decent. Little did the British know how their dispersal of food was radically altering the blackcaps' evolutionary patterns and drying out other habitats.[1]

Why begin our discussion on demand for innovation with blackcaps? Because it helps illustrate an important point about our adoption of new technologies. Many of us tend to think we're independent, spontaneous, free-spirited, and unique. But in the grand scheme of things, what if we are somewhat similar to the blackcaps? What if we are predictable and malleable? So much so that an algorithm can reveal our identity from several data points (including our geolocation data) and can divine our secrets, which we believe are closely guarded, with enough of our Likes on Facebook and our online interactions, to then influence our behavior.

What if we, like the blackcaps, primarily serve the amusement, enjoyment, or strategic gain of others? At least the British care about the blackcaps and take joy in feeding and observing them. But what if the Tech Barons look at us as the means to extract value? They spread the birdseed around their ecosystem and value chains. While we believe we're snowflakes—unique, unpredictable, and autonomous—our value is in our predictability and manipulability that serve the Tech Barons' ends.

This chapter considers how the Tech Barons can impact our demand for disruptive innovation. Here we see the flip side of the nowcasting radar and three torpedoes. This side of the story is essential. While the Tech Barons can exclude the disruptive Tech Pirates from their ecosystems, they cannot permanently eliminate all Tech Pirates from the digital or brick-and-mortar economy. However, they can deprive them of scale by dictating the direction in which we migrate.

The Demand for Innovation

Earlier generations often took decades to adopt game-changing technologies, like landline telephones and automobiles. By contrast, today it typically takes only years, if not months, to adopt major technologies, such as tablets and the latest smartphones. Of course, no one can accurately predict which innovations will succeed or fail or the adoption rate for a particular invention. And yet, at times, a technology, despite being beneficial *and having potential demand*, never takes off or is delayed in its adoption. Why? Part of the answer may be found in the Tech Barons' ability to distort the demand for innovation.

To illustrate this power, we turn to Everett M. Rogers's seminal five stages of users' adoption, which many business students may recall.[2] Adoption, as outlined in Figure 4.1 below, begins with knowledge and persuasion, leading to decision, implementation, and confirmation:

Figure 4.1

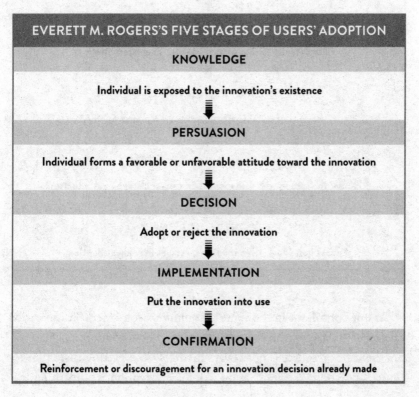

EVERETT M. ROGERS'S FIVE STAGES OF USERS' ADOPTION

KNOWLEDGE

Individual is exposed to the innovation's existence

PERSUASION

Individual forms a favorable or unfavorable attitude toward the innovation

DECISION

Adopt or reject the innovation

IMPLEMENTATION

Put the innovation into use

CONFIRMATION

Reinforcement or discouragement for an innovation decision already made

Using Rogers's seminal framework, we'll illustrate how today's Tech Barons can encourage us to quickly adopt the innovations that fortify or expand their ecosystem and dissuade us from using the Tech Pirates' products and services (even though these disruptive innovations may offer us more options and significantly benefit us).

In Figure 4.2, we modify Rogers's five stages to reflect the power of the Tech Barons to distort the demand for innovation.

Figure 4.2

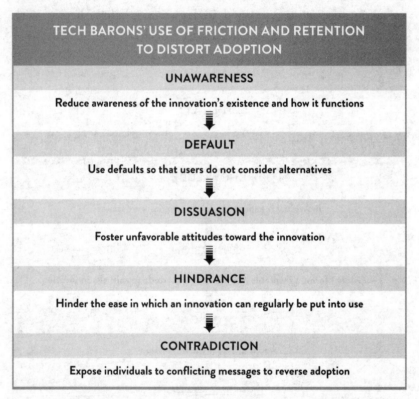

TECH BARONS' USE OF FRICTION AND RETENTION TO DISTORT ADOPTION

UNAWARENESS

Reduce awareness of the innovation's existence and how it functions

DEFAULT

Use defaults so that users do not consider alternatives

DISSUASION

Foster unfavorable attitudes toward the innovation

HINDRANCE

Hinder the ease in which an innovation can regularly be put into use

CONTRADICTION

Expose individuals to conflicting messages to reverse adoption

As one consultant in the venture community observed, "it can easily take a start-up two to three years to cross a technology-adoption chasm."[3] So, the scarce resource is not always the R&D, but getting customers to notice and adopt the innovation. And our attention is something the

Tech Barons often control. The more time we spend within their eco-systems, the more information the Tech Barons collect about us, the more experiments they can conduct, and the better they can predict and manipulate our behavior. As they do, they can reduce our adoption rate of many potentially disruptive innovations.

Two fundamental forces that affect the adoption of innovation in the digital economy are *friction* and *retention*. So, to reduce the adoption rate of the Tech Pirates' innovations, the Tech Barons increase retention of users, reduce friction to the complementary sustaining innovations that fortify their ecosystem, and increase friction to the potentially disruptive innovations. The path to the Tech Barons' creations is frictionless (think, for example, how Amazon's Buy Box reduces friction for purchasing items). In contrast, our path to the Tech Pirates has many obstacles, enough to deprive the Tech Pirates of scale and experimentation.

Granted, the technologies anointed by a Tech Baron will not al-ways prevail. But a Tech Baron through the retention/friction levers can increase the odds of a given technology's adoption or failure, not-withstanding our conviction that we are making our choices freely and choosing the technology strictly "on the merits."

The retention/friction levers help explain why it took so long for us to effectively use ad-blocking technology while surfing the web on our smartphones. As we'll see, Apple and Google for years stifled this tech-nology, using the five "friction" stages. Let's start with the first stage.

From Knowledge to Unawareness

The easiest way to prevent us from adopting an innovation is to make it harder to find. Our time and attention are finite. The more time we spend within the Tech Barons' ecosystems using the technologies they encourage us to use, the less time and attention we can devote to alter-natives.

To exist in today's digital economy, companies need visibility within GAFAM's ecosystems. How many apps have you used that were either: (1) not preloaded on your phone or (2) that you did not find in Google's or Apple's app stores? Probably none. To adopt an innovation or seek it outside of the Tech Barons' ecosystems, we first must know about the innovation and how it functions.

By controlling the ecosystem, the Tech Barons have the power to shape our awareness in their favor. Take, for example, behavioral advertising. One supposed benefit of behavioral advertising and its attendant surveillance and profiling is the personalization of recommendations. The Tech Barons can identify innovations relevant to our preexisting needs by accumulating a significant volume and variety of personal data. Thus, the Tech Barons can use the behavioral advertising tools to identify likely adopters of the innovation, increase their awareness of the particular innovation, and help persuade them to use it. So, the Tech Barons will reduce our search costs to discover and use the favored innovations (those that fortify their ecosystem). Consider, for example, how Google used its search engine to increase our knowledge of its favored technologies—whether they are comparison shopping tools, browsers, or maps.

As their ecosystem expands and we rely on the Tech Barons for news and entertainment, the Tech Barons can suggest a story about the favored innovation in their news feed or a targeted ad. As we spend more time interacting with the Tech Barons' digital assistants, whether in our home, car, or on the run (with our smartwatches or smart glasses), the Tech Barons will have more opportunities to recommend our trying a favored innovation. Currently, we can spend days with the two hundred–plus innovation-related skills on Alexa and Google Home, listening to hours of innovation-related podcasts such as "game-changing—killer innovations."[4] These digital assistants will eventually recommend specific innovations for us to consider, explain how the innovation can help us, and win us over on the technology. Even if the innovation wastes our time, that is still a victory, as we had less time to discover and experiment with the Tech Pirates' innovation.

On the flip side, the Tech Barons can make it harder to find the pirates' disruptive innovations. For any company, besides those with famous brands, if they are not easily found within the Tech Barons' ecosystem, they might as well not exist. Consider driving cross-country on the highways. What we see on Google Maps, Waze, or Apple Maps often reflects our reality of nearby gas stations, coffee shops, and restaurants. Likewise, if most people start (and stop) their shopping on Amazon, that means for many third-party merchants that they might as well not exist if they are not on Amazon.

So, if a Tech Baron wants to kill an innovation that threatens its profits or business model, it doesn't necessarily have to kick it out of its ecosystem. It just has to make it a little harder to discover. The increase in friction can be remarkably minuscule. In theory, we could still find the innovation. But in reality, we will unlikely have the incentive to embark on this time-consuming search.

Think for a second: How much energy is required to scroll to the second or even third page of search results? Very little. But few of us have the time or attention to venture beyond the first page of the search results.

For example, in the *Google Shopping* case, the European Commission accused the dominant search engine of favoring its comparison-shopping website. Google recognized internally that its comparison shopping website was inferior in quality to rival offerings.[5] So, to increase traffic to its shopping service, Google positioned it at the top of the search page. At the same time, it degraded rivals' shopping websites to the fourth (or subsequent) page of search results, which few people visit. As a result, many of us stopped using the rivals' services and began using Google's inferior service.

The commission's findings are telling: on the first page of Google's generic search results (on a desktop computer), the ten highest-ranking generic search results generally received approximately 95 percent of all clicks (with the top result receiving about 35 percent of all the clicks). On page 2 of Google's search results, the first result received "only about 1 percent of all clicks."[6] So while Google might list twenty-five pages of results, the first page of search results gets nearly all the clicks. Even on the first page, the ranking is critical. Simply moving the top result (even if it's more relevant) to the third position reduces the number of clicks "by about 50 percent."[7] Degrading search results is worse on mobile devices because of the small screen size. As the commissioner for competition in Europe wryly noted, if one wants to hide a product or service, just put it on the fourth or fifth page, precisely because few people make it to that page.

Google argued that its innovations in updating search results sought "to improve the user experience."[8] But the commission and European General Court rejected Google's justification, finding instead that the company's self-preferencing enabled it to dry out traffic to rivals and reduce their innovation efforts (Google's appeal before the European Court of Justice is pending).[9] The commission stated that competitors "will have an incentive to invest in developing innovative services, improving the relevance of their existing services and creating new types of services, only if they can reasonably expect that their services will be able to attract a sufficient volume of user traffic to compete with Google's comparison shopping service."[10]

What Google argued was an "innovation" designed to improve the quality of its search service for users and advertisers[11] was instead an innovation-killer. Vertical search had the potential to upend Google's value chain. It could divert more valuable advertisements—such as travel and hotels—to the verticals, leaving Google with the less profitable advertising segments.

Now consider an app seeking to be discovered. According to Google, one out of every four users finds an app through its search engine.[12] And because Google Search is the overwhelmingly dominant search engine in most of the world, app developers rely on it to reach customers. So, the Tech Baron, by using the retention/friction levers, can help us discover the favored (and possibly inferior) offerings within its ecosystem and reduce the likelihood that we discover superior disruptive innovations.

While the Tech Pirate may be a few clicks away, competition isn't. Innovation and society pay the price for this self-preferencing, as Congress heard from numerous market participants:

[S]elf-preferencing and discriminatory treatment by the dominant platforms forced businesses to lay off employees and divert resources away from developing new products and towards paying a dominant platform for advertisements or other ancillary services. . . . Without the opportunity to compete fairly, businesses and entrepreneurs are dissuaded from investing and, over the long term, innovation suffers.[13]

From Persuasion to Default

Suppose we somehow discover the Tech Pirate's innovation despite the Tech Barons' efforts to the contrary. Next comes *persuasion*, when we form a favorable or unfavorable attitude toward the innovation.

We might think we are critically evaluating whether to adopt an innovation, with the same discernment as choosing a wine for our meal. But our choices can be easily manipulated. Why have us deliberate when the Tech Baron can simply choose for us?

Ever wonder why Google pays Apple billions of dollars (estimated to be $15 billion in 2021[14]) to remain Safari's default search engine? Certainly not for its enhanced privacy features.

Most of us are not rational, self-interested individuals with willpower, as the field of behavioral economics established. Daniel Kahneman and Amos Tversky, two pioneers of this field, quantified what every good advertiser and car salesperson already knew. We have cognitive biases, which refer to our tendency to react, think, or operate in a certain way, which diverges from assumed rationality. Because deliberative thinking requires effort, we also engage in mental shortcuts (heuristics). Businesses and governments can trigger consumers' biases and heuristics to achieve specific goals. So too the Tech Barons can target our weaknesses—our optimism bias, overconfidence, and illusion of control—to nudge us to the technologies that benefit them and away from the technologies that threaten their power or value chain. It can be as simple as the default setting.

Policymakers have long recognized how defaults can affect behavior. If you want employees to contribute to their retirement plans, make that the default. Same with organ donations. Through defaults, Tech Barons can affect our behavior while we retain our sense of independence and autonomy—allowing us to believe that we are making our own choices. For example, we can easily change the default search engine on our Apple devices, but few of us do so. (Google's worldwide market share for search

has never fallen below 89 percent between 2009 and August 2021.[15])
And this default impacts what products, services, and listings we see and
will likely click when using the search engine.

Because few of us change the default, Google has more opportunities
to gather data and train its search engine's algorithms, which make them
better, especially in identifying relevant responses for uncommon ("tail")
queries. That also means we spend less time on other, more privacy-
friendly search engines, such as DuckDuckGo (which has less than a
1 percent worldwide market share), which means fewer opportunities
for their search algorithm to discover relevant responses and improve,
and fewer opportunities for the Tech Pirates to be found on these other
search engines.

That's also why Google demands that Android phone manufacturers
preload its apps on their phones.[16] In securing the defaults—whether
for its search engine app, mapping app, Chrome browser, or YouTube
app—Google crowds "out placement for other apps while also taking
up significant memory."[17] Indeed, Google was receiving complaints from
mobile phone manufacturers that their users were panning their Android phones. Why? Because Google preloaded so many of its apps on
the phones (about thirty apps), less than half of the phone's 16 gigabytes
of memory was actually available.[18]

So how did Google preload so many apps on these Android phones?
Through another strategy called "tying," which achieves the same outcome as defaults. Google tells Android phone manufacturers that if they
want the Play Store and the Google Search app, then they must also preinstall Google's Chrome browser and suite of other Google apps. Plus,
the phone manufacturer must make it impossible for us to delete or remove many of these Google apps.[19] This further reduces our incentive to
add other competing apps (especially if our phone has limited memory).
Plus, the phone manufacturer has to place *all* of the Google apps on the
device's home screen or very next screen (as we'll more likely stick with
the default and use Google's apps more). As the European Commission
found, this bundling reinforces Google's dominant position, increases
entry barriers, and deters innovation.[20]

As a result, while we maintain the illusion of control, the Tech Barons steer us away from disruptive technologies and providers.

From Decision to Dissuasion

Ordinarily, in the decision stage, we experiment with the innovation to decide whether to adopt or reject it. Here we might ask peers who tried the product or service, which can provide us a "vicarious trial."[21] For apps or games, it might be the recommendation of a friend on Facebook. It can also be a YouTube video that demonstrates the use of the innovation.

The favored innovators will rely on the Tech Barons to help them identify early adopters and persuade them to experiment with the innovation. Early adopters exchange information with the innovator (to improve the product or service) and educate the adopters' followers (to persuade them to also use the technology). Here the Tech Barons have blurred the functions of the "mass media channels," which historically generated general awareness of the innovation, and the "interpersonal channels," where peer networks (such as one's friends) historically were more important at the persuasion and decision stages.[22] The Tech Baron already uses its comprehensive profiles of users to predict and manipulate their behavior. It can also highlight how the innovation is relevant to that person's particular needs. Thus, through defaults, advertising, or "organic" placements, innovators will rely on the Tech Barons to persuade individuals to try their products and services.

But the disfavored technologies, at best, will get the silent treatment or, at worst, be subjected to a dissuasion campaign.

In the previous chapter, we discussed the difficulty of sideloading, which is downloading an app on your smartphone outside of Google's and Apple's app stores. While sideloading is impossible within Apple's closed ecosystem, it could be done on Android devices (with much effort). But here is where dissuasion plays a role. To prevent you from sideloading an app on your Android phone, Google creates and imposes broad practical, technological, and contractual impediments. It effectively closes the Android app distribution ecosystem. As the state attorneys general allege in their monopolization complaint, Google increases friction by

- imposing needlessly broad restrictions on direct downloading of apps and app stores,

- using contracts with Android device manufacturers to prevent the manufacturers from modifying the operating system to circumvent the sideloading or code restrictions imposed by Google,

- blocking competing app stores from distribution on the Play Store, and

- preventing non-Play app stores and apps from purchasing advertising on key Google properties including YouTube and the Google search engine results page.[23]

If you have an Android phone, try downloading Fortnite or another app directly. You will likely encounter, as the state AGs note, "superfluous, misleading, and discouraging security warnings."[24] For example, Google will warn you that "This type of file can harm your device. Do you want to keep [name of app] anyway?" If you persist, you will get a more dire warning:

> Your phone and personal data are more vulnerable to attack by unknown apps. By installing apps from this source, you agree that you are responsible for any damage to your phone or loss of any data that may result from their use.

Plus, to discourage you further, Google will require that you grant permission multiple times for a single app installation. Of course, if you download the same app in the Google Play Store (where Google gets 30 percent of the in-app revenues), you won't encounter these warnings and hurdles.

These and other hurdles and warnings are known as "dark patterns."[25]

The Tech Barons have many subtle tools to manipulate our decision-making, choices, and search habits. We encounter these strategies frequently on the web, although we may not always realize their significance to our decision-making. The list of dark patterns is long. Some examples from the industry and literature include:

- Hidden information (using small print or difficulties in locating the information)

- Obstruction (making it difficult to exercise your will)

- Misdirection (distracting you from the information you seek)

- Confirm-shaming (guilting you for opting to use one option rather than another)

- Roach motel (making it very hard to navigate your way on the platform and exercise your choice)

- Trick questions (for example, using two "negatives" in a question, thus making it hard for you to understand which option [continue or cancel] reflects your will)

- Bait and switch (forcing another option that you never chose)

- Sneak into the basket (using defaults and opt-outs to add items as you check out)

- False hierarchy (present similar options in a hierarchical manner)

- Forced registration (trick you into thinking registration is necessary)

- False urgency and scarcity (countdown timer or indications that demand is high and supply low)[26]

Once a Tech Baron takes these or other dark patterns, adds more friction and defaults, and supplements with a dash of manipulation, most of us simply give up and pursue the path set for us.

Now suppose you want to load a rival app store on your Android phone, like Aptoide. The dark patterns are even darker. Google first hides the Aptoide app on your phone. But suppose undeterred you go to the settings on your Android phone to launch the app store. Google describes the app as potentially harmful and asks you to uninstall it.[27] But suppose you override Google's warning by clicking "keep app (unsafe)." The app store "still won't work because Google blocks Aptoide from installing apps."[28] As a result of Google's actions, Aptoide's cofounder and CEO Paulo Trezentos estimated that it lost between 15 and 20 percent of its user base since June 2018.[29]

But suppose you overcome Google's obstacles to sideloading. You will now face additional difficulties when updating the sideloaded app or app store. As the state attorneys general alleged, "Google prevents sideloaded apps and app stores from updating in the background."[30] What this means is that you would have to manually approve every update via a multistep process—all designed to further discourage you from using alternatives to Google's Play Store.

On the other hand, Tech Barons can nudge our adoption of the favored technologies. In 2021, Facebook said it would stop using its facial-recognition software. Previously, if you decided to opt out of Facebook's facial recognition software Facebook would highlight the benefits of the privacy-invasive technology and downplay (or not even mention) all of the technology's privacy risks. Moreover, Facebook would warn you of the danger of someone impersonating you should you turn off the technology:

> Help protect you and others from impersonation and identity misuse, and improve platform reliability. For example: We may be able to detect if you appear in someone else's profile picture and send you a notification. If you review the profile picture and think someone is impersonating you, you can report that profile.[31]

How significant is this risk? Facebook never told you. Nor did it tell you all its uses for this technology, including for behavioral advertising purposes. As a result, Facebook probably held "'the largest facial dataset to date'—powered by DeepFace, Facebook's deep-learning facial recognition system."[32]

Thus, the Tech Barons can use dark patterns and enlist others to persuade us to opt for the chosen, nonthreatening technologies and further dissuade us from using the Tech Pirate's technologies.

From Implementation to Hindrance, from Confirmation to Contradiction

By the fourth phase, there are few, if any, threatening innovations for us to implement. But if we could find the Tech Pirate's innovation, reject the default options, and are not hindered by the dark patterns, we finally come to the implementation phase where we put the innovation to use. Here the Tech Pirate will want to address any operational issues about the technology, feedback from other users, etc.

So, for the favored innovations, the Tech Barons can use the data collected within their ecosystem to better understand how customers are using the products and ways to improve them. Again, the aim is to minimize friction to facilitate our implementation. Indeed, friction is a buzzword for online sellers. An Amazon executive identified the following questions developers should ask:

- How many decisions are between a customer and completing a task?

- Is each of these decisions absolutely necessary?

- If so, can you make the decision for the customer by pre-selecting an option?

- If not, and the customer absolutely needs to make that decision, how can you simplify the decision process?

- If there are multiple decisions, could you combine them into one decision?

- Can you present the most important decision first to the customer?

- How can you preserve the decision once it's been made so that you don't have to ask the customer again in the future?[33]

Just as it can reduce friction to keep us using its favored innovations, the Tech Baron can dissuade us from experimenting with disfavored innovations by making it harder to use them. Thus, Apple's other products, such as the Apple Watch and AirPods, reportedly "'lose significant functionality when paired with a smartphone other than the iPhone,' locking iPhone users into the iOS ecosystem."[34]

So if an innovation performs poorly, we will likely blame its developer for the sluggish performance (especially when we don't experience this with the Tech Baron's competing services). We will be unlikely to blame the Tech Baron for hindering interoperability.

Consider, as another example, Google's subtler nudges with Zoom:

> More recently, as remote work became commonplace during the COVID-19 pandemic, Google attempted to manipulate users into using its Google Meet videoconferencing tool instead of upstart competitor Zoom. As Zoom emerged as the market leader during the early stages of the pandemic, Google introduced a new widget for Meet inside Gmail. A similar message could be found inside Google Calendar, which prompted users to "Add Google Meet video conferencing" to their appointments. "For people with the Zoom Video Communications Inc. extension on their Chrome browsers, the prompt sits directly above the option to: 'Make it a Zoom Meeting.'"[35]

By reducing friction to Google Meet (making it the default and having it work seamlessly with the other services within Google's ecosystem) and increasing the friction for Zoom (by requiring users to exit Google

Distorting the Demand for Innovation

77 ∎

calendar, log in to Zoom, copy and paste the invite link, and send it out as a calendar invitation, text, or e-mail), the Tech Baron sought to reduce the odds of our using Zoom. And while Zoom still had the lead in 2021, Google Meet was the leading Google app downloaded in the Google Play Store.[36]

Using these strategies, the Tech Barons can affect our implementation and confirmation, pushing us closer to their favored innovations and causing us to second-guess our continued use of the disfavored innovation.[37] We're more likely to follow the path of least resistance by using the technology that the Tech Barons favor.

Mobile Ad Blockers

It is hard to prove the counterfactual, namely all the innovations that we might have been using but for the Tech Barons' manipulation of demand. But let's look at one example that illustrates how the Tech Barons can affect (negatively and positively) the demand for innovation that many of us favor—ad blockers on mobile devices.

Most of us dislike behavioral advertising and the underlying surveillance and manipulation. But we have very little control. Here there clearly was a pent-up demand for this technology. Many smartphone users complained about unwanted ads. These ads were annoying, consumed data, slowed downloading times, and cluttered the small screen.[38] Nonetheless, Google (and to a lesser extent Apple) effectively hampered for many years the development and adoption rate for ad-blocking technologies for smartphones.

More people in 2017 were using ad-blocking technology on their laptops (68 percent of US ad blocker users) and personal computers (51 percent) rather than smartphones (22 percent).[39] Many smartphone users had a favorable attitude toward the technology (so the issue was not *persuasion*, the second stage of the innovation adoption process). Instead, the initial hurdle was *knowledge*. Even though many were employing this ad-blocking technology on their laptops and PCs, few were aware of whether the ad-blocking technology could be installed on their smartphones and how to install it.[40] Neither Apple nor Google promoted the technology for iOS or Android smartphones. Instead, Google, which relies primarily on advertising revenue, in 2013 removed some of the ad-blocking apps from its Android app store.[41] But this was not a sin of omission. Google also made it harder for users to *implement* ad-blocking technology on their Android phones.

In 2015, Apple finally announced that its new iOS 9 operating system would permit users to download ad-blocking extensions through the mobile Safari browser. After Apple's Safari allowed ad-blocking extensions, many people added the technology to their iPhones.[42] But Google still did not accept ad-blocking plugins for Chrome, the default Android browser. Instead, users had to download another browser, such as Firefox, for their Android smartphone and use an ad-blocking extension.[43]

A key barrier to mobile ad-blocking technology, a 2017 survey found, was the need for Android users to download another browser, like Firefox, to block ads.[44] Thirty-five percent of the surveyed smartphone owners said that they used their default browser and never considered using a different browser. Only 14 percent used an additional browser.[45]

Only in 2018 did Google enable its browser Chrome to block certain annoying ads that ran on sites that repeatedly violated standards set forth by the Coalition for Better Ads.[46] By 2023, Chrome might even phase out support for third-party cookies.[47]

The bottom line: despite the consumer demand, the Tech Barons can affect our ability to adopt a given innovation.

Now, you probably wonder why we have witnessed a change in their attitude toward ad blockers. Why the turnaround for Google? One explanation is that the seemingly privacy-friendly measure weakens rivals in the online display advertising markets and strengthens Google's grip over advertisers. So, this move is very much in keeping with the Google ecosystem's value chain.

As for Apple, the move was arguably driven by its desire to further distinguish itself as the privacy-oriented mobile operating system. And while the company emphasizes its privacy-enhancing features, one should not ignore its close collaboration with Google that exposes its users' privacy (more on that in chapter 8).

In the end, we return to the same principle that drives the Tech Barons' strategies. Regardless of how they present their actions, the Tech Barons seek to fortify their ecosystem and protect their value chain. Disruptors are not invited.

Reflections

Just as the blackcaps spend more time in Britain, so too we are now spending more time within the Tech Barons' ecosystems—whether on Facebook, Instagram, YouTube, Apple, Microsoft, or Amazon.[48] And as we use the leading digital assistants (Google's, Amazon's, Microsoft's, and Apple's), phones and tablets (likely Apple's or Android), and a range of services online and on our wearables, the Tech Barons carefully drive us toward their favored offerings, and away from pirates' innovation.

In the digital platform economy, what we demand may well be what we were primed to demand. Granted, we still have some degree of autonomy. If consumers had balked at the iPhone, Apple would unlikely be the world's largest company in 2022 (based on market capitalization).[49] Just consider the Google Graveyard websites, where Google Buzz and Google Glass now reside.[50] If consumers balk, the innovation will fail. But in designing the ecosystem, a Tech Baron can choose which defaults to employ, which products to feature, and the degree of interoperability of these products or services. While we may first resist, we do get habituated and accept what is offered to us over time. Professor Shoshana Zuboff described this habituation process as a "combination of agreement, helplessness and resignation." At the end of this process, she notes, "the sense of astonishment and outrage dissipates. The incursion itself, once unthinkable, slowly worms its way into the ordinary."[51] Of course, the Tech Barons will not impede all disruptive innovations. Nonetheless, their influence over the supply and demand of innovation can slow down our adoption rate of the Tech Pirates' technologies and further diminish the diversity of innovation.

Before we conclude this chapter, one important caveat is in order. Our discussion highlights the power to manipulate user demand to favor the Tech Barons' interests and hinder Tech Pirates when they threaten disruption within the Tech Barons' ecosystem. It should not be confused with legitimate attempts by Tech Barons to advance their technology and, in doing so, educate us as to its benefits. After all, even if innovation doesn't slavishly follow consumers' tastes, it may anticipate consumer demand. One quote attributed to Apple's cofounder Steve Jobs is:

> Some people say, "Give the customers what they want." But that's not my approach. Our job is to figure out what they're going to want before they do. I think Henry Ford once said, "If I'd asked customers what they wanted, they would have told me, 'A faster horse!'" People don't know what they want until you show it to them. That's why I never rely on market research. Our task is to read things that are not yet on the page.[52]

Although the Tech Barons will never be omnipotent in forcing us to accept every innovation, no matter how toxic, they don't have to be. They just use their multiple levers to impede our adoption of the Tech Pirates' innovation.[53] Even beyond their ecosystems, the Tech Barons can increase the odds of our adopting the favored innovations and avoiding the disfavored ones. Let's examine how.

Distortions beyond the Tech Barons' Ecosystems

IN EARLY 2020, *Protocol* reported that "around 200 venture capital investors, academics and regulators gathered at Stanford University's law school to debate whether big tech companies stifle innovation, and what role antitrust should play in leveling the playing field."[1] The antitrust enforcers by then had heard concerns that the Tech Barons were stifling innovation within their ecosystems. Indeed, few, if any, Tech Pirates have taken on the current Tech Barons, or even managed to destabilize their value chain.

But what about start-ups operating far outside the Tech Barons' ecosystems? Seemingly they were safe. Some participants agreed, noting that these pirates could eventually disrupt the Tech Barons, just as Google displaced Yahoo. A few argued that the real kill zones come from regulations and government intervention. But several venture capitalists were less sanguine. One noted how privacy-focused start-ups were dying off, even though they tried to give individuals new and better ways to control their data. "That's as much of a kill space as you can imagine, depending on the idea," said Switch Ventures partner Paul Arnold (who is also the grandson of the famous antitrust trustbuster Thurman Arnold). "You're getting to the core value proposition of extremely powerful and entrenched companies that do not want to cooperate with that idea, so how do you pull it off? I haven't seen a company yet." Nor have we.

Even when Tech Pirates enter markets far beyond the Tech Barons' ecosystems, their future, nonetheless, may depend on the Tech Barons' value chain. The "kill zone" extends outside the Tech Barons' ecosystem. This chapter looks at four key areas where the Tech Barons can wield power beyond their ecosystem to crush disruptive innovation (Figure 5.1).

Figure 5.1

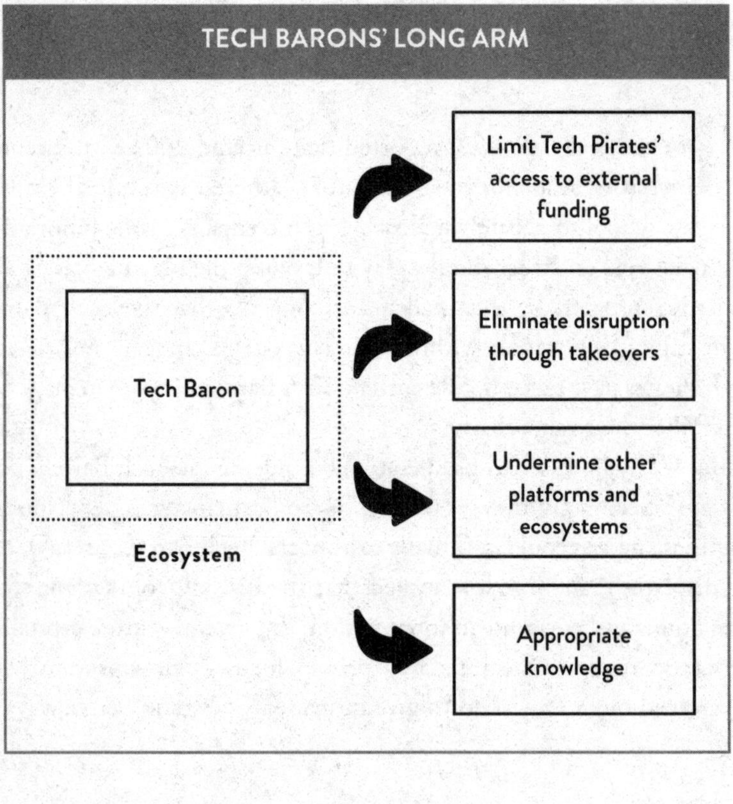

TECH BARONS' LONG ARM

Tech Baron

Ecosystem

Limit Tech Pirates' access to external funding

Eliminate disruption through takeovers

Undermine other platforms and ecosystems

Appropriate knowledge

First, Tech Barons can limit the Tech Pirates' opportunities to access long-term funding. While the Tech Barons wield this power within their ecosystem, they can also chill the financing of Tech Pirates seeking to disrupt industries outside their ecosystem. One example is when the Tech Barons signal their intentions to develop future platforms, products, or services that compete with the emerging disruptive innovation, thus chilling the incentives to finance these Tech Pirates.

Second, the Tech Baron may acquire the Tech Pirates. This may be an attractive "exit strategy" for the aspiring disruptor delighted to join the navy and fortify the ecosystem.[2] The problem, however, is that some of these transactions (sometimes referred to as "killer acquisitions") reduce innovation plurality, eliminate innovation paths, and widen the Tech Barons' protective moat.

Third, Tech Barons can prevent alternative ecosystems from developing. Recognizing that innovation is often a collective rather than isolated individual effort, the Tech Barons can force those within their ecosystem to shun Tech Pirates and third-party platforms. Those who help develop another ecosystem that threatens the Tech Barons' value chain will be cut off—whether from data, interoperability, or critical services—leading to their demise.

Last, the Tech Barons can use their power to colonize the "knowledge economy." Since knowledge sharing is key to innovation, Tech Barons can direct innovation efforts to support their commercial interests and hinder research that might disrupt their ecosystems. Innovation and knowledge are funneled into the Tech Barons' ecosystems and redeployed to where they add more value to the Tech Barons (but not necessarily society). Just as prior colonists extracted gold and minerals, the Tech Barons can extract knowledge and redeploy it wherever it is cheaper (or where the Tech Barons can extract more value). So, a Tech Baron can close a research center in one country and redeploy the knowledge to a center in another lower-wage country without transferring humans or physical assets.

In the end, the start-ups find that they're more likely to survive in fighting over the scraps left by the Tech Barons than in challenging them.

Funding, or the Lack of It

Most start-ups fail, as do most attempts to innovate. Only 24.6 percent of the US start-ups that began in 1994 were still operating seventeen years later.[3] Moreover, disruption can advance gradually through trial-and-error learning.[4] The innovative process can take years, if not decades, from inception to disruption, and to survive and flourish, the Tech Pirates will need capital. They must attract investors or buyers. And most of the venture capital money only comes when the company reaches the late stages, as opposed to the early or seed stages.[5]

This financial dependency affects commercial strategy and innovation paths, noted Roger McNamee, author of *Zucked: Waking Up to the Facebook Catastrophe*. He was an early investor in Facebook and a long-time mentor to Mark Zuckerberg but has since become one of Facebook's fiercer (and more knowledgeable) critics. As they look for funding, start-ups have difficulties applying a different business model or value chain that is not compatible "with the business models that have made the Internet platforms so successful."[6] So the Tech Barons need not even exert their influence and power. Their ecosystem already acts as an undertow, pulling in millions of developers, advertisers, and websites that complement their ecosystem. Any start-up with an alternative vision of AI that is not based on behavioral advertising would have to compete against this undertow, including having to "compete on price to get that talent." This puts the Tech Pirate at an even further disadvantage and makes it an even riskier proposition for venture capitalists.

When thinking of investments in new technologies and innovation, it shouldn't come as a surprise that venture capitalists think twice before backing a disruptor who challenges the prevailing ecosystems' value chain. After all, they invest when they expect handsome returns. If the risk and uncertainty are too high, investments will not follow. A managing partner at Union Square Ventures, Albert Wenger, reflected: "Kill Zone is a real thing. The scale of these companies and their impact on what can be funded, and what can succeed, is massive."[7] Another venture capitalist noted how he only invests "in things that are not in Facebook's, Apple's, Amazon's or Google's kill zone."[8] Switch Ventures' Paul Arnold shed further light on the disincentives to invest:

> Venture capitalists are less likely to fund startups that compete against monopolies' core products. . . . As a startup investor, I see this often. For example, I will meet yet another founder who wants to disrupt Microsoft's LinkedIn. They will have a clever plan to build a better professional social network. I always pass on the investment. It is nearly impossible to overcome the monopoly LinkedIn enjoys. It is but one example of an innovation kill zone.[9]

One aspiring innovator noted, "People are not getting funded because Amazon might one day compete with them."[10] As the industry says, there is no point in investing on the elephant trail (the giants will likely quash you). The 2019 Stigler Report on Digital Platforms notes how the effects of dominant firms become apparent when looking at sub-industries (rather than aggregated industry data).[11] Investment patterns in start-ups in subindustries have "fared poorly compared to the rest of software for Google and Facebook, the rest of retail for Amazon, and the rest of all VC for each of Google, Facebook, and Amazon. This suggests the existence of so-called 'kill-zones,' that is, areas where venture capitalists are reluctant to enter due to small prospects of future profits."[12]

When a Tech Baron announces its intention (or is widely seen) to expand its ecosystem to a new market segment, funding for disruptors that collide with its value chains will likely dry up. As a result, companies aspiring to innovate in the digital economy shouldn't only inquire whether their technologies will disrupt the Tech Barons' current ecosystem but need to anticipate where the Tech Barons will expand. Start-ups, innovators, and investors must constantly adjust as the Tech Barons expand their "economic waters." Their ecosystems now include supermarkets, clothing and private label products, gaming, digital assistants, smart appliances, wearables, self-driving cars, and health care.

The result? A pirate might have a great team of people. There might be significant pent-up demand for its technology. And the target market space might be far away from that of the Tech Barons. The only thing missing is financing. And yet, as the Tech Barons' ecosystems expand, so too will the innovation kill zones, as venture capitalists will be reluctant to fund disruption in these segments.

Mergers and Acquisitions

How can funding dry up when the digital economy is buzzing with merger activity? After all, Google, Amazon, Facebook, Apple, and Microsoft collectively purchased over seven hundred companies over the past twenty years.[13] Google alone "purchased well over 260 companies—a figure that likely understates the full breadth of Google's acquisitions, given that many of the firm's purchases have gone unreported."[14] A 2021 FTC study considered acquisitions by GAFAM that were not subject to antitrust reporting obligations. The study found that in the ten years between 2010 and 2020, the companies completed over six hundred such acquisitions, many of which targeted nascent competitors.[15] FTC Chair Lina M. Khan commented on the "systemic nature" of GAFAM's acquisition strategies, noting that the study "captures the extent to which these firms have devoted tremendous resources to acquiring start-ups, patent portfolios, and entire teams of technologists—and how they were able to do so largely outside of our purview."[16]

On the upside, these acquisitions offer valuable capital injections to start-ups. The Tech Barons can offer the target companies access to markets, resources, and know-how, help accelerate growth, and integrate breakthrough innovation into their ecosystem. These acquisitions might help supplement the Tech Barons' incremental innovation efforts and in-house R&D with disruptive innovation, which cannot quickly be developed within the established organization's processes, values, or culture.[17] These acquisitions also help bring talented individuals from the start-up into the ecosystem. Their creative minds can now advance the Tech Barons' strategy, and they and the target shareholders are rewarded accordingly. Furthermore, the prospect of acquisition helps stimulate research and development by these start-ups and forms an attractive "exit" strategy that offers a return on their investment, risk-taking, and efforts.[18] An active market with viable "exit" options helps fuel investment in both sustaining and disruptive technologies.

So, where's the problem?

When it comes to disruption, these acquisitions do not beget greater innovations. Instead, the opposite often happens. The Tech Pirate, after being acquired, will no longer be a disruptive Tech Pirate. After all, a Tech Baron acquires these pirates to integrate or quash their disruptive innovation. Thus, from a *market perspective*, these acquisitions further deplete the ranks of Tech Pirates.

While not necessarily typical,[19] "killer acquisitions" are among the Tech Baron's weapons to minimize the risk of disruptive innovation. After acquiring a Tech Pirate, the Tech Baron simply removes their creations from the market.[20]

But even where the Tech Pirate's product remains, its innovations will shift from disruptive to sustaining.

We'll begin with Instagram.

As Facebook CEO Mark Zuckerberg expressed in one of his emails: "it is better to buy than compete."[21] That proved true when Facebook was caught unprepared for the shift to mobile. Its initial mobile offering was weak. To make matters worse, in 2010, Facebook rewrote its mobile app's native applications in HTML—"The language used for pages designed to be viewed in a web browser"—which Zuckerberg would later call "the biggest mistake we made as a company."[22] Its mobile Facebook app warranted only a two-star rating. Zuckerberg knew Facebook was vulnerable on mobile.[23]

Meanwhile, the start-up Instagram took advantage of the smartphone's camera and was scaling quickly. It gained "25,000 users on its first day in 2010; 100,000 users in a week; one million users in less than three months; and ten million users in less than a year."[24] And that was when Instagram was available only on Apple's iOS devices. Thus, Zuckerberg internally warned how Instagram "could be 'very disruptive' to Facebook." But as Zuckerberg previously noted: "one thing about start-ups though is you can often acquire them."[25]

In its monopolization complaint against Facebook, the FTC noted how this strategy addressed its failure "to compete on business talent," which drove Facebook to develop "a plan to maintain its dominant position by acquiring companies that could emerge as or aid competitive threats."[26] As Zuckerberg noted of start-ups like Instagram, "The businesses are nascent but the networks are established, the brands are already meaningful and if they grow to a large scale they could be very disruptive to us."[27] In 2012, Facebook acquired Instagram for $1 billion. Instagram's cofounder Kevin Systrom reportedly feared that "Facebook would go into 'destroy mode' if he did not sell Instagram."[28]

All in all, the acquisition enabled Facebook to eliminate this disruptor and neutralize its innovation threats. As Zuckerberg recognized, it also hindered other firms' ability to access or purchase Instagram's technology and infrastructure. (Facebook feared Apple or Google acquiring it.[29]) In addition, by squelching the direct threat from Instagram, the transaction reduced the competitive and innovation pressure on Facebook.

Under its control, Facebook prevented Instagram from disrupting its entrenched social network. For example, Facebook "limited promotions of Instagram that would otherwise have drawn users away from Facebook Blue."[30] This disappointed Instagram's cofounder, who complained in a November 2012 email: "you keep mentioning how you can't promote Instagram until you understand it's [sic] effect on FB engagement. Who decided this?"[31] Of course, it was Facebook. As its vice president of growth responded: "Chris [Cox, vice president of Product,] voiced the concern (which btw I agree with) about instagram's feed cannibalizing our own / training users to check multiple feeds—which is why we want to first measure the impact of instagram's usage on our engagement / wire things up to make sure it is all accretive." Basically, to grow, not disrupt, Facebook's ecosystem.

So even when they're not classic "killer acquisitions," they can eliminate a disruptor. They stifle competition and innovation precisely because start-ups "play a critical role in driving innovation, as their prospective entry may dislodge incumbents or spur competition."[32] Once acquired, many innovators, like Instagram, recognize that they need to align their innovations to complement, rather than disrupt, the Tech Baron's ecosystem.

Consider another example, Waze. Google acquired the navigation app for $966 million (most of which—$847 million—was goodwill).[33] The role of Waze after that changed—from being a potential disruptor to a complementor. In 2021, Waze's CEO left Google. As he wrote after his departure, "I was the naive start-up leader believing that I can build out Waze within Google to its full potential and conquer the beast, regardless of its nature. This irrational belief is critical for a start-up leader but challenging in the corporate environment."[34] Google simply began integrating Waze's distinguishing features into Google Maps, including real-time user reports on crashes, speed traps, and traffic slowdowns.[35] Rather than a disruptor, Waze now serves as a protective moat for Google. As Waze's former leader remarked:

> Any idea we had was quickly co-opted by Google Maps. The Android app store treated us as a 3rd party, there was no pre-installation option and no additional distribution. We did have a lot more marketing dollars to spend but had to spend them like any other company, except we were constrained in what we could do and which 3rd parties we could work with due to corporate policies. All of our growth at Waze post acquisition was from work we did, not support from the mothership. Looking back, we could have probably grown faster and much more efficiently had we stayed independent.[36]

For the Tech Baron, these acquisitions buy time, prevent the disruptive threat, and eliminate the risk that another Tech Baron acquires the technology (and user base). (Both Apple and Facebook, for example, were reportedly interested in Waze.)

These acquisitions can also increase the Tech Baron's power, thereby decreasing the remaining firms' incentives to innovate. This debunks the myth that acquiring one Tech Pirate incentivizes other start-ups to assume that role. A 2021 discussion paper by the International Monetary Fund reviews the empirical market data and observes that when "market leaders strengthen their lead over followers through M&As, the latter can become discouraged from competing, and invest less in R&D. Likewise, potential entrants may get discouraged, and new firm entry may fall. As the competitive pressure on market leaders diminishes, they may, in turn, lower their innovation effort, further amplifying the decline in business dynamism."[37] Likewise, economists found that major acquisitions by large tech companies lead to less investment in start-ups in the same sector.[38]

Of course, mergers and acquisitions come in different shapes and forms and generate a range of effects. While some bring benefits, others lessen competition. When it comes to the Tech Baron's acquisitions, the threat to disruption is hard to ignore.

Preventing the Emergence of Alternative Ecosystems

Tech Barons kill not just individual Tech Pirates but emerging ecosystems that may challenge them. Learning from the demise of old ecosystems that failed in expansion and self-renewal,[39] the Tech Barons will fiercely protect their value chain.

Innovation, as economists recognize, is a collective endeavor requiring different companies interacting across sectors.[40] Developing an alternative ecosystem also requires collaboration. A Tech Pirate's virtual reality gaming platform, for example, must work seamlessly on all the devices where one could play that game. This emerging ecosystem must also attract developers, equipment manufacturers, and users. To counter the threat from emerging ecosystems, Tech Barons can prevent others from helping the Tech Pirates and hinder the collaborative effort.

Consider Google's Android mobile operating system. Unlike Apple's devices and software, which "form a 'closed ecosystem' in which Apple controls every aspect of the user experience for iPhones and iPads,"[41] Android, in theory, is an open-source project. Android's goal, according to its website, "is to avoid any central point of failure in which one industry player can restrict or control the innovations of any other player."[42] If this were true, why is there only one principal version of Android (which Google controls)? And how did Google make Amazon's Android phone and any other significant variant of Android disappear?

For that, we turn to the European Commission's case against Google, where it was fined 4.34 billion euros for its exclusionary behavior. (The US and most state attorneys general challenged this same behavior in 2020, and all the cases are still being litigated as of early 2022.)

As the European Commission found, smartphone manufacturers only have one viable choice—Android—when it comes to operating systems. (Apple doesn't license its operating system.) And when it comes to app stores, smartphone manufacturers again have only one choice—Google Play Store. No other Android app store has "the quantity and popularity of apps available on the Google Play Store" and "the automatic update functionalities of the Play Store," as the European Commission found. So, Google wields this power to prevent the development of alternative Android ecosystems.

First, as we saw in chapter 4, Google imposes technical barriers to effectively prevent third parties from distributing apps outside the Google Play store (limiting sideloading). Google also prevents original equipment manufacturers (OEMs) from circumventing its technical barriers to hinder sideloading.

Second, to prevent the formation of rival app stores, Google uses its dominant position with Google Play and its must-have apps. If smartphone manufacturers support alternative versions of Android (competing forks), they cannot get Google Play Store, other must-have apps (like Google Search), and access to Google's APIs. (The majority of the top paid and unpaid Android apps employ APIs found only in Google Play Services.) Specifically, if the mobile phone manufacturer wants a license to the Play Store and the Google Search app, it must agree to Google's "anti-fragmentation" requirements.

Third, Google uses contracts to block app developers from forming or supporting competing app stores. As a condition of appearing in the Google Play Store, app developers must agree not to compete with Google's app store or help others develop and monetize a competing app store.[43]

Fourth, Google hinders the ability of any rival app store to advertise within Google's ecosystem. To attract app developers to one's app store, one needs to attract users. To attract users, one needs to advertise. To prevent alternative app distribution channels from forming, Google prevents app developers from promoting these alternative channels through Google's marketing properties. If the app wishes to participate in Google's advertising campaigns program—"a critical program for many app developers"—Google requires the app developers to distribute their apps in the Google Play Store, which requires them to agree to all of the above restrictions.[44]

Finally, to further disincentivize alternative ecosystems from forming, Google skews incentives. It shares its monopoly profits with the larger OEMs and mobile network operators to disincentivize their helping competing app stores. Google, for example, offered to buy off Samsung to keep it from developing its competing app store.

These anti-fragmentation obligations were not necessary for the Play Store and Google Search app to exist. They were unrelated, the European Commission found. Android forks represented a significant competitive threat to Google's control over an "open" operating system. If Amazon, for example, created a better version of Android or offered better features, then Google would no longer control the leading mobile operating system and app store. Amazon could support an alternative search engine like Bing, weakening Google's dominance over search advertising. One can imagine more versions of Android with more options for app developers and more innovations beyond Google's control.

Without the smartphone manufacturers' and popular app developers' support, no alternative Android forks of significance emerged. With

Google directing Android's innovation path, it ensures that its apps remain the defaults on the Android phones, which continue to collect more first-party personal data to better surveil us, which helps Google maintain its dominance in online behavioral advertising.

What's remarkable is that even without these anti-forking agreements, network effects already insulated Google from many threats. App developers develop for platforms with many users (namely Google and Apple). Users want phones with many apps. So, a new version of Android would need an app store already stocked with popular apps (including Google's apps and APIs) to attract users. But without many customers already willing to buy the new Android phone, app developers would be unlikely to incur the time and expense to develop apps for the Android fork. So, we revisit the "chicken and egg" problem where network effects already insulated Google's dominance, leaving app developers and phone manufacturers all stuck with Google's version of Android. But to eliminate any pirate's chance of actually opening up Android's network, Google forced the smartphone manufacturers, app developers, and mobile network operators to shun any would-be disruptor.

Now few, if any, will invest in apps that Google would reject. Few will go up the chain and develop a competing app store to Google's Play Store because one would also need a competing version of Android, which none of the leading smartphone manufacturers and apps would support. As the US explained:

> Distributors know that any violation of an anti-forking agreement could mean ex-communication from Google's Android ecosystem, loss of access to Google's must-have GPS and Google Play, and millions or even billions of dollars in lost revenue sharing . . .[45]

Google's strategy hindered both would-be Tech Pirates and the growth of other giants, like Amazon's mobile phone and Fire systems. The threat from Google chilled major manufacturers that simply "declined to support Amazon's phone out of fear doing so would risk their lucrative deals with Google." As the US alleged in its complaint, these practices undermined "innovation in new products that could serve as alternative search access points or disruptors to the traditional Google search model [and insulated] Google from significant competitive pressure to improve its general search, search advertising, and general search text advertising products and services."

It isn't just Android. Any Tech Baron can leverage its power to inhibit competing threats and the emergence of alternative ecosystems. Facebook, for example, is an important distribution channel for third-party apps, "with features like the Find Friends API serving as a valuable growth tool."[46] Between 2011 and 2018, Facebook made its Facebook Platform "available to developers only on the condition that their apps neither competed with Facebook nor promoted its competitors."[47] Who were Facebook's competitors? Anyone who provided personal social networking services, provided mobile messaging functions, provided promising social functionality, or connected with or promoted other personal social networking providers. As the FTC argued, Facebook imposed these conditions to deter any competitive threats to its ecosystem.[48] (As we'll discuss later, a federal district court dismissed these claims, holding that a monopoly can deny interoperability absent a very narrow exception.)

The Tech Barons' strategies send a clear signal to anyone seeking to challenge their hegemony—if you intend to rely on the help of others, such as app developers, hardware manufacturers, or advertisers, to develop your innovation and establish a competing ecosystem, think again.

Appropriation of Knowledge

European countries started colonies to channel the natural resources to their home countries. It was extractive—bringing the gold and other assets home. What is the equivalent of gold in today's economy? Knowledge, which the Tech Barons can access, appropriate, and redeploy.

How can Tech Barons access knowledge?

Knowledge sharing is key to innovation. As a 2020 survey of the business literature found, an organization "that encourages knowledge sharing is likely to produce new ideas and facilitate innovative capabilities."[49] Important innovation drivers are spillovers from other technologies and the total scientific knowledge pool.[50] And to increase their capacity to innovate, firms can increase their involvement in knowledge networks. In their book *Corporate Innovation in the Fifth Era*, Matthew Le Merle and Alison Davis share tactics that leading innovators use to harness and direct external innovation efforts.[51] These include, among other things:

Grants and scholarships to academic institutions that enable access to thinking and scientific breakthrough. Identifying and supporting up-and-coming researchers at an early stage of their career may enable developing a relationship before these individuals are pursued by other competing players.

Collaborative innovation networks offer a valuable mechanism to gain access to a large number of individuals with relevant expertise and research focus. These may be particularly beneficial when they offer exclusive access to important innovations and researchers and subsequently a competitive advantage.

Joint research and development agreements offer long-term funding to partnerships with innovation institutions. Such partnerships may provide privilege access, shared ownership of the innovation output, and the right to pursue commercial applications.

Developer networks bring together and support large groups of developers and ensure that they prioritize the interests of the company and "build their own solutions and products leveraging the platforms and standards that are important to your company."[52]

Funding and investment offer an important lever to capture innovation. Efforts may include third-party or corporate incubators and accelerators, angel investment funds, and venture capital funds.

Using these tactics, a Tech Baron can increase their access to disruptive and frontier innovation clusters and support the absorption of innovation.[53] The tactics also enable the Tech Barons to direct innovation efforts to support their commercial interests and their ecosystem's value chain.

How do Tech Barons appropriate knowledge?

Having obtained access to knowledge clusters and collaborations, next on the Tech Baron's agenda is appropriation. The Tech Barons often strategically compartmentalize the research so that the collaborating public universities and other entities only see the subparts. In contrast, the Tech Barons see the whole (and its value).

Scholars Cecilia Rikap and Bengt-Åke Lundvall, for example, analyzed science and technology collaborations and innovation systems driven by Google, Amazon, and Microsoft. They next contrasted each of these efforts with patent co-ownership. What they found is that tech giants use these collaborative efforts to appropriate knowledge from third-party organizations.[54] They note how these leading firms organize and control the collaborative efforts while the other participants will rarely be privy to the research's overall implications and monetization. As Rikap told us:

> The overall organization of the R&D effort is driven by the dominant tech giants. In addition to them being able to distort the overall orientation of research efforts, the collaborating researchers often do not get access to data held by the big tech companies. Each third-party innovator only focuses on one aspect of the development.

In controlling the research path and selectively sharing knowledge and information with third parties, the Tech Baron can appropriate the collectively created knowledge.

These predatory practices of rent-seeking also affect the ownership rights in the innovation. Tech Barons will generally patent alone or with employees as co-owners, despite knowledge being developed through collaborations. Rikap's analysis of hundreds of scientific publications, which Google, Amazon, and Microsoft coauthored with third parties and academic institutions, reveals a distinct asymmetry, with less than .3 percent co-ownership of patents following collaborations.[55] Knowledge is aggregated at the Tech Barons' end, with other innovators deprived of the whole data and scope. With the Tech Barons' deep pockets, ongoing hiring of talent, accumulation of data, control over deep learning, and advanced analytics at a scale unmatched by others, we witness an ongoing process of appropriation and monopolization of knowledge.[56] In those cases, the celebrated innovation attributed to the particular Tech Baron merely represents the appropriation of the collective efforts of many others.

How do the Tech Barons redeploy knowledge?

Suppose a Tech Baron finances an innovative design center in your city, state, or country. One might dream of this developing into a regional innovation cluster, like Silicon Valley. But based on our conversations with industry participants, it also fosters a dangerous process of knowledge redeployment out of the state or country and into the Tech Baron's ecosystem.

Rather than a brain drain (which involves the mass migration of people out of a city, state, or country), we are witnessing an "innovation drain," where design and innovation centers funnel innovation and knowledge into the Tech Barons' ecosystems. This goes beyond hiring talent out of universities. Innovation drain creates a knowledge transfer without the physical migration of individuals. For some countries, these processes result in the cross-border appropriation of knowledge.

Once appropriated, this knowledge will often be redeployed to other lower-cost countries where the Tech Baron can extract more value. So, if you work at the Tech Baron's design center, you likely will be training your counterpart one day in a lower cost country. Indeed, it can be cheaper to transfer knowledge than production facilities. So, while the rust belt might have taken decades in shifting physical infrastructure, knowledge is nomadic—not connected to the land. Once it's extracted from one colony, the Tech Baron can discard the individuals and territory.

For the Tech Barons, these strategies to access, appropriate, and re-deploy knowledge are completely rational. These strategies help them control the path of innovation (for example, by supporting research that promotes the Tech Barons' interests and diverting funds away from dis-ruption) and, where possible, appropriate and monetize the rewards. But these strategies will have a significant long-term effect, and here again society ultimately will pay the price. After all, today's applications of AI stem from the basic research done thirty years ago.[57] Similarly, future in-novation (and applications of AI) will depend on today's research, which the Tech Barons are dominating.

No doubt, the private sector plays a significant role in promoting innovation. The free market can offer efficiencies that the state cannot, and innovators may need to internalize many rewards for their efforts.[58] However, the architectural advantage created and maintained by the Tech Barons enables high levels of knowledge appropriation and tips the scale away from contestability. One should not confuse market power (which may be necessary for innovation's cause and effect) with the Tech Barons' significant control over innovation paths, access to knowledge, and much of the monetization.

The current trajectory supports a "cyclone effect," which enables Tech Barons to aggregate and appropriate diffused knowledge and intangible assets at a velocity unmatched in history. The control over the ecosystems, the access to data, and big analytics may herald the colonization of in-creasingly large segments of knowledge by a select few. Tech Barons can absorb seemingly open innovation efforts,[59] appropriate them, and in-corporate them in closed innovation processes. Over time, the increased concentration of aggregated knowledge and intellectual property rights at the hands of the few Tech Barons would leave little room for disrup-tive Tech Pirates. With enhanced absorption capacity,[60] the Tech Barons are on a trajectory to emerge as the *knowledge monopolies* of the future.

Reflections

Tech Barons can wield power beyond their ecosystems to stifle innovation that threatens their value chain.

Essential here for policymakers, would-be Tech Pirates, and companies seeking to compete in the digital economy is that current and future Tech Barons are not passive players who just happen to operate in markets tipped in their favor. Instead, the Tech Barons' tentacles reach distant innovation corners. This brings to mind the Standard Oil octopus image, which the political satire magazine *Puck* published in 1904. One tentacle controlled the U.S. Capitol, another the shipping industries, another the steel and copper industries, and another tentacle was about to grip the White House.

As the U.S. Department of Justice, supported by eleven states, explained in their complaint, "new companies with innovative business models cannot emerge from Google's long shadow." Potential innovations and competitors will continue to align with the Tech Barons' value chain. As one Google engineer noted, the strategy is "to make them do things we want."[61]

Consider the pioneer of wireless home smart speakers, Sonos. Its mission is to give "people access to the content they love and allowing them to control it however and wherever they choose."[62] So, the manufacturer developed the capacity to include multiple digital assistants (some potentially more privacy-friendly than the Tech Barons') in its speakers. But the Tech Barons did not share the enthusiasm for this open platform. As Sonos's CEO Patrick Spence told Congress:

> These companies have gone so far as demanding that we suppress our inventions in order to work with them. The most recent example of this is Google's refusal to allow us to use multiple voice assistants on our product simultaneously. . . . I think the whole spirit of trying to encourage small companies, encourage new innovations and new startups is at risk, given how dominant these companies are.[63]

But we are still in the infancy of the Tech Barons' reign. As the digital economy expands, the innovation landscape under the current policies will become even more barren. As Tech Barons build out their ecosystems, they direct the innovation paths, suppress disruption, and actively tip future innovation in their favor. As a result, the diversity of innovation efforts and funding will diminish. Tech Pirates will become rarer. While many start-ups might proclaim themselves to Tech Piratehood, their spirit will be institutionalized. They will align with the prevailing Tech Baron's value chain. To put it differently, in all but uniform, they will have joined the navy.

We are left with less innovation diversity, less disruption, and less choice. And what else are we left with when these innovation paths narrow? Some genuinely frightening innovations, as the next chapter explores.

CHAPTER 6

Toxic Innovation Galore

AS THE TECH BARONS thin the ranks of pirates and narrow their possible innovation paths, what happens to the *value* and *type* of innovation?

The Tech Barons' growing power, as we'll see, increases the likelihood that the resulting innovation within its ecosystem will serve the Tech Barons' interest, not ours. What does that mean? More innovations that extract value (siphoning more money into the Tech Barons' pockets) or destroy value with some truly privacy-invasive technologies.[1]

To appreciate the rising toxicity, one must first understand the relationship between the increase in power over the ecosystem and the diminishing value of the implemented innovation. As Figure 6.1 reflects, the more concentrated the market becomes, the less likely its innovations will maximize our interests. To illustrate, let's first look at competitive markets.

Figure 6.1

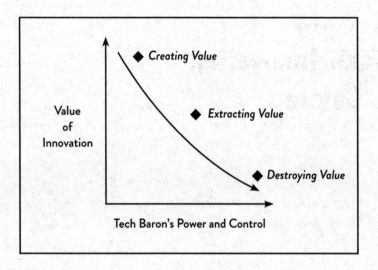

Competition and Value Creation

In competitive environments one would rightly expect sustaining and disruptive innovations that create value. Neither the Tech Pirates nor established firms can promote innovations that primarily extract or destroy value since they'll lose sales to rivals or other pirates. Consumer demand and interests will drive innovation.

As with many economic theories, this expectation rests on several assumptions.

One is that the competition is healthy (rather than toxic) and therefore benefits us. As we explore in our book *Competition Overdose*, competition, while ubiquitous, can take different forms, not all of which are beneficial. Competition, at times, can be a race to the bottom that harms both rivals and customers (in *Competition Overdose*, we illustrate this by looking at college admissions). At times, firms make more money exploiting our weaknesses (as we explore with Las Vegas hotels' drip pricing and online dating). At other times, the competitive pressure causes a degradation in quality, safety, and the environment (as we discuss with the horsemeat scandal). When competition is toxic, the innovations can also be toxic, in that they extract or destroy value. So, the issue is what kind of competition exists, and whether it is toxic, zero-sum, positive-sum, or noble.[2]

A second assumption is that the supply of disruptive pirates, waiting in the wings, never depletes. As long as innovators are tinkering away, have sufficient access to funding, knowledge, and technology, and can reach the market, there will be dynamic disruption.

A third assumption is that innovators will benefit from the fruits of their efforts. Suppose competition is too fierce (where price equals marginal cost). In that case, the margins will be too low for them to recover their investment in R&D. But in most real-world markets, firms have some market power, unlike the economic model of perfect competition.

These three assumptions underpin much of the prevailing debate about innovation. If you trust them to be correct, you can expect the ensuing innovations will create significant value.

And while this is often the case in competitive markets, there are many examples where innovations do not create value even in competitive environments. Consider, for example, the 2008 financial crisis. The economist Joseph Stiglitz discussed how the subprime mortgage industry, with its innovative products, worsened, rather than solved, borrowers' problems.[3] Subprime mortgages increased costs and risks for consumers while providing mortgage brokers and lenders larger fees. These products, however, increased risk to the institutions that acquired the ensuing credit default swaps and collateralized debt obligations. Among the losers in the financial crisis were supposedly sophisticated investors who failed to appreciate these assets' risks. Moreover, these financial innovations made speculation easier.[4]

To summarize—we should expect value-creating innovation only if the three underlying assumptions are true. (But even in competitive markets, like the subprime mortgage industry, competition can still yield innovations that destroy or extract value.)

From Value Creation to Extraction

As we move away from a competitive landscape to where the number of Tech Pirates and their impact dwindle, and where a few Tech Barons can affect the supply and demand of innovation, the nature and value of innovation will change. There will be relatively more sustaining, rather than disruptive, innovations. Value-creating innovations will be gradually displaced by innovations that focus on extracting value from the downstream users or upstream suppliers and primarily benefit the Tech Barons. There will be relatively more innovations that destroy value.

Of course, this is not an all-or-nothing scenario. As the Tech Barons' power increases, we won't be inundated with just value-destroying innovations. Instead, it reflects a material but subtle change in the value and nature of innovation. We will still get value-creating innovation when it disrupts industries outside the Tech Barons' current ecosystem—such as driverless cars and innovative health care. But we will get far fewer innovations that might potentially disrupt the Tech Barons' ecosystem. Within the ecosystem, the incentives change to focus on *sustaining* rather than *disruptive* innovations. And since every Tech Baron develops its ecosystem to ensure that it profits from the competition, one can expect more extractive innovations.

To illustrate this trend, let's take a look at personal data. Initially, personal data was acquired from consumers to primarily benefit consumers. Back in 1998, when they presented a prototype of their search engine, Google's founders Sergey Brin and Lawrence Page warned how advertising could distort a search engine's incentives. They predicted that "advertising funded search engines will be inherently biased towards the advertisers and away from the needs of the consumers."[5] Given the "insidiousness" of the resulting search bias, the young entrepreneurs argued "that it is crucial to have a competitive search engine that is transparent and in the academic realm." Google initially wasn't dependent on advertising revenues, and its search engine collected personal data to improve its search engine results.

Likewise, in 2006, with eight million users, Facebook acknowledged the value of championing privacy. After privacy concerns were raised about its News Feed feature, Facebook quickly reiterated its commitment to users' privacy.[6] Mark Zuckerberg publicly apologized, saying, "We really messed this one up . . . this was a big mistake on our part, and I'm sorry for it."[7] Facebook subsequently agreed to tighten its privacy controls. Why? Because users were unhappy, and more importantly, they had viable alternatives (outside options). They could have walked away.

In winner-take-all markets with multiple network effects, like search engines and social networks, once the market tips in the Tech Baron's favor, it is harder for consumers to switch to a different or nascent offering. As the competitive pressure dampens, the Tech Baron's incentives shift—from creating to extracting value. So, the Tech Barons collect far more data *about* us, but not necessarily *for* us. Yes, consumers get more personalized services, but the data is increasingly compiled to better profile us, target us with behavioral ads, and predict and manipulate our behavior. As the Tech Baron's power increases, our privacy erodes.

One study, for example, reviewed copies of Facebook's privacy policies from 2005 to 2015.[8] In ranking each Facebook privacy policy based on its compliance with thirty-three privacy criteria, the study found a decline in twenty-two of the thirty-three standards. As Facebook's power increased, its privacy policies no longer fully described under what circumstances data are externally disclosed or Facebook's use of internet-monitoring technologies, such as beacons, weblogs, and cookies. "Drops in these measures suggest that privacy policies became less informative over time, even as word count soared."

While we might derive some value from the Tech Barons' innovations, the Tech Barons extract even more value from us. Consider the behavioral advertising ecosystem (where even Apple is complicit). We may get the "free" app, but the surplus goes to the Tech Barons. Consider, for example, the value that Facebook extracts from users. As Table 6.2 reflects, Facebook extracted significantly more revenues per user over the past decade.

Table 6.2

FACEBOOK'S AVERAGE REVENUE PER USER AS OF FOURTH QUARTER 2020, BY REGION (IN U.S. DOLLARS)			
	U.S. and Canada	Europe	Asia Pacific	Rest of world
Q4 '11	$3.20	$1.60	$0.56	$0.41
Q4 '12	$4.08	$1.71	$0.69	$0.56
Q4 '13	$6.03	$2.61	$0.95	$0.84
Q4 '14	$9.00	$3.45	$1.27	$0.94
Q4 '15	$13.70	$4.56	$1.60	$1.10
Q4 '16	$19.81	$5.98	$2.07	$1.41
Q4 '17	$26.76	$8.86	$2.54	$1.86
Q4 '18	$34.86	$10.98	$2.96	$2.11
Q4 '19	$41.41	$13.21	$3.57	$2.48
Q1 '20	$34.18	$10.64	$3.06	$1.99
Q2 '20	$36.49	$11.03	$2.99	$1.78
Q3 '20	$39.63	$12.41	$3.67	$2.22
Q4 '20	$53.56	$16.87	$4.05	$2.77

Source: Facebook[9]

Can one justify Facebook making about sixteen times more in revenues in 2020 per US and Canadian user than what it was making in 2011? Perhaps, if these users were getting significantly more in value over this same period. But, arguably, they haven't.[10]

Why haven't the Tech Pirates prevented the Tech Barons from degrading privacy or disrupted their monopoly profits? The answer is market power and the anticompetitive strategies outlined in the preceding chapters. The elimination of potential competition and disruption (which leave customers with fewer options) enabled the shift from value creation to value extraction.

When the Tech Barons' ecosystem relies on behavioral advertising, the first frontier is to better predict our behavior. Under the guise of personalization, the Tech Barons and those within their ecosystem innovate in finding better ways to harvest data and predict our behavior. Among the many patents and innovations to implement these strategies, you could find, for example:

- Technologies that scan your private communications to learn more about you, your interests, and your needs; [11]

- Mechanisms that enable third parties to access your correspondence; [12]

- Technologies that use available microphones, including on your smartwatch, to listen to your environment; [13] and

- "Sniffer" algorithms that listen to background conversations (at times, without requiring a "wake word"). [14]

The Tech Barons continuously run experiments on us to see how we react to subtle changes and to better predict our behavior. Facebook, for example, reportedly uses an artificial intelligence–powered engine to predict user behavior. The technology enables Facebook to predict user loyalty to a particular brand and the likelihood of switching to a competitor's. Third parties and advertisers use Facebook's "loyalty prediction" to "target people on the basis of decisions they haven't even made yet" and "to alter a consumer's anticipated course." [15]

Of course, advances in predictions can add value. New technologies that predict our demand can be used to increase efficiencies in production and distribution, speed up delivery times, and lower return rates. But the Tech Barons often harness these advancements against our interests. Why? Their incentives are not always aligned with ours and the lack of pushback from potential competitors and disruptors offers them the freedom to exploit. Instead of working for us, the innovations now serve its new barons.

From Predicting to Manipulating Our Behavior and Emotions

Even with behavioral ads, it can be hit-or-miss. One study found that "98% of all advertising information is not perceived at all, and the average duration of an advertisement perception is only 2 seconds."[16] Why then predict our behavior when greater profits can be had from manipulating our behavior and emotions? In getting us to buy things we otherwise wouldn't want at the highest price that we are willing to pay, Tech Barons can profit even more.

As we saw in chapter 4, we are more like the blackcaps than the autonomous creatures we might imagine. In the behavioral advertising environment, autonomy is a rather slippery concept. And so, to increase profits, the Tech Barons' ecosystems move beyond personalized ads and services. They aren't simply showing you shirts, cars, or shoes that interest you but making you want that particular polo, EV-car, or pair of sneakers. And that gap between predicting and manipulating is closing, as AI systems and devices "will soon recognize, interpret, process, and simulate human emotions."[17]

Critical here is the stealth mode of these manipulations. Your personal device, as one researcher noted, could "know more about your emotional state than your own family."[18] Machine learning is now discovering what events and stimuli trigger specific emotions and is "already at or beyond human-level performance in discerning a person's emotional state on the basis of tone of voice or facial expression."[19] Once an algorithm can predict what stimuli will make you happy or sad, it can manipulate particular emotions for desired results, whether to buy or endorse a product, vote for a specific candidate, or refrain from voting. In line with these technologies, we will see advances in refining ways to better manipulate our feelings and behavior. Currently, marketers rely on eye-tracking research for "a more objective approach to assessing consumer's perception of advertising."[20] We are often oblivious to these manipulations, and underestimate the extent to which they affect our behavior. As these neuro-technologies and neuromarketing techniques improve, our autonomy, control, and well-being will decline.

One early example was Facebook's "Emotional Contagion Study." Researchers manipulated 689,003 users' News Feeds to see whether it would influence the users' emotions.[21] It did. Facebook controlled the number of positive and negative posts their users received and measured how this affected their moods. Those receiving fewer positive posts were, in turn, less positive themselves.[22] Those who received less negative content were less negative. The study concluded that "emotions expressed by others on Facebook influence our own emotions, constituting experimental evidence for massive-scale contagion via social networks."

One 2019 study examined whether it is possible to accurately predict consumers' personality traits solely from their online browsing behavior in real-time.[23] Could they assess whether you are agreeable or neurotic simply by how you moved your mouse across the screen?

Yes. Using data fed from Google Analytics trackers, the machine learning algorithm could accurately predict in real-time multiple personality traits of the study's participants, namely their (1) need for cognition, (2) need for arousal, (3) lay rationality, and each of the so-called Big 5 personality traits: Openness to experiences, Conscientiousness, Extraversion, Agreeableness, and Neuroticism (OCEAN). If you are a consumer with a high need for arousal, you will buy more impulsively and "react more favorably to violent, sexual, and fear-provoking content." If you are a consumer high in neuroticism, you likely shop less online, but when you do, "it is often for the purpose of mood management."[24]

This study involved a commercially available tracker (Google Analytics), which monitored particular events (such as whether the participant's mouse indicator hovered over a picture of one of the products). The data set was relatively small (38,840 recorded events from 770 participants), which was fed into the study's "personality trait prediction" algorithm. But it offers a glimpse into the formidable analytical power of data, how it can be used to manipulate our behavior, and the potential for abuse. The study's algorithm predicted fairly accurately some personality traits even when the study's participant viewed only one web page or spent just ten seconds in the shop.[25] So, while the consumer is browsing the shop, the online retailer could "quickly determine a consumer's personality traits and then dynamically adjust their online shop accordingly." Now imagine what the Tech Barons can unleash with more data that trains more sophisticated deep learning algorithms.[26] They will improve their behavioral advertising apparatus so that e-tailers can focus on those consumers for whom those predictions are most likely to be accurate and most profitable.

Companies continuously invest in innovative ways to decode our psyche. New technologies are not limited to communications, eye movements,[27] or body language[28] to gain insights as to our behavior. Facebook, for example, can already infer our relationship (whether we're single, married, in a relationship, etc.) and sentiment based on our interactions, profile image, and contacts, even if we opted not to make that information public.[29] Our personality characteristics can now be inferred from our social networking interactions on Facebook, Instagram, or WhatsApp.[30] To do so, linguistic data is extracted from our status updates, notes, messages, posts, comments, or any other communications and is analyzed with additional data (such as our age, gender, number of contacts, frequency, and range of interactions) to identify our personality characteristics such as "extroversion, agreeableness, conscientiousness, emotional stability, and openness."[31] But Facebook burrows deeper by developing technology that may enable it to read our emotions by analyzing the speed and pressure applied as we type on our keyboard.[32]

Facebook is not alone. Microsoft has patented technology that classifies our emotions for targeting purposes.[33] Microsoft's technology explores what external stimuli prompt our particular "happiness, sadness, anger, fear, disappointment, or pride" and cognitive states such as being "focused, engaged, distracted, bored, sleepy, confused, or frustrated."[34] As one patent states, "advertisers provide targeting data that includes the desired emotional states of users it intends to target. . . . The computer system monitors the online activity of users. . . . In turn, the computer system assigns emotional states to the users based on the tone of the content and the indications of the users' reactions. Advertisements are selected for delivery . . ."[35] Similarly, IBM's technology provides search results based on the user's browsing history and emotional state.[36] New technology from Amazon will allow Alexa to recognize and classify your emotional state—"happiness, joy, anger, sorrow, sadness, fear, disgust, boredom, stress"—and react with targeted promotions and advertising.[37] Your new voice-activated digital helper may change its "emotional" tone when communicating with you based on your mood.[38]

When information is missing, new technology can infer it based on your interactions with others. Facebook now has technologies that enable it to detect your emotions by analyzing imagery from smartphone cameras or webcams.[39] Innovations now can examine the quality, tempo, and tone of your speech to offer insights into your emotional state[40] or reveal your underlying attitudes and thoughts.[41]

We might think we have a pretty good poker face, but researchers have found otherwise. They discovered that tracking subtle, fleeting changes in forty-four facial muscles can reveal unconscious "emotional leaks."[42] These micro-expressions of disgust, for example, during marriage counseling sessions were "a reliable sign that the marriage would fail."[43] The *Harvard Business Review* predicted in 2019 that the "affective computing market" would grow to "$41 billion by 2022, as firms like Amazon, Google, Facebook, and Apple race to decode their users' emotions."[44] As one pioneer of AI noted, "In the not too distant future, your iPhone may not only be asking you why you're upset; it may also be helping you to calm down."[45]

Our privacy and autonomy have already taken a toll from innovations developed to maximize behavioral advertising revenue, such as how long our mouse lingers over an image, what we search, what we Like on Facebook, where we go, and what we say and do—all observed from our smart appliances, wearables, digital assistants, phones, computers, cars, and home security cameras.[46]

Thus, the current frontier is our emotions, where algorithms will predict our feelings better than our closest family members and friends with the likely goal of manipulating us. Our personalities and weaknesses are being converted into code. As the futurist Richard van Hooijdonk notes, "If a marketer can get you to cry, he can get you to buy."[47]

But it will become even more intrusive, as we'll see next, with the convergence of neurotechnology (where the Tech Barons are investing in machine learning to better decipher human thoughts), neuromarketing (which studies "unconscious sensorimotor, cognitive and human emotional reactions to external stimuli") and the metaverse—all fueled by behavioral advertising.[48]

"I am very good."

In 1876, Alexander Graham Bell, seeking to develop hearing devices for the deaf, transmitted the first words over his invention, the telephone: "Mr. Watson, come here. I want to see you." Fast forward to July 2021, where an algorithm successfully decoded for the first time speech from brain activity. When the study's participant, who, because of paralysis, could not speak, was asked, "How are you today?" AI was able to decode from the participant's brain activity his response: "I am very good."

Researchers at UC San Francisco in 2021 successfully developed this "speech neuroprosthesis" that enabled someone "with severe paralysis to communicate in sentences, translating signals from his brain to the vocal tract directly into words that appear as text on a screen."[49] An electrode was implanted into the person's brain. The person sought to say fifty specific vocabulary words many times while the electrodes recorded the brain signals from his speech cortex. When the person tried to speak, the computer algorithm distinguished the "subtle patterns in brain activity to detect speech attempts and identify which words he was trying to say."[50] After about twenty-two hours of recording the person's neural activity, the algorithm could decode the participant's thoughts from his brain activity "at a rate of up to 18 words per minute with up to 93 percent accuracy (75 percent median)."

No doubt, these innovations can create significant value, particularly for those with speech paralysis. The critical point is that with market power, control over the ecosystem, and existing value chains, these technologies will likely be implemented in ways that do not necessarily serve our interests. In an environment where the Tech Barons eliminated disruption and potential competition, they will likely drive the innovation to deliver the ultimate goal—profits. With power comes the ability and incentive to implement new innovations to exploit us. As more participants' internal thoughts are converted into code, algorithms can more accurately predict what we are thinking. Just as our DNA has been mapped out, so too will our emotions, thoughts, and thought processes. So, who is sponsoring UCSF's "speech neuroprosthesis" AI? Facebook, which emphasized the multiple applications from decoding our thoughts:

> This work illustrates how applying new machine learning techniques can accelerate brain-computer interface (BCI) development for many different applications. At Facebook Reality Labs, we're focused on exploring how non-invasive BCI can redefine the AR/VR experience. New research helps illuminate the path forward in our mission to develop a non-invasive silent speech interface for the next computing platform. We are proud to sponsor and support academic research groups like UCSF.[51]

This research aligns with Facebook's goal of transitioning from a social media company to a metaverse company. The speech neuroprosthesis technology in decoding our thoughts is part of Facebook's investment in its virtual reality ecosystem, "to let you experience anything, anywhere, with anyone."[52] As Facebook's CEO told investors in mid-2021:

> So what is the metaverse? It's a virtual environment where you can be present with people in digital spaces. You can kind of think about this as an embodied internet that you're inside of rather than just looking at. We believe that this is going to be the successor to the mobile internet.
> You're going to be able to access the metaverse from all different levels of fidelity—from apps on phones and

P.C.s to immersive virtual and augmented reality devices. Within the metaverse, you're going to be able to hang out, play games with friends, work, create, and more. You're basically going to be able to do everything that you can on the internet today as well as some things that don't make sense on the internet today, like dancing.

The defining quality of the metaverse is presence—which is this feeling that you're really there with another person or in another place. Creation, avatars and digital objects will be central to how we express ourselves, and this is going to lead to entirely new experiences and economic opportunities.[53]

For Zuckerberg, the metaverse "is the ultimate expression of social technology."[54] It's not just the Tech Barons. Fortnite's developer, for example, is pursuing "a realistic 3D world in which participants have both social experiences, like sitting in a bar and talking, and also game experiences."[55] So, your virtual avatar can watch a Netflix show with other gamers: "All in the virtual 3D world. You can stand there and watch Netflix with your friends, and it's different than watching it in front of the T.V. You can talk to your friends, and you can emote and throw tomatoes at the screen. And so it is a very different experience than either a game or Netflix."[56]

If the metaverse represents Big Tech's ultimate expression of social technology, what does that portend for us? A look at the current use of some technologies can give us a glimpse to the way in which third parties could abuse them. As Facebook's internal reports acknowledge, drug cartels use the Tech Baron's platforms to recruit, train, and pay hitmen.[57] A Mexican drug cartel's Instagram account had a "video of a person with a gold pistol shooting a young man in the head while blood spurts from his neck."[58] The next Instagram post was "a photo of a beaten man tied to a chair; the one after that is a trash bag full of severed hands."[59] Facebook employees internally record "their embarrassment and frustration, citing decisions that allow users to post videos of murders, incitements to violence, government threats against pro-democracy campaigners and advertisements for human trafficking."[60] Internally, Facebook employees recognize that the company's current mitigation strategies, especially outside of the US, are insufficient.[61]

Now imagine Facebook developing this "non-invasive silent speech interface" for the next computing platform, the metaverse. This could present a nightmare scenario: Facebook can't protect us currently from the sex traffickers and drug cartels on their platforms. So, expect those who currently promote on Facebook's platforms violence, exacerbate ethnic divides, and delegitimize social institutions[62] to also be in Facebook's metaverse. Also, Facebook is seeking to decipher our thoughts while we experience this discord in the metaverse. To envisage how Facebook's metaverse can harm our well-being, let's consider Instagram, once it came under Facebook's control.

Toxic Innovations That Destroy Value

One rarely sees US senators across the political spectrum pummel one company so vigorously.[63]

What prompted the outcry?

As Senator Richard Blumenthal said, "Facebook seems to be taking a page from the textbook of Big Tobacco—targeting teens with potentially dangerous products while masking the science in public."[64]

In 2016, according to former Instagram executives, Facebook directed its employees "to focus on winning what they viewed as a race for teen users."[65] It worked. By 2021, over 40 percent of Instagram's users were under twenty-three years old, and about twenty-two million teens logged on to Instagram in the US each day.[66] On average, teens in the US spent 50 percent more time on Instagram than on Facebook.[67]

The impact this usage has on their mental health is of great concern.[68] But Facebook's Zuckerberg downplayed any concern, testifying before Congress that "[t]he research that we've seen is that using social apps to connect with other people can have positive mental-health benefits."[69] That was deceptive.

Internally, Facebook knew of the harmful effects of its Instagram platform on millions of young adults, as a *Wall Street Journal* series on the company revealed.[70] Facebook studied the issue extensively and found that some of the problems were specific to Instagram and not social media more broadly.[71]

Among Facebook's internal findings were:

- "Thirty-two percent of teen girls said that when they felt bad about their bodies, Instagram made them feel worse," Facebook's researchers said in a March 2020 internal slide presentation. "Comparisons on Instagram can change how young women view and describe themselves." "We make body image issues worse for one in three teen girls," said another internal slide from 2019.

- According to one internal Facebook study of teens in the US and UK, the feelings of having to create the perfect image, not being attractive, and not having enough money were most likely to have started on Instagram. Over 40 percent of Instagram users who reported feeling "not attractive" said the feeling began on the app.

- "One in five teens say that Instagram makes them feel worse about themselves, with UK girls the most negative."[72]

- "Teens who struggle with mental health say Instagram makes it worse."[73]

- "Teens blame Instagram for increases in the rate of anxiety and depression," said another Facebook slide. "This reaction was unprompted and consistent across all groups."

- Among the ways that Instagram harms their mental health is "[i]nappropriate advertisements targeted to vulnerable groups."[74]

- Among teens who reported suicidal thoughts, 13 percent of British users and 6 percent of American users traced the desire to kill themselves to Instagram.

As Facebook internally noted, teens regularly reported wanting to spend less time on Instagram. Still, they lacked the self-control to do so: "They often feel 'addicted' and know that what they're seeing is bad for their mental health but feel unable to stop themselves." Indeed, Facebook researchers warned "that the Explore page, which serves users photos and videos curated by an algorithm, can send users deep into content that can be harmful." Although the research was shared with top management, the internal documents also show that "Facebook has made minimal efforts to address these issues and plays them down in public."[75] Why? "We're standing directly between people and their bonuses," one former researcher said.

The Tech Baron is also targeting preteens, including finding ways to engage toddlers during playdates. As one Facebook official asked, "Is there a way to leverage playdates to drive word of hand/growth among kids?"[76] According to the *Wall Street Journal*, which reviewed the company's internal files, the Tech Baron "formed a team to study preteens, set a three-year goal to create more products for them and commissioned strategy papers about the long-term business opportunities presented by these potential users."[77] It is not surprising that teenagers are warning their younger siblings of the dangers of social media. As one Facebook employee noted, "If it is common that teens are discouraging preteens from sharing, there are obvious implications for creation and the ecosystem both in the near and longer-term as preteens are the next generation coming onto the platform."[78] It is also not surprising that Facebook is developing an Instagram product targeting children under thirteen. After the 2021 Senate hearings, Facebook said it would temporarily suspend launching the app to hear more from parents, experts, and lawmakers.

One senator asked a Facebook official a fundamental question: "Are teenagers safe on any of your platforms?"[79] Facebook's vice president of

Privacy & Public Policy equivocated, "We're working really hard to make that the case." The Facebook executive testified that there was no more important priority than the well-being and safety of its users. That set off the senator. "I really can't believe you're saying that. I mean really."[80] The Tech Barons "always dissemble. You always mislead. I can't believe that given the research you have conducted that you can sit there and say that teens' health and security and safety are your top priority. Clearly, it's not, and you won't share any of the data. You're stonewalling every member of this [Senate] committee."[81]

Now imagine children navigating the Tech Barons' technological advances in neuromarketing, neurotechnology, and the metaverse, where the incentives are skewed by behavioral advertising. If Tech Barons' platforms are purposefully addictive now, consider their toll on mental health and well-being when the last bastion of privacy—mental repose—collapses.

The innovations within the Tech Barons' ecosystem are invariably skewed to attracting and sustaining our attention—whether watching Apple TV, YouTube, or Prime videos, posting on social media sites, texting, playing online games, or browsing the web. That means less time for other activities—like sleep, studying, and doing things with other people that can actually improve our well-being.[82] Millennials, reportedly, spend an average of 5.7 hours using their smartphones each day, of which 48 minutes are dedicated, on average, to texting.[83]

So encompassing is our reliance on our phones that psychologists have coined a word for the fear of being without one's phone: *nomophobia* (no mobile phone phobia).[84] Symptoms include "regular and time-consuming use, feelings of anxiety when the phone is not available, 'ringxiety' (i.e., repeatedly checking one's phone for messages, sometimes leading to phantom ring tones), constant availability, preference for mobile communication over face to face communication, and financial problems as a consequence of use."[85] Psychologists have defined as disorders "social network site addiction" and "Facebook addiction,"[86] in which users are "overly concerned about social media, driven by an uncontrollable motivation to log on to or use social media, and devoting so much time and effort to [social network sites] that it impairs other important life areas."[87]

Thus, how did so many of us get hooked on our phones? "Your kid is not weak-willed because he can't get off his phone," one neuroscientist noted. "Your kid's brain is being engineered to get him to stay on his phone."[88] The same could be said of all of us. The Tech Barons and apps within their ecosystem foster this addiction through dopamine rewards. As one Stanford professor explained, the problem is that "the brain's set-point for pleasure changes. Now we need to keep playing games, not to feel pleasure but just to feel normal. As soon as we stop, we experience the universal symptoms of withdrawal from any addictive substance: anxiety, irritability, insomnia, dysphoria, and mental preoccupation with using, otherwise known as craving."[89]

The Tech Barons' ecosystems incentivize companies to make their apps and games as addictive as possible, thereby eroding our capacity for free choice.[90] As explained by the early Facebook investor and mentor Roger McNamee, the company's business model "depends on advertising, which in turn depends on manipulating the attention of users, so they see more ads."[91] Between late 2012 and 2017, Facebook "experimented constantly with algorithms, new data types and small changes in design, measuring everything."[92] The goal was to use the company's best minds to figure out better ways to exploit our psychological weaknesses.[93] Our need for connection and validation is constantly used to addict us. "Instead of technology being a tool in service to humanity," McNamee noted, "it is humans who are in service to technology."[94] The result, as a former Facebook employee pointed out, is "a business model designed to engage you and get you to basically suck as much time out of your life as possible and then selling that attention to advertisers."[95]

Former Facebook executives also voiced misgivings about "the company's role in exacerbating isolation, outrage, and addictive behaviors."[96] Sean Parker, an early investor in Facebook who served as its first president, confirmed that Facebook's strategy and technology seeks to "consume as much of your time and conscious attention as possible. And that means that we need to sort of give you a little dopamine hit every once in a while . . . it's a social validation feedback loop. . . . You're exploiting the vulnerability in human psychology. And I think the inventors, creators—and it's me, Mark [Zuckerberg] . . . —understood this, consciously, and we did it anyway."[97] In an interview, he was clear about the fact that Facebook's founders "knew they were creating something people would become addicted to," adding "God only knows what it's doing to our children's brains."[98] Now Facebook knows, from its internal studies.

Aza Raskin, who is credited with inventing the habit-forming infinite-scroll feature (that allows you to endlessly swipe down through content without clicking), said in a BBC "Panorama" interview:

We're in the largest behavioral experiment the world has ever seen. You're being tested on it all the time. . . . We do things like changing the color of your 'like' button . . . there is this shade of blue—should it be a little bit more red? And they'll keep trying a different button on you, at different times, until they find the perfect shape and the perfect color that most maximizes your continuing scrolling. Behind every screen on your phone, there are literally a thousand engineers who try to make it maximally addicting. It is as if they are taking behavioral cocaine and just sprinkle it all over your interface.[99]

And the reason behind this drive couldn't be more straightforward:

In order to get the next round of funding, in order to get your stock price up, the amount of time that people spend on your app has to go up. . . . So, when you put that much pressure on that one number, you're going to start trying to invent new ways of getting people to stay hooked.[100]

In search of some respite, some of us may try to evade tracking and profiling by not visiting the Tech Barons' ecosystems. But it will be even harder to hide as the brain hacking technologies burrow into our thoughts and fears.

Reflections

The shift from predicting to manipulating behavior doesn't have to be toxic. The innovations, with our knowing and voluntary consent, could nudge us in ways to increase our well-being, such as eating healthier, sleeping more, saving for retirement, getting us off the screen, and directly interacting with our community.

But in the Tech Barons' ecosystems, expect these innovations to extract even more value from us (and expect the Tech Barons to disavow their toxicity). Facebook's CEO already told investors that behavioral advertising will likely be "a meaningful part of the metaverse."[101] Indeed, the metaverse offers more opportunities to manipulate us into buying things we might not otherwise have wanted at the highest price we will pay. As Zuckerberg told investors:

> . . . I think digital goods and creators are just going to be huge, right, in terms of people expressing themselves through their avatars, through digital clothing, through digital goods, the apps that they have, that they bring with them from place to place.
>
> A lot of the metaverse experience is going to be around being able to teleport from one experience to another. So being able to basically have your digital goods and your inventory and bring them from place to place, that's going to be a big investment that people make.[102]

So, from Google, Facebook, and Amazon, where revenues from behavioral advertising and sales are the driver, expect more innovations to decode your emotions, identify what prompts those emotions, and trigger the particular feeling for the desired action. For Apple, expect more innovations that keep you within its walled ecosystem. For Microsoft, to build its gaming, intelligent cloud and intelligent edge platforms, expect innovations to help it and its clients find better ways to engage users (by manipulating their behavior).

And what about the disruptive pirates? By now, you should know the answer. If they threaten the value chain, they will be crushed.

As the Tech Barons' ecosystems expand to the metaverse, health care, smart cars, and smart appliances, the means of surveillance will likely change. Once a Tech Baron can effectively decode and manipulate our thoughts and emotions, it may not require us to spend as much time on its platform. After all, a casino does not require you to spend all your time playing the slots. Just enough time to extract most of your wealth this time while giving you enough excitement for you to return—again and again—over your lifetime.

In decoding our thoughts and emotions, the victorious Tech Baron will already know what we'll likely buy or consume tomorrow morning and why we'll want it before we even open our eyes. So, once current or future Tech Barons perfect brain hacking, they may not need as much data about what videos you watch or what you are searching. Protecting our data will be yesteryear's battle. Absent a change in policies, you might be reading this book in 2030, thinking your privacy and autonomy are restored. After all, the Tech Barons of 2030 may no longer nudge you back to their ecosystems, and you may have time for more recreational things—like reading this book.

But consider your last forty to fifty purchases, your recent interactions, and your view of the world. What emotions or thoughts prompted them? Were they as serendipitous as you initially thought? And were they yours or those of the overseers of the metaverse?

CHAPTER 7

Ripple Effects

FACED WITH INCREASED TOXICITY, one might want to avoid the Tech Barons' ecosystem as much as possible. Granted, the seas have narrowed to lakes and ponds for Tech Pirates and the rest of us. But there are still millions of lakes around the world to explore.

Of course, such a proposition is naive. It ignores the ongoing expansion of the Tech Barons' ecosystems, the interconnections between innovation efforts, and the broader impact the Tech Barons have on innovation paths, funding, and knowledge.

But even if we could ignore this toxicity within and around the Tech Barons' ecosystems, we still face the broader consequences of their innovations—the ripple effects of toxicity.

We will not catalog all the harmful effects (which will change as the toxic innovation evolves). Instead, we make a simple point: *What happens online doesn't stay online.* The ripple effects from toxic innovation extend far beyond the Tech Barons' ecosystems, the digital economy, the user experience, and the impact on Tech Pirates. These toxic innovations ultimately corrode our social and political fabric and harm our autonomy, democracy, and well-being.

To illustrate, we consider three ripple effects (Figure 7.1), each with different consequences: first, how the Tech Barons' toxic innovations undermine our social fabric in spreading emotional contagion; second, how advanced targeting and manipulation harm democracy and governance; and finally, how dynamism diminishes overall.

Figure 7.1

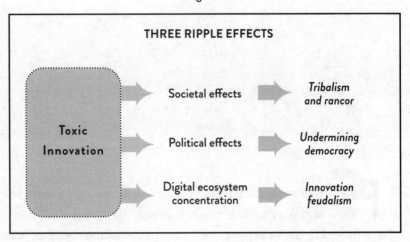

One caveat is in order. Tech Barons and their toxic innovation, while important factors, are not the only variables. For example, the legal framework; social, political, and ethical norms; and business strategies also contribute to the political and societal effects we'll examine (and impact disruptive innovation). Our point is that there are no seawalls to contain the harm from these toxic creations; we pay the price in our autonomy, well-being, and democracy.

Tribalism and Rancor

"If you feed the beast, that beast will destroy you." This warning came from former Facebook vice president for user growth Chamath Palihapitiya. Speaking at Stanford University's Graduate School of Business,

Chamath, who's now the founder and current CEO of Social Capital, warned about the toxic innovations designed to addict us:

> [W]e have created tools that are ripping apart the social fabric of how society works. That is truly where we are.... The short-term dopamine-driven feedback loops that we've created are destroying how society works. No civil discourse, no cooperation. Misinformation, mistruth. And it's not an American problem—this is not about Russian ads. This is a global problem.... It is eroding the core foundations of how people behave by and between each other.
>
> . . . bad actors can now manipulate large swathes of people to do anything you want . . . and we compound the problem . . . we curate our lives around this perceived sense of perfection because we get rewarded from short term signals—hearts, likes, thumbs-up, and we conflate that with value, and we conflate it with the truth. And instead, what it really is, is fake brittle popularity. That's short-term, and that leaves you even more . . . vacant and empty before you did it. Because then it forces you into this vicious circle where you like what's the next thing I need to do now . . .[1]

Once triggered by a post, video, or story, our anger and fear do not stop with us. They create a ripple effect, where we spread our anger and fear to others through the pictures, posts, videos, or stories we share and comment on. Facebook's emotional contagion study confirms this. Indeed, an internal study by Facebook warned how its News Feed algorithms "exploit the human brain's attraction to divisiveness."[2] "If left unchecked," it would feed users "more and more divisive content in an effort to gain user attention and increase time on the platform."[3] Facebook's social media platforms also lower the costs for extremist groups to identify, communicate, and enlist members. The Tech Baron helped these extremist groups grow. An internal 2016 Facebook study found that "64% of all extremist group joins are due to [Facebook's] recommendation tools."[4]

These effects are not limited to social networks. Take, for another example, YouTube's video recommending algorithm. Over 70 percent of the time we spend on the platform is dedicated to recommended videos.[5] Designed to increase our engagement by favoring disagreeable and controversial content, the algorithm "propagates inflammatory content, leaving honest content-makers in the dust."[6] As the algorithm experiments on content to retain us longer, it amplifies extreme content and contributes to the formation of filter bubbles.[7] These effects did not go unnoticed within Google. Employees sought to address these filter bubbles and increase the diversity of content by changing YouTube's recommendation algorithm. But that improvement reduced viewers' retention (which would eventually reduce advertising income), and Google subsequently suspended that change.[8]

This is unsurprising when behavioral advertising finances Google's and Facebook's ecosystems. Attention and personal data are the two vital inputs to maximize ad revenues. If fear, rancor, anger, and antagonism increase our engagement, expect the algorithms throughout the Tech Barons' ecosystems to recommend even more divisive content. Thus, the Tech Baron's algorithm "isn't actually rewarding content that drives meaningful social interactions" but "bad content" that exploits racial divisions, "fad/junky science," "extremely disturbing news," and gross images.[9]

And the Tech Barons know this. A former Facebook AI researcher discussed the internal research by Facebook:

> [They] conducted "study after study" confirming the same basic idea: models that maximize engagement increase polarization. They could easily track how strongly users agreed or disagreed on different issues, what content they liked to engage with, and how their stances changed as a result. Regardless of the issue, the models learned to feed users' increasingly extreme viewpoints. "Over time they measurably become more polarized," he says.[10]

Even if you avoid social media platforms, the Tech Platforms affect billions of users each day. (Facebook alone has more than 1.9 billion daily users; YouTube is second and attracts at least a 50 percent share of all social media users, with numbers of daily active users reaching 225 million in India and 197 million in the US.[11]) So, the emotional contagion will likely spread to you and your family, friends, and community.

Just consider India, which is Facebook's largest market in terms of users. The company knew that its social network and WhatsApp messaging app were helping disseminate "content that encourages conflict, hatred and violence."[12] Muslims were asking Facebook to protect them from this hatred. And Facebook researchers knew some of the key propagators of this hate and violence (its researchers found that two Hindu nationalist groups with ties to India's ruling political party were posting inflammatory anti-Muslim content on its platform). But Facebook did little to prevent the hate its platforms were spreading, even though people told Facebook researchers that they were fearing for their life. One Muslim man told Facebook researchers that "if social media survives 10 more years like this, there will be only hatred," and India will be a "very difficult place to survive for everyone."

The unavoidable outcome is increased tribalism and hate. Algorithm-driven recommendations have been linked to increased radicalization. Even before India, the sharing of fake reports and rumors on Facebook led to riots and brutal killings of Muslim minorities in Myanmar. Riots in Sri Lanka, which were also triggered by false rumors, led a presidential adviser to comment: "The germs are ours, but Facebook is the wind."[13]

The Tech Barons warrant blame for fueling the tribalism and rancor. But the central culprit is not the Tech Baron per se, but its value chain. As FTC Commissioner Rohit Chopra noted:

> The case against Facebook is about more than just privacy—it is also about the power to control and manipulate. Global regulators and policymakers need to confront the dangers associated with mass surveillance and the resulting ability to control and influence us. The behavioral advertising business incentives of technology platforms spur practices that are dividing our society. The harm from this conduct is immeasurable, and regulators and policymakers must confront it.[14]

To compete with the Tech Barons for our attention and data, other social media platforms, like Twitter or Twitch, also propagate conspiracy theories, extreme views, and ultimately violence.[15] Likewise, one wouldn't think Amazon would need to employ these tactics as they control over 70 percent of book sales. But its recommendation algorithm could drive people from one conspiracy to the next, as the Institute for Strategic Dialogue found:

> One of the effects of Amazon's recommendation algorithm is to cross-propagate conspiracy theories. Users who view a book about one conspiracy theory are not only likely to be recommended more books about that conspiracy theory, but also books about other conspiracy theories. Amazon's recommendation algorithms can thus drive users deeper into conspiratorial content and cross-pollinate conspiracy theories.[16]

The Tech Barons and those who compete within their ecosystem do not necessarily create falsehoods, propaganda, or conspiracy theories. Still, they profit from them.[17] A vicious cycle emerges: with the Tech Pirates crushed, the innovations mainly complement and fortify the prevailing value chain and business model. Thus, for ecosystems that rely primarily on behavioral advertising, it becomes harder for any company, including the Tech Baron, to buck this value chain, especially when the ensuing innovations—under the guise of personalization—seek better ways to grab our attention and data and manipulate behavior.

The anomaly does not stop there. Following public outrage over their platforms' content, the Tech Barons now pursue a schizophrenic effort to curb the tribalism their ecosystems promote. After the January 2021 attack on the U.S. Capitol, for example, the Tech Barons sought to temper some of this extremism by delisting groups. Figure 7.2 shows a warning received by Facebook users in mid-2021.

The irony is hard to ignore, since Facebook's recommendation algorithm helped these extremist groups grow. So, these Tech Barons employ warring algorithms: one that rewards outrage and lies to attract and sustain our attention; another that seeks to censor that content.[18]

Figure 7.2

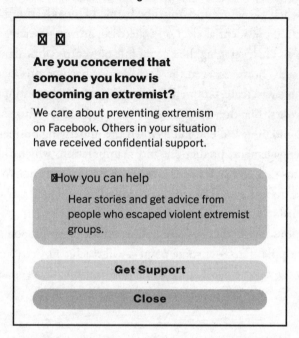

But because misinformation and online radicalization spread faster than truth on social media platforms, the Tech Barons cannot contain the wildfires they foster.[19] Moreover, Facebook's CEO resisted efforts to further tamper the attention-grabbing algorithm. Why? Because "he was worried they might hurt the company's other objective—making users engage more with Facebook."[20]

We can expect the Tech Barons to continue to battle extremist content and misinformation, which their platforms (and value chain) reward. Nuanced, deliberate, and rational debate is crowded out while the toxic innovations from the Tech Barons' ecosystems tear our social fabric apart, day after day.

Moreover, in seeking to temper these wildfires, the Tech Barons' algorithms will also marginalize or suppress disfavored voices, a concern among some conservative lawmakers in the United States.[21] Facebook, as its internal documents reveal, does not enforce its content moderation rules evenly.[22] So the risk of private censorship increases. While some cheered when Facebook and YouTube banned Donald Trump (after he lost the 2020 presidential election), there is a growing concern that the Tech Barons are leveraging their economic power to political power.

Ultimately, however, even the Tech Barons become prisoners to the ecosystems they create. Granted, Facebook and Google continue to reap record profits. But they can't convert their fight clubs into something more enlightening and ennobling when the underlying business model rewards engagement, prediction, and manipulation, which their toxic innovations seek to maximize. So, the Tech Barons continue to feed the beast, and that beast will destroy a lot around us—including trust in our institutions.

Regardless of whether you are online, offline, or sailing on a remote lake, this ripple effect—at some point—will reach you. As we have seen the COVID vaccine debate, this social polarization affects us all.

Undermining Democracy

"It's no good fighting an election campaign on the facts," Cambridge Analytica's managing director told an undercover reporter, "because actually it's all about emotion." The UK political consultants knew from the research coming from the University of Cambridge's Psychometrics Centre that "Facebook profile information could be used to successfully predict an individual's personality traits according to the 'OCEAN' scale."[23] As we saw in the last chapter, this psychometric model measures an individual's openness to experiences, conscientiousness, extraversion, agreeableness, and neuroticism. Cambridge Analytica needed to train its algorithm to predict and map personality traits to target voters and appeal to their hopes, neuroses, and fears. That required lots of personal data. So, to build these psychographic profiles, the self-described "global election management agency" enlisted a Cambridge University professor, Aleksandr Kogan, whose app, called thisisyourdigitallife, collected

Facebook data on the app users in the United States and data about their Facebook friends.[24] The information helped train the company's algorithm, which then generated personality scores for each person. Cambridge Analytica then matched these personality scores with US voter records to target them and manipulate their behavior. As the company's CEO, Alexander Nix, elaborated, "we were able to use data to identify that there were very large quantities of persuadable voters there that could be influenced to vote for the Trump campaign."

Cambridge Analytica also deployed these microtargeting methods in other democracies to identify and persuade swing voters and influence them through bespoke targeting.[25] As its managing director, Mark Turnbull, explained:

> The two fundamental human drivers when it comes to taking information on board effectively, are hopes and fears, and many of those are unspoken and even unconscious. You didn't know that this was a fear until you saw something that just evoked that reaction from you. And our job is to get . . . to drop the bucket further down the well than anybody else, to understand what are those really deep-seated underlying fears, concerns . . .[26]

So, what underlies the Cambridge Analytica scandal? Many were disturbed at how Facebook disclosed not only the personal data involving the 250,000 to 270,000 app users but also personal data about their 50 to 65 million Facebook friends. Others were disturbed by how easily the toxic innovations arising from the behavioral advertising ecosystem were redeployed to other areas, like political elections. While falsehoods and manipulation were always part of politics, the toxic innovations struck at our autonomy. "We use nearly 5 thousand different data points about you to craft and target a message," said Cambridge Analytica's CEO in a 2016 interview. "The data points are not just a representative model of you. The data points are about you, specifically."[27]

Cambridge Analytica is only one example of the microtargeting, manipulation, and deception of voters spawned by these toxic innovations.

The story represents one symptom of a spreading problem. Other political consultants will develop more advanced analytics to manipulate voters' fears to swing political outcomes.[28]

If the simple personality app thisisyourdigitallife could be used to harness some of the data of millions of Facebook users, imagine the power of the Tech Barons, through ongoing trial and error, to shape public opinion and behavior.

Take, for example, the story on Facebook prodding users to vote by feeding them pictures of friends who had already voted and creating an "I Voted" button. This simple nudge reportedly boosted turnout by hundreds of thousands of voters. "It became a running joke among employees that Facebook could tilt an election just by choosing where to deploy its 'I Voted' button."[29]

Facebook also offers political parties some of its advertising tools, such as Lookalike Audiences, which automatically finds and refines audiences similar to those who visited a page's website or liked that page. This is reportedly how the German nationalist and right-wing party AfD "was able to strategically reach out to a diverse set of people that are similar to their existing voter base in one way or another."[30]

Ultimately, a surveillance economy cannot be quarantined to the advertising sector. Political campaigns may not even need Facebook's data. Just think about the use of mouse tracking technology (mentioned in chapter 6), which enables an algorithm to analyze the way you move your mouse across the screen to measure you against the same five OCEAN personality traits. E-tailers can already use this "psychometric profile" to influence what you purchase. Thus, the successors of Cambridge Analytica will likely use similar, yet enhanced, tools to frame messages to manipulate your wraths, views, and voting (or whether to vote at all).

Many national elections are won by small margins. In swinging hyper-targeted groups, these innovations can and will determine political governance.[31]

The incentives also change. Why appeal to reason when political campaigns are all about emotion? Why have truth when microtargeting allows messages tailored to each voter's emotions? And why even have elections when those currently in political power and in possession of these toxic innovations can wage more insidious disinformation campaigns? The surveillance economy is fundamentally anti-democratic.

The power to microtarget enables politicians to move away from single coherent messaging (typical to public platforms) and engage in personalized, polarized campaigning. When the political ads you see differ from those of your neighbors, politicians become less accountable, as each ad might appeal to that voter's particular biases or fears. This targeting will increase social divisiveness with limited political accountability.[32]

In this already polarized environment, the toxic innovations arising from the Tech Barons' ecosystem will further undermine societal cohesion and stability. Political campaigns will fine-tune images, words, or phrases that trigger the desired emotional reaction for that voter. So, if you are among those with a high need for arousal, expect more violent, sexual, and fear-provoking content. The ability to target, divide, and influence, peppered with false information and arguments that "the game is rigged," risks eroding public trust in liberal democracy.[33] As one critic noted, "What started as a way for businesses to connect directly with potential customers has transformed into a disinformation machine at a scale that autocratic governments of the past could only imagine."[34]

We are already feeling these ripple effects as political parties tailor their messages to the Tech Barons' algorithms. According to Facebook's internal documents, some political parties in Europe told Facebook that its News Feed algorithm "had made them shift their policy positions, so they resonated more on the platform."[35] Many political parties, "including those that have shifted to the negative, worry about the long term effects on democracy," read one internal Facebook report, which didn't name specific parties. Two Facebook researchers in April 2019 internally reported how a political party in Poland shifted the proportion of its Facebook posts "from 50/50 positive/negative to 80% negative, explicitly as a function of the change to [Facebook's] algorithm."[36] Political parties told Facebook that as a result of its algorithm that favors reshares, they go really negative or sensationalistic to make their Facebook posts travel as far and fast as possible through reshares: Spain's political parties, for example, "have learnt that harsh attacks on their opponents net the highest engagement," an internal Facebook report notes. "They claim that they 'try not to,' but ultimately 'you use what works.'"[37]

So, the profiling and manipulation advertising tools spawned in the Tech Barons' ecosystems are now wielded by others—including foreign autocracies seeking to undermine the integrity of democratic political systems and erode our trust in democratic institutions. The scale of distortions cannot be ignored. Recent polls show a clear trend, as increasing numbers of citizens in Western countries question the foundations of democracy. The Tech Barons can only offer Band-Aids, like requiring certain political ads to include disclaimers with the name and entity that paid for the ads.[38] But since fear, uncertainty, and doubt are their ecosystems' friends (rather than the enemy), the Tech Barons cannot prevent their platforms from being weaponized or their toxic innovations from being deployed to undermine democracy. They must feed the beast, and that beast is destroying us.

Innovation Feudalism

With democracies at risk, one might hope for a Tech Pirate to alter the overall trajectory of toxic innovation. But you know better. With the Tech Barons' increasingly controlling the supply and demand of innovation within their sprawling ecosystems, they are reducing the diversity of innovators and impeding any potential innovator not aligned with their value chains. Welcome to the third ripple effect, where the Tech Barons' strategies are marginalizing Tech Pirates and thereby reducing the overall levels of dynamism.

There is no survey data of the number and types of Tech Pirates. (Even the pirates may be unaware initially of the potentially disruptive effect of their innovations.) But we can use more general data on small and medium-sized enterprises (SMEs) and start-ups, many of which are essential drivers of innovation in many sectors, to illustrate the trend.[39]

Overall, there has been a noticeable slowdown in the creation of new businesses,[40] with top firms capturing more market share.[41] For example, the percentage of younger companies—less than one year old—in the United States has declined by almost half over the last generation. And those declines swept across industries, including tech. An analysis of trends between 1978 and 2012, carried out by the Kauffman Foundation and Brookings Institution, found that the number of companies less than a year old had declined as a share of all businesses by nearly 44 percent.[42] The U.S. Congressional Report similarly noted how "[t]he entrepreneurship rate—defined as the share of start-ups and young firms in the industry as a whole—fell from 60% in 1982 to a low of 38% as of 2011."[43]

With reduced dynamism and disruption, leading companies can entrench their position. Indeed, the concern is that America and Europe have a significant market power problem beyond the digital economy. A 2021 IMF Discussion paper, "Rising Corporate Market Power," offers a broader view of increasing market power and declining business dynamism: corporate market power has increased significantly since 1980 in advanced economies around the world and negatively affected, among other things, investment and innovation.[44] Incumbent firms face less competitive pressure as fewer new firms enter the market. Markets are characterized by fewer firms with high-speed growth and less market experimentation.[45]

And with market power comes greater profitability. In the technology sector, corporate markups reportedly increased over 30 percent between 1995 and 2016. That increase in markups, the IMF found, was more than three times larger than among firms in the industrials and consumer goods industries. Winner-takes-all dynamics driven by powerful network effects supported this trend. The conventional wisdom is that industries with corpulent monopoly profits are ripe for disruption as they attract entrants.[46] That's false, the IMF noted from its detailed empirical analysis across industries at the country-industry level. Instead, the IMF found a strong association between falling business dynamism and rising market concentration.

Entrenched powerful companies with deep pockets can mount even more effective strategies against Tech Pirates, leading to marginalization and exclusion. The US Congressional Report noted the high entry barriers—attributable in significant part to the Tech Barons' anticompetitive conduct. As entry barriers increased, entry declined, and the average age of technology firms has skewed older.[47] The European Commission observed how in digital markets, the "weak market contestability and gatekeepers' sustained market position" led to "longer-term societal losses in terms of products' and services' prices, consumer choice and suboptimal innovation opportunities." As the Commission explained:

> Gatekeepers control the conditions for innovation and entry by independent firms. An important effect of the exercise of control by gatekeepers is that they can inhibit innovation by potential alternative platforms or by applications providers operating on their platform. Potential competitors, which might offer an alternative route to customers, may find it challenging to gain a foothold in markets with gatekeepers.[48]

Notably, the decline in SMEs and start-up activities is not offset by an increase in investment by dominant and established firms in disruptive technologies. Quite the opposite. Several economists, each of whom has considered different empirical data about research and development funding, noted how increased market concentration (and decline in competition) could be partly responsible for a lower overall investment rate.[49] This is in line with earlier theoretical work and empirical observations that find that as markets become more concentrated and firms increase in market power, they will tend to reduce their level of investment in innovation, despite greater profit margins.[50]

This cycle of power and exclusion increases the Tech Barons' control over the ecosystem. Furthermore, with the Tech Barons' deep pockets, their ecosystems can further expand to capture knowledge and new markets. Interconnected innovations align with the paths set by the Tech Barons. The risk of Tech Pirates' disruption is further marginalized.

It will only be natural then for society to increasingly rely on a few companies for its future prosperity. Monopoly profits and controlled ecosystems may be accepted as an essential part of the innovation arms race with other countries. As we'll see in the next chapter, the Tech Barons often argue that only their leading ecosystems can countermand foreign threats. After all, who else could take on the Chinese government's quest for AI supremacy? Who else has the data and knowledge in deep learning necessary to compete? Who controls all the relevant levers? And if we go down this path, industrial policies, rather than promote disruption, will instead strengthen the Tech Barons as they compete against foreign companies to ensure they lead the innovation race.

The Tech Barons' ecosystems reflect "innovation feudalism," where many companies and individuals become the serfs toiling away. Here lies the crux of the matter—by crushing Tech Pirates and distorting innovation paths, the Tech Barons prevent any significant disruption to their value chain. Beyond the obvious increase in market concentration, beyond the reduction in investment in innovation, we see increased control and the rise of innovation feudalism.

We already see how the rise of these giants defies the power and foundations of the state.

They already extract value and impose taxes on their serfs. App developers, for example, pay a monopolistic 30 percent tax on in-app revenues to Google and Apple. Google collects anywhere between a 22 and 42 percent tax of US ad spending that invariably goes through its network.[51] Amazon collects a hefty tax on third-party sellers (in addition to copying some of their innovations).[52] Facebook appropriates even more value from its users.

Once distorted, the digital economy will not quickly self-correct, and our grandchildren may still be waiting for creative destruction.

Following this trajectory, illustrated in Figure 7.3, the Tech Barons will set themselves up as the primary engine for investment and innovation while extracting or destroying even more value.

Figure 7.3

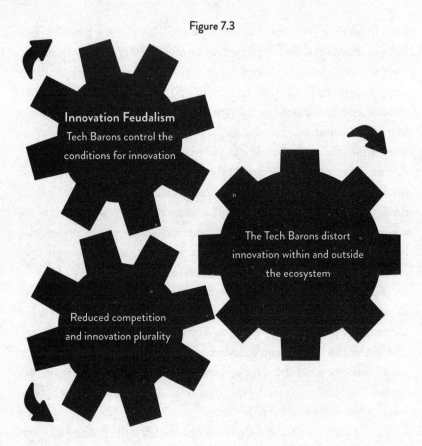

Reflections

If this sounds dystopian, ask yourself this: *Are the Tech Barons' interests aligned with our interests?*

At times they are. But the spate of toxic innovations reflects how their ecosystem's value chain defines the Tech Baron's interests. They and others in their ecosystem will deploy innovations that extract and destroy value. The Tech Barons will view any attempt to rein in their toxic innovations as a threat. Think, for example, about behavioral advertising. In its 2020 Annual Report, Google identified how data protection and privacy laws, which we want (and Californians voted in 2020 to strengthen and Europeans are seeking to further fortify), can harm its business. So, what we may perceive as good, namely, "[n]ew laws further restricting the collection, processing and/or sharing of advertising-related data," Google perceives as a threat to its data-driven behavioral advertising business model.[53]

Frances Haugen, a former Facebook data scientist turned whistleblower, released, in late 2021, thousands of internal documents outlining the Tech Baron's failure to keep harmful content off its platforms.[54] Reflecting on the evidence, tech ethicist Tristan Harris noted how the issue goes beyond the documents proving the harms generated by the Tech Giant. The most significant insight, according to Harris, is that Facebook knew about these harms to society, democracy, and individuals, but still refrained from taking action as it prioritized its profits.[55]

Evidence released by another whistleblower reveals the depth of disregard to the societal impact. According to the leaked information, as Facebook sought to quell the controversy surrounding the US elections, its communications official Tucker Bounds reportedly said:

> It will be a flash in the pan. Some legislators will get pissy. And then in a few weeks they will move onto something else. Meanwhile we are printing money in the basement, and we are fine.[56]

So, what can be done? The first thing to do is to examine the conventional wisdom that supports the status quo. When we asked one US policymaker about the Tech Barons' toxic innovation, she replied, "Do you want cabbage or steak?" Welcome to the ideological platter, which we'll sample next.

CHAPTER 8

The Innovation Narrative

WHEN WE RAISED THE concept of toxic innovation with competition officials, one US policymaker waved us off. When she was fourteen years old, she traveled through the then-Communist-governed Eastern Bloc countries and ate cabbage every night. "When you limit the freedom of companies to operate and innovate, you'll get a centrally planned economy," she warned us. "You'll end up eating cabbage every night. I prefer the steak in a free-market economy."

So do we. But that's not a choice society needs to make.

The alternative to the Tech Barons' innovation feudalism is not the absence of innovation and Soviet-era meatloaf and cabbage.

And yet, even when the Tech Pirates are being eradicated, and the innovation kill zones expand, our policymakers and enforcers still hesitate. We have become anesthetized to the toxic innovation flowing from the Tech Barons' ecosystems. Often, policymakers and enforcers are wary about chilling innovation and refrain from acting.

The innovation rhetoric's impact is pervasive. Many people are troubled by the Tech Barons' growing power and abuse; nonetheless, they assume that GAFAM promote innovation. In a 2019 Pew Research

Center study, many Americans distrusted two groups in particular: the leaders of tech companies and members of Congress. Americans rated technology leaders and members of Congress far lower in empathy, transparency, and ethics than others in a position of power (such as military leaders, public school principals, police officers, or even local elected officials).[1] Most Americans believe that tech leaders and members of Congress often behave unethically and can get away with it. But when it comes to innovation, many Americans' views change. Notwithstanding the evidence, most Americans believe that tech leaders are highly likely to fulfill their mission of building products and services that enhance our lives. (Many Americans, however, were pessimistic about members of Congress accomplishing their mission, such as promoting laws that serve the public.)

Even when we look at antitrust enforcement, which has intensified in recent years (more on this in the next chapter), the cabbage/steak imagery still captivates the debate.

How were we, as a society, so easily fooled? Well, the same fallacies, if told repeatedly, take on the truth. Psychologists call this the "illusory truth effect."[2] As experiments show, "people tend to rate items they've seen before as more likely to be true, regardless of whether they are true or not, and seemingly for the sole reason that they are more familiar."[3]

The effectiveness of repetition is increased if each fallacy contains some grain of truth.[4] The recipe is old, yet effective: start with undisputed facts or beliefs and stretch them to fit your agenda. Tailor the message to your listener's ideology, biases, and fears. To increase its appeal, have different groups (many of which might be on your payroll) repeat the message and even sprinkle a few commissioned studies and reports to complete the picture. And while you are at it, add a few doubts or critiques of the industry to not appear to be proselytizing.

The result is an ideological platter that appears substantive but consists of empty calories. We'll sample six mantras about innovation that you might have heard so frequently that you accept them as true.

What the Tech Barons Deliver, Others Cannot

When we asked economists about myths involving innovation, most identified this one: the belief that the large digital platforms are the most innovative companies in the world. The economists note how the Tech Barons' own innovations are primarily sustaining and have added relatively little value in recent years.

Nonetheless, when Epic Games challenged Apple's exclusionary and restrictive practices involving its App Store, Apple replied that its "App Store encourages vigorous competition between apps and is an engine of innovation."[5] With 957,390 gaming apps and 3.42 million non-gaming apps within Apple's ecosystem, all competing for us to download, we benefit.

Platforms are indeed central to the digital economy. They offer important matchmaking functions and can deliver efficiencies by, among other things, lowering the cost to innovate. But we have also seen how a Tech Baron's control over the demand and supply of innovation and its ability to affect innovation paths kill disruptive innovation and foster toxic innovation. Once we account for the decline in innovation plurality, the Tech Barons no longer appear as the engines of innovation.

And then there is the reference point. The steak-versus-cabbage story posits the current scenario with an even worse scenario, a centrally planned economy. But Communist and Socialist countries can point to the innovations from their economy and how they are better than other despotic regimes. After all, no matter how bad things are, undoubtedly, one can point to a worse situation (or worse place to live).

The problem with disruptive technologies is that it is hard to predict the counterfactual. Since the Tech Barons dominate across so many jurisdictions, we cannot say how the technological landscape would appear with more Tech Pirates today. For example, that only two app stores predominate does not mean that only Apple and Google can provide app stores. Other app stores exist, and absent Apple's and Google's restraints, these app stores would likely contain far more apps than they currently offer.[6]

The fact that Apple's and Google's app stores are growing does not mean the market is competitive. Network effects work in the Tech Barons' favor. In limiting access to other app stores on their platforms, Google and Apple ensure that we turn to their app stores, which requires app developers to use Google and Apple. So, the fact that the Google and Apple app stores grew in size does not mean customers are rewarding the Tech Barons for their innovations (or, more accurately, the innovations they allow into the ecosystem). Instead, it can simply represent the lack of viable competitive alternatives.

Nor are the Tech Barons the primary originators of digital innovation. Instead, as a 2021 *Harvard Business Review* article notes, "much of the technology we rely on every day runs on free and open-source software (FOSS). Phones, cars, planes, and even many cutting-edge artificial intelligence programs use open-source software such as the Linux kernel operating system, the Apache and Nginx web servers, which run over 60% of the world's websites, and Kubernetes, which powers cloud computing."[7] One concern is that the Tech Barons are appropriating the free open-source software that creates value for the whole community, and walling it off so that "they were the only ones who could capture value from it."[8]

A third crack in the ideology is that we don't see the Tech Pirates' disruptive innovations that have been killed or stifled. Nor do we see any of the Tech Barons' innovations that could potentially disrupt their ecosystems. Consider Bell Labs, which was once the research and development arm of AT&T. As Professor Tim Wu recounted, it collected "seven Nobel Prizes, more than any other corporate laboratory, including one awarded in 1956 for its most renowned invention, the transistor, which made the computer possible."[9] But we never saw the many innovations that AT&T stifled (like magnetic tape and the answering machine). As Wu recounts:

For when the interests of AT&T were at odds with the advancement of information, there was no doubt as to which good prevailed. And so, interspersed between Bell Labs' public triumphs were its secret discoveries, the skeletons within the imperial closet of AT&T. And here we clearly see the long-term costs of industrial rule by a single firm.[10]

So, we do not see the closet of shelved technologies that the Tech Barons perceived as threatening their ecosystem's value chain or all the Tech Pirates buried in the backyard.

Innovation and competition, as a result, suffer. Let's revisit app stores. As Europe's top antitrust enforcer, Margrethe Vestager, said in 2021:

> By setting strict rules on the App store that disadvantage competing music streaming services, Apple deprives users of cheaper music streaming choices and distorts competition. This is done by charging high commission fees on each transaction in the App store for rivals and by forbidding them from informing their customers of alternative subscription options.[11]

Indeed, as their app stores grew, so too did Apple's and Google's profits. Apple's revenues from services, where its app store is a key driver, reached $16.9 billion in the second quarter of 2021. Its gross profit margins from services reached a record 70 percent in 2021. That is twelve percentage points higher than its 2018 fiscal year (when the company first began disclosing service margins).[12] Apple's operating margins for its app store are estimated to be even higher (over 75 percent) for 2018 and 2019.[13] A 75 percent gross margin dwarfs what other monopolies and oligopolies enjoy—such as tobacco products (44.2 percent) or even Apple's products segment, which had 36 percent gross margins in 2021. So, when Apple imposes a 30 percent tax on app developers, we ultimately pay with higher prices and receive less innovation.[14]

Consequently, while the Tech Barons innovate, their innovations on their core products have been primarily incremental, sustaining innovations within their value chain. Many of their innovations, as we saw in the last chapter, extract or destroy value. Plus, we lose when they kill the Tech Pirates, shelve their own disruptive innovations that threaten their value chain, and reorient the innovation paths to fortify their ecosystems. We should not resign ourselves to the Tech Barons' self-interested claims that innovation can only flourish within their closed ecosystems.

What Tech Barons Deliver, the State Cannot

Another myth is that private firms innovate and create much of the wealth in our society, while governments have a limited role. We've been conditioned to consider innovation as arising solely in the private sector. Since the Tech Barons support innovations, we are told, any interference by the state in their ecosystems will weaken (if not kill) innovation. So, the biggest threat is the government, not the Tech Barons.

Under this mindset, the government has a limited, indirect role in protecting innovation: protect intellectual property and well-defined property rights through well-functioning courts that uphold rule-of-law ideals, lower regulatory burdens, limit corruption, and invest at the margins (such as education or tax credits). Any more meddling will hamper innovation.

Here again is the steak-or-cabbage fallacy, which posits the current scenario (a hierarchical ecosystem dominated by private monopolies) with an even worse one (a hierarchical ecosystem dominated by an inefficient, corrupt government). It intuitively fits into our capitalistic ideology that innovation cannot be left entirely to the government. As John Stuart Mill cautioned, "where everything is done through the bureaucracy, nothing to which the bureaucracy is really adverse can be done at all."[15] But the same can be said about entrusting innovation to a handful of Tech Barons.

The first crack in this ideology is *spillovers* and *positive externalities*. Basically, why invest in innovation when others will monetize and capture many of the benefits? Spillovers can be good for innovation and society. The social returns to R&D from spillovers are typically much higher than the private returns to the firms (some suggest four times greater).[16] The problem, however, is that private firms will not engage in private research when they cannot recover a sufficient private return on their efforts. Thus, if R&D is left entirely to private firms, there will be an underinvestment in R&D generally and basic research in particular.[17] Therefore, governments play a crucial role in funding "higher risk, basic research that private investors are often reluctant to take on," which "tends to produce higher value, high-spillover inventions over a longer period of time."[18]

A good example of spillover effects is universities, whose basic research can play a critical role in fostering regional innovation clusters.[19] Indeed, Silicon Valley benefited from research from the local universities (such as Berkeley and Stanford) and the U.S. Defense Advanced Research Projects Agency. Most of the innovations on your smartphone, for example, were the fruit of government-sponsored research:

> If you've ever used a GPS system, you have the Defense Department's research to thank. What about your smartphone? Although the government didn't directly fund the exact phone you own, NASA, the National Science Foundation (NSF), and the CIA were integral in creating crucial elements of today's smartphones—such as microchips and touch screens. Even the internet, which makes reading this story possible, began as the Advanced Research Projects Agency Network (ARPANET), a computer network first made by the U.S. Defense Advanced Research Projects Agency (DARPA).[20]

The economist Mariana Mazzucato debunks the "public sector inferiority" myth and underscores innovation as a collective process. She notes how many innovations, including the internet, Google's search algorithm, GPS, voice activation, touch screens, and more, originated through efforts driven by public institutions. By investing in the early, risky stages of development, the government effectively reduces the risk for venture capitalists.[21] As Mazzucato puts it, "risks in the innovation economy are socialized, while the rewards are privatized."[22]

While the private sector has a significant role, it is not alone in this quest. Furthermore, it is rewarded handsomely, even when it appropriates value created by public funds.[23]

Second, the government has an essential role in preventing the intellectual capture of innovation. One cannot innovate without access to the necessary raw ingredients. No government would countenance a monopoly of chemicals, test tubes, and microscopes, much less one that could dictate for which research efforts its equipment and raw materials could be used. But as we saw in earlier chapters, that is the situation in the digital economy, where a significant amount of innovation comes from deep learning, which requires large data sets as the raw ingredient. Why should we entrust the research path in deep learning to a few firms' wisdom (and discretion)?

The fact that the private sector can drive innovation does not justify the monopolization of the raw ingredients (such as large data sets). John Stuart Mill aptly summarized the role of government as "the greatest dissemination of power consistent with efficiency, but the greatest centralization of information, and diffusion of it from the centre."[24] Although Mill wrote this over 160 years ago, it contains several essential lessons on the government's role in the digital economy.

In recognizing the government's "special duty" of "making the knowledge acquired in one place available for others,"[25] Mill grasped data's non-rivalrous nature. Multiple people can derive insights from large data sets without the data losing value. Just consider all the researchers worldwide who at this very moment are mining the data from the U.S. Bureau of Labor Statistics and the U.S. Census Bureau. Moreover, while data is non-rivalrous, there are costs in its collection and dissemination. Finally, as we saw, powerful firms have the incentive to hoard data (and knowledge). Thus, the government plays a central role in collecting and disseminating the information while safeguarding individuals' privacy interests.

Next is the issue of the platform's real contribution to our society. Silicon Valley's genius combined with limited corporate regulation promised a new age of technological innovation; entrepreneurs would create companies that would in turn fuel unprecedented job growth. In his book *The Great Reversal*, Thomas Philippon examines the economic footprint of the big tech platforms Microsoft, Apple, and Google. While they benefit from significant profit margins and account for nearly 10 percent of the stock market, their labor footprint is small and amounts to only .23 percent of employment. Their limited integration in the economy, from input purchasing to employment, supports his conclusion that "the notion that the biggest tech firms are somehow the pillars of the US economy is false on its face. The defining feature of the new stars is not how much they make or how high their stock market values are. If we exclude Amazon, the defining feature of the new stars is how few people they employ and how little they buy from other firms."[26]

So, the government serves many essential functions in the digital economy to spur innovation, including its investments, disseminating data, preventing the slaughter of the Tech Pirates, and deterring the spread of toxic innovation.

Tech Barons Are Essential to Attract and Invest in Innovation

Here the mantra is that investment in innovation is booming, with the Tech Barons leading the way. Of course, from a quantitative perspective, as we saw in chapter 1, the Tech Barons invest heavily in research and development. And when it does not disrupt its ecosystem's value chain, the Tech Barons will invest in and support disruptive innovations.

The problems, as we have seen, are several-fold.

First, there is no perfect measure for innovation. The input measures, such as research and development expenses, are not always reliable. To see why, let us return to how GAFAM define research and development expenses. Google and Microsoft, for example, include as R&D expenses depreciation and stock-based compensation to their engineers and technical employees responsible for R&D.[27] So, giving stock options counts as a research expense. Same for Facebook, where 27 percent of its 2020 R&D expenses were stock options.[28] And the same for Apple, where 19 percent of its 2018 R&D expenses were stock options.[29] So, putting aside any diminishing returns to R&D investments, increasing stock options does not necessarily correlate with more disruptive innovations that provide us significant value.

Looking at patents, we cannot say that GAFAM are awarded the most patents in any year. Annex A[30] lists the fifty organizations that annually received the most patent grants from the U.S. Patent and Trademark Office between 2011 and 2020. Based on that metric, IBM is the clear leader, followed by Samsung Electronics and Canon. In looking at GAFAM's rankings over that period, Microsoft was consistently in the top ten. As for the rest, only Apple broke the top fifty in 2011. Other than Google, none of the three other tech platforms broke the top five, and Facebook made the top fifty in only three of the ten years.

But the number of patents is also an imperfect measure of innovation. While one might think higher R&D effort and investment will cause faster technological improvements, a 2021 study found otherwise. Examining all US patents issued over forty years, the study found no correlation between the number of patents in a technological field and the annual performance improvement of that field (so technology areas with more patents did not necessarily improve quicker than fields with fewer patents).[31]

The number of patents does not reflect how disruptive the patented innovation is or whether it's toxic or beneficial. Moreover, the Tech Barons' number of patents does not capture those innovations, which resulted from knowledge appropriation and monopolization, as discussed in chapter 5. Their patent number also hides their cannibalizing other innovation efforts that preceded its appropriation. Furthermore, patent numbers do not account for the Tech Barons' distorting the innovation paths and monopolizing knowledge. Even if the Tech Barons double the number of patents, their patents will likely complement, rather than disrupt, their prevailing ecosystems' value chains.[32]

So, when the Tech Barons analogize their interlocking platforms to coral reefs that attract organic innovation, consider the warnings by Margrethe Vestager: the government must watch "the expansion of platforms into new markets" so that it "doesn't undermine competition as it goes, like a bloom of algae that kills off every other form of life as it expands."[33] Vestager warned that "the biggest threat to competition and innovation comes from platforms that are not just a single business, but the center of large empires."[34]

The Tech Barons can play an important role in promoting innovation. But they will not necessarily promote the innovations that deliver the most value. If the Tech Barons are left unchecked, instead of vibrant coral reefs, we'll get putrid red algae.

Disruptive Innovation Is Around the Corner

Few of the Tech Barons acknowledge that they are monopolies. For them, the digital economy is dynamic and ruthlessly competitive. So, when Epic Games challenged Apple's 30 percent app tax, Apple disclaimed its monopoly power. "For starters, Apple is not a monopolist of any relevant market. Competition inside and outside the App Store is fierce at every level: for devices, platforms, and individual apps. Fortnite users can dance their Floss, ride their sharks, and spend their V-Bucks in no fewer than six different mobile, PC, and game-console platforms."[35] Surprisingly, one district court agreed despite finding that Apple behaved in many ways like a monopolist. (We'll examine in the next chapter how the current state of antitrust law led to her contradictory findings.)

But even if the Tech Barons dominate their market, they will always remind you that they are still exposed to competition *for* the market. One common theme in GAFAM's financial reports is that market power is transient, disruptive innovation is just around the corner, and competition remains fierce regardless of how large the platforms become. Citing competition twenty-nine times in its 2020 Annual Report, Google warns: "Our business is characterized by rapid change as well as new and disruptive technologies. We face formidable competition in every aspect of our business, particularly from companies that seek to connect people with online information and provide them with relevant advertising."[36] Citing competition sixteen times, Facebook's 2020 annual report warns that its "business is characterized by innovation, rapid change, and disruptive technologies," and how it faces "significant competition in every aspect of [its] business."[37] So, the threat of creative destruction incentivizes the Tech Barons to innovate with the consumer in mind.[38] As Eric Schmidt, then Google's CEO, said, "Google faces such strong incentives to treat its users right, since they will walk away the minute Google does anything with their personal information they find 'creepy.'"[39]

You will likely appreciate the irony: the Tech Barons say the Tech Pirates check their power while killing them off. Although no monopoly lives forever, it is hard to ignore the cracks in their disruption narrative.

Even if we put aside all the evidence, the Tech Barons' claims are contradictory. Take, for example, Apple's dire warning to investors: "The markets for the Company's products and services are highly competitive, and are characterized by aggressive price competition and resulting downward pressure on gross margins."[40] But wait. In that same filing, Apple reports that its gross margins on its services, which includes revenues from its 30 percent app store tax, are 70 percent. If the market were as fiercely competitive as Apple claims, such outsize profits should have attracted many entrants.[41] Apple never seeks to reconcile this contradiction, nor can it. Companies do not enjoy such extraordinarily high-profit margins in competitive markets.

Next, let us consider the durability of their dominance. Most US companies live short lives. As one study found, the average half-life of US publicly traded companies is close to 10.5 years, meaning that half of all companies that began trading in any given year have disappeared in 10.5 years.[42] Nor are platforms guaranteed long lives. One study calculated that 209 platforms had failed and died over the past 20 years. Most of them (85 percent) were transaction platforms, which had shorter lives (on average 4.6 years) than the innovation platforms (5 years) or hybrid platforms (7.4 years) in the survey.[43]

So, suppose many companies and platforms die within ten years of their birth. In that case, it is all the more remarkable that GAFAM have successfully dominated multiple markets for years and seem poised to continue their domination over the next decade.

Consider Microsoft. It was the dominant operating system for personal computers, and its anticompetitive conduct embroiled the monopoly in litigation in both Europe and America for over two decades. While Apple was always a rival and Apple's market share has increased over the years, Microsoft in December 2021 still controlled 73.75 percent of the global desktop operating system market.[44] And in 2021, Microsoft was using Windows to fuel its cloud business and Microsoft 365 strategy to develop new categories of devices—both its own and third-party. The result—in early 2022, Microsoft was the second largest company in terms of market capitalization (after Apple) and before Alphabet (ranked third), Amazon (ranked fifth), and Meta (Facebook) (ranked seventh).[45]

So, while the threat of creative destruction remains, the Tech Barons have far less to fear with their nowcasting radar and other weapons.

Market Power Supports Innovation Efforts

The flipside to the "ruthless competition" narrative is that monopoly profits are needed to undertake the risk to innovate and explore. Even if GAFAM's profit margins are several times larger than the average for US firms, the thinking goes that these Tech Barons should be rewarded for their effort. The ability to appropriate the benefits of innovation is key to increased investment. The conventional wisdom is that monopoly power is the crucial reward for the more efficient, innovative firm that prevailed in the competitive struggle.[46] As the Supreme Court surmised in 2004:

The mere possession of monopoly power, and the concomitant charging of monopoly prices, is not only not unlawful; it is an important element of the free-market system. The opportunity to charge monopoly prices—at least for a short period—is what attracts "business acumen" in the first place; it induces risk taking that produces innovation and economic growth.[47]

The lower courts repeatedly cite that dicta—over fifty times by 2021. While they disavow possessing monopoly power, the Tech Barons also quote this language to swat away competition concerns.[48] Their trade association also raises national security concerns about losing to China if the Tech Barons' power is checked.[49]

Granted, in an intensely competitive market, the margins might be so slim that firms cannot afford to invest in R&D. If they do invest, they need to appropriate the benefits of their investment. That is why countries protect patents and copyrights.[50]

But while intensely competitive markets may hinder innovation, the fallacy is to assume that monopolies are a boon to innovation. Most economists today would agree that greater market power does not necessarily support more innovation.[51] From the empirical economic literature, the reality is more complex than to say monopoly profits help or hinder innovation.[52]

First, as the antitrust scholar Jon Baker aptly points out, "the modern economic and business literatures consistently and convincingly demonstrate that enhanced competition leads to greater productivity and that the exercise of market power reduces it."[53] Why would any Tech Pirate want to invest its time and money to expand markets and take business away from a Tech Baron by improving privacy, quality, and features; developing new and better products and production processes; or enhancing the value for customers, when they will likely be stamped out?

Second, monopolies can hinder innovation. Several studies posit an *inverted U-shaped relationship* between innovation and market power.[54] However, the subsequent academic debate over the "inverted

U" hypothesis is even more unfavorable for the Tech Barons' rheto-ric.[55] A 2020 economic study, for example, found that the rate of in-novation plateaus rather than declines as competition increases.[56] As Baker concludes:

> Given the unpersuasiveness of arguments for the innovation benefits of market power and the strong arguments for the innovation bene-fits of competition, we should feel safe concluding that greater com-petition generally enhances the prospects for innovation, while the exercise of market power tends to slow innovation and productivity improvements.[57]

Moreover, one economic study found that stricter antitrust standards and enforcement in the 1950s to 1970s cracked down on the ability of dominant firms to acquire nascent competitive threats. As a result, that fostered more innovation by larger firms to grow organically.[58]

What is clear is that healthy competition has been squeezed out of many technology markets, and disruptive innovation has taken a hit. Indeed, as we saw, the empirical data indicates an ongoing decline in the entry rate of new firms and a decrease in market experimentation. As Kristalina Georgieva, managing director of the International Mone-tary Fund, said, "when you have that high degree of concentration, why bother to invest and innovate when you can just charge a little bit more and get the same or even better profitability?"[59]

The final rejoinder is that we need these monopolies in order to com-pete against China's Tech Barons. But China has been cracking down on its tech giants. With its state-media outlets describing online games as "opium for the mind," China in 2021 enacted new regulation that will ban minors (those under eighteen years of age) from playing online video games entirely between Monday and Thursday, and only for one hour each day on the other three days of the week, and public holidays.[60] China doesn't find addictive technologies necessary to prevail, and our Tech Barons will not always protect us.

Tech Barons Compete with Each Other

Our last innovation myth is that oligopolies are better than monopolies. After all, the Tech Barons can exert competitive pressure on each other. As Rome saw, triumvirates present uneasy alliances. According to this narrative, as the Tech Barons expand their ecosystems, they'll inevitably challenge each other's power. Envision the Tech Barons' ecosystem platforms as shifting tectonic plates. As their plates expand, the rival platforms will occasionally get stuck together at their edges due to friction. As the stress along the platforms' edges increases, so too does the level of innovations. So, we'll be rewarded with vibrant oligopolistic competition as the Tech Barons duke it out across industries.[61]

Indeed, when Apple allowed users to avoid being tracked, Facebook saw this not only as an affront to the many small advertisers on its platforms but as a direct competitive threat. As Facebook told investors:

> [W]e think the impact of the Apple approach is really much bigger than this particular update around third-party data usage. Apple has a number of private APIs on hardware and software that advantage their own products and services in ways that are challenging, and we face that issue with—in places like our messaging products and even with the hardware products we're launching. So we generally don't think that this closed approach is the best one for the industry from an innovation perspective.[62]

In early 2022, Facebook's stock dropped 26 percent in one day, losing more than $230 billion in market capitalization. It was, as the *Wall Street Journal* reported, "the biggest one-day loss in market value for a U.S. company ever."[63] Part of the disappointing news that caused the stock's decline was that Apple's privacy policy would cost Facebook about $10 billion in ad sales in 2022.

On the other hand, Apple can justify privacy considerations as a strategic goal to ensure consumer trust, gain a competitive advantage, and weaken rival dominant platforms.[64]

In early 2021 the *Economist* rejoiced that the days of monopolies are over. Instead, we have oligopolies, where the second and third firms compete vigorously against the incumbent. As the magazine declared, "an oligopoly of rivals is much better than a monopoly."[65]

No doubt, the Tech Barons will clash as their ecosystems expand.[66] But oligopolies are nothing to celebrate. Instead, every country's merger law seeks to prevent mergers that yield oligopolies precisely because they typically lead to less competition, higher prices, poorer-quality products and services, and fewer innovations. Moreover, it is never a good policy to rely on a few powerful firms for either competition or innovation.

Take, for example, Apple and Google, which compete on many levels. Yet, despite the rivalry, the companies also have a history of collaboration—from illegally agreeing not to poach each other's employees[67] to their ongoing revenue-sharing agreement (fifteen years strong), which incentivizes Apple to feature Google as the default search engine on Safari and Siri. While Apple publicly proclaimed how privacy was built into the company's DNA, its revenue-sharing agreement with Google aligns the companies' interests. As one senior Apple employee wrote to a Google counterpart, "our vision is that we work as if we are one company."[68] As a result, in 2019 Google reportedly paid Apple $12 billion to be the default search engine on Safari,[69] which is significant by itself relative to Apple's 2019 net income of $55.256 billion.[70] As Disconnect's Casey Oppenheim told us:

> If iPhone users knew how much tracking was taking place in apps, they may install fewer of them. Or if Apple forbids app tracking altogether, app developers would likely make less money. In either event tighter privacy controls might mean fewer app developers would create iOS apps, and potentially fewer iPhones would be sold, which is an existential threat to Apple. So Apple may not profit directly from sharing or collecting your data, but they make a ton of money from allowing other companies to track your every move.

Some of the Tech Barons' recent acknowledgments of privacy do not represent a change in their value chains. Quite the contrary. They still rely on behavioral advertising. As we saw, the Tech Barons will phase out technologies (like third-party cookies) that they no longer require, or when the move doesn't materially hamper their profits and power. When specific tools to manipulate our behavior become obsolete, we should not celebrate. As long as the value chain persists, the Tech Barons and those competing within their ecosystems will intensify their efforts to manipulate our behavior with superior technologies.[71] While the means of extracting value might change, the Tech Barons' incentive to extract value won't. As the value chains of the Tech Barons' ecosystems converge, there will be even less incentive to disrupt each other's ecosystems. So, we may not want to break out the champagne glasses in celebrating oligopolies.

Reflections

The ideological platter, even when exposed, remains hard to resist. It fits into a broader free-market narrative that assumes large players won the competition fairly and have the edge over others. The Tech Barons have poured a lot of money into trusts, grant providers, think tanks, and academic institutions to propagate this ideological platter.[72]

When some academics warn of regulatory capture, they rarely point to their home institutions. And yet, increasingly, universities are being harnessed and used by the Tech Barons to advance their narrative. One example is George Mason University's Antonin Scalia Law School. While the FTC was investigating Google from 2011 to 2013, "Google contributed at least $762,000" to the public university's Law and Economics Center, "which was used to support numerous GMU studies and academic conferences backing the search giant's position that the company had not acted anticompetitively."[73] For these purported academic conferences, George Mason's dean (a state employee) reportedly coordinated with Google as to the speakers, who unsurprisingly endorsed a hands-off approach.[74] Google, Amazon, Facebook, and Qualcomm were also substantial funders of George Mason's Global Antitrust Institute, another university center "that routinely defends the companies on antitrust issues."[75]

The criticism is that the Tech Barons fund these centers to churn out policy papers favorable to their position and send professors and graduates to critical jobs at agencies like the FTC. In reporting on the findings by the Tech Transparency Project, Bloomberg's David McLaughlin noted how George Mason helped shape the FTC's workforce and "infused it with a laissez-faire philosophy favorable to the school's tech donors."[76] George Mason also provides training programs for judges and antitrust enforcers from the US and elsewhere that promote a simplified narrative that "the best way to foster competition is to maintain a hands-off approach to antitrust law."[77]

A congressional hearing on "Reviving Competition" underscored the distorting effect of this intellectual capture.[78] After listening to a presentation by Tad Lipsky, a director at George Mason's Global Antitrust Institute, New York congressman Mondaire Jones was remarkably frank:

If we wanted to hear the views of Amazon, Google, or Qualcomm we would have invited them. When a CEO comes before this committee, I understand that they are going to advocate for their own interest. . . . But when your institute is funded by secret donations from big tech companies, you today come as a wolf in sheep's clothing, and I would submit that the American people deserve to know the truth. The truth is that secret corporate funding, like yours, has distorted our discourse for far too long. For decades institutes like yours have massed corporate money to protect monopoly power. Institutes like yours have worked to "teach" judges and regulators to let their guard down as corporate funders, like yours, came to dominate our economy. The American people, of course, are paying the price. The corporations who wrote your paychecks are now not only the gatekeepers for our economy, they are the gatekeepers for our democracy . . .[79]

Big tech companies also support other universities, policy groups, and NGOs. The Google Transparency Project, for example, "identified 330 research papers published between 2005 and 2017 on public policy matters of interest to Google that were in some way funded by the company."[80] The Tech Barons "flood" the marketplace with scholarly papers that support their narratives and question the validity of reform policies. Of course, financial support does not always affect the path and output of research. Yet, with increased reliance on funding, academic freedom and objectivity inevitably take a back seat.

Academic conferences are supposed to be an open exchange of ideas. Many still are. But for the industry-supported conferences, one of our colleagues offered this apt insight: the cash-rich Tech Barons are the ideology sellers. They pack the discussion with their paid or supported speakers, who then pummel the one or two scholars not on the payroll who present contrary research. The policymakers and enforcement officials in attendance are the (unsuspecting) buyers; and the sponsored institutions and universities in the US, Europe, and elsewhere serve as the lubricant.

But surely, the policymakers must know something is amiss. Some do. But many don't. One academic paper found, for example, that judges targeted in such seminars "were more likely to approve mergers, rule against environmental protections and organized labor, and use economic language in rulings compared to judges who did not attend."[81] When all you need as a Tech Baron is to raise marginal resistance to change (or sufficient doubt), the money is well spent.

The result? Even though competition authorities around the world by 2022 were challenging most of the Tech Barons, as we'll see next, the lethal cocktail of ideology and lobbying have led the courts to marginalize antitrust; some repeat these half-truths without ever critically examining them. Welcome to the world of CSI Antitrust, where the courts have come to expect from the antitrust agencies the unrealistic forensic techniques and science seen on the *CSI: Crime Scene Investigation* television shows.

CHAPTER 9

Current Antitrust Enforcement

WHEN THE CEOS OF Google, Apple, Facebook, and Amazon testified before Congress in 2020, they all agreed that the current laws and policies in the US foster the entrepreneurial spirit.

Amazon's CEO testified, "We [America] nurture entrepreneurs and start-ups with stable rule of law, the finest university system in the world, the freedom of democracy, and a deeply accepted culture of risk-taking."[1]

Likewise, Facebook's CEO testified:

Our story would not have been possible without U.S. laws that encourage competition and innovation. I believe that strong and consistent competition policy is vital because it ensures that the playing field is level for all.[2]

Why would the Tech Barons celebrate the current antitrust policies, which are supposed to crack down on mergers that may create a monopoly and prevent monopolies from acquiring or crushing nascent competitive threats? As you might expect, the current antitrust framework generally works in the Tech Barons' favor.

Here's why. The current antitrust policies exhibit at least four inter-related problems:

First is CSI Antitrust—namely, its focus on what is quantifiable (price and output) rather than what is essential in the digital economy (innovation, quality, and privacy).

Second is antitrust's focus on narrowly defined antitrust markets rather than on ecosystems.

Third is antitrust's focus on past (rather than current or future) anti-competitive practices.

Finally, antitrust focuses on what the defendants did, not why they did it. Basically, antitrust does not account for the ecosystem's value chain, namely, why the Tech Baron or those within its ecosystem behave the way they do.

As a result, despite the recent flurry in antitrust enforcement, the existing antitrust policies will not significantly deter the Tech Barons nor halt the spread of toxic innovation.

Confusing What Is Measurable with What Is Important

Ask a roomful of economists what is most responsible for advances in our standard of living, and the likely response is innovation. According to the Organisation for Economic Co-Operation and Development (OECD), a highly influential intergovernmental institution with thirty-six member countries, innovation is vital to economic growth and overall well-being. It "is responsible for most of the increase in material standards of living that has taken place since the Industrial Revolution."[3]

Consequently, innovation should play a central role in competition policy. Ostensibly it does. Most antitrust policymakers, like economists, agree that innovation, at times, can improve well-being far more than lower prices will, and that dynamic efficiencies are often more important than prices. So, the premise is that competition "often spurs firms to innovate"[4] and that "competitive markets play an important role in promoting and incentivizing innovation that benefits consumers."[5] Mergers, for example, can lessen innovation, even when the merger will not impact prices (such as when the products are free to consumers).[6] The 2010 US merger guidelines even have one section dedicated to how mergers may hamper innovation and product variety.[7]

Given innovation's significant role in competition policy, precisely because it fosters economic growth and overall well-being, antitrust enforcement should be, in theory, seeking to promote innovation.

So, when a Tech Baron uses its nowcasting radar to eliminate a nascent competitive threat, like Facebook acquiring Instagram or WhatsApp, alarm bells within the competition agencies should be ringing—even more so when the tone from the top, per Facebook's CEO, is that "it is better to buy than compete."[8] Enforcers should also know, as the *Economist* and others reported, how the Tech Barons can quickly identify nascent competitive threats. You would expect enforcers to stand guard, especially as "the Agencies have made combatting anticompetitive conduct in the technology sector [as] a top priority."[9]

Now may be a good time to set your expectations aside and do some quick math. Over one hundred jurisdictions have competition laws, including the power to review mergers. While several Tech Barons are not in China, Google, Amazon, Facebook, Apple, and Microsoft operate in most jurisdictions. In chapter 5, we looked at the strategic acquisitions by GAFAM. And how many of these seven hundred–plus acquisitions did the antitrust authorities block before 2021?

None.[10]

How many did they investigate?

Before 2021, very few.[11]

How many did they condition?

Before 2021, even fewer.[12]

Even if we put aside GAFAM and broadened our review, how many mergers did the competition authorities block solely or primarily because of their adverse effect on innovation? The answer again is relatively few cases. While innovation is often mentioned and identified in decision-making, it is rarely acted upon.[13]

If innovation is so important and these acquisitions risk creating innovation "kill zones," why haven't *any* of the one hundred–plus competition authorities worldwide blocked any of the seven hundred–plus acquisitions by GAFAM during the above period?

Some of these transactions may be benign or pro-competitive, but many others raised concerns. As one study found, in 60 percent of GAFAM's 175 acquisitions over three years, the brand of the target firms was killed within one year of the merger.[14]

Many factors contributed to the antitrust agencies' collective failure to back the "innovation championing" rhetoric with meaningful action. In essence, as we will illustrate, they are like the weather forecaster in making predictions. But unlike the weather forecaster, they use imperfect tools for the job and operate within a system that is ill-designed to properly assess innovation effects. Also, unlike the weather forecaster, they have no idea how often they accurately predict the merger's impact on competition or innovation, as they seldom conduct post-merger reviews. The result—while competition agencies strive to promote innovation, they can do little in most cases.

Shift to CSI Antitrust for Merger Review

Let's first focus on mergers and acquisitions by the Tech Barons. When it comes to merger review generally and innovation specifically, the agencies are in a prediction game, and it is tough to predict a merger's impact on innovation. The competition agencies typically review significant mergers before they occur. They must predict the merger's likely anticompetitive effects. However, the law does not require clairvoyance.[15] The agency need not establish "with certainty" that anticompetitive effects would occur.[16] Despite the law, the courts and agencies have come to expect detailed forensic-like analysis—sometimes referred to as "CSI

Antitrust," where antitrust enforcers, like the forensic investigators, gather detailed evidence to prove anticompetitive harm.[17]

To see why, let's consider white bread. If you live in America, you probably have seen the supermarket bread aisle dominated by soft, sliced bread loaves of different colors, flavors, and textures. In one of his early cases at the DOJ's Antitrust Division, back in 1995, one of us, Maurice, was involved in a merger of the leading producers of sliced white bread, including the Wonder and Butternut brands. In any merger, the issue is whether the merger may substantially lessen competition or tend to create a monopoly. To determine that, the agency typically defines the relevant product and geographic markets, measures market share and concentration levels, and assesses the difficulty in entering those markets. Ordinarily, market definition is quite contentious. If the market is defined narrowly—for example, branded white pan bread sold in the greater Los Angeles area—then the market shares and concentration levels are problematic. Define the market broadly—all types of bread, including the artisan baguettes sold at the farmer's market—then the market shares, concentration levels, and antitrust concerns decrease.

But the agencies typically go beyond concentration levels and assess how this particular merger will likely harm competition. One theory is coordinated effects. With fewer rivals, it becomes easier to tacitly or expressly collude. The other is that the merging parties can unilaterally raise prices post-merger. Because consumers perceive the merging parties' brands as close substitutes, the company, for instance, could profitably increase the price of Wonder bread post-merger. Loyal Wonder bread customers would pay more, and of the customers who switch, many would go to the merging party's other popular white bread brands, such as Butternut. The issue is how do you prove this? And must the agency do so to prevail?

The 1995 bread case, while a success, helped foster CSI Antitrust and the decline in merger review. In building the case to establish the likely harm, the Department of Justice could procure weekly scan data that the supermarkets collected. (When you are checking out, the clerk scans each item's Universal Product Code, which retailers and manufacturers rely upon.) That scan data, for the DOJ economists, was like gold. Since we typically buy bread weekly, the economists could measure how changes in price affected changes in demand. When pumpernickel bread, for example, was on sale, did it significantly impact the sales of white bread? Ditto for bagels and baguettes. The DOJ economists could quantify the cross-elasticity of demand (and determine to which products customers switched when white bread prices increased). More importantly, the economists could also quantify the merger's harm. Using diversion ratios, the estimated consumer demand at post-merger prices, and the profit margins of the merging parties' products, the DOJ could prove that the merger *would* lessen competition and quantify how much prices would likely increase post-merger. This was exciting.

Unilateral effects theory became the opium for merger review. Once the agency could predict the likely post-merger price increases for bread, it was expected to do the same in the subsequent consumer products merger involving facial tissue, toilet paper, and baby wipes.[18] As one DOJ official noted at that time, "What is noteworthy is the improvement in our ability to collect and analyze data, which allows us to predict with greater confidence when a transaction is likely to give the merged firm the ability to raise the price by itself, without regard to the actions of the remaining competitors."[19]

But the heady sensation soon faded. In one merger case, there was scan data only for some of the distribution channels but not for other significant retail outlets. Thus, the data gave an incomplete picture; the economists could not repeat the magic and prove the likely anticompetitive effects with the same certainty as in the bread and toilet paper cases. The internal debate was whether to accept a weak settlement or challenge the merger in court. Fearing a loss, the DOJ chose the inadequate settlement. Even though the law did not require certainty, the merging parties and courts began demanding this CSI Antitrust for every merger. As one DOJ official observed in 1996:

More and more when we go to court, the judges seem to be asking for concreteness; the anecdotal evidence seems less important to them than surveys, which seem systematic, but may be flawed. If the issue is product market, the courts seem to want to know exactly how many customers would be willing to switch. And if it's competitive effects, they want to know how big an effect will result. More and more, in order to persuade a court that a merger is going to be harmful, we feel the need to do the best we can to quantify.[20]

By the early 2000s, the US agencies challenged most mergers under a unilateral effects theory,[21] where they could likely quantify the anticompetitive effects and win. Of all the mergers that the FTC reviewed between 1989 and 2016, for example, 82 percent were horizontal (where the companies directly competed) as opposed to vertical (where a powerful platform might acquire a seller or app) or conglomerate (where the acquirer is a perceived or actual entrant).[22] And the focus in these horizontal mergers was unilateral effects.[23] As a result, the agencies focused on what was quantifiable—namely whether the merger will lead to higher prices—and less on what was important (but harder to quantify), like quality, privacy, systemic risk (in bank mergers), or innovation.

The result? Agencies can tackle problems under the lamppost, but CSI Antitrust increasingly restricts their ability to look beyond.

How CSI Antitrust Marginalizes Innovation

One casualty of CSI Antitrust is innovation. The antitrust officials still recognized the importance of innovation, but proving that a merger will lessen it is challenging for several reasons.

First, it is hard to predict disruptive innovation. As Clayton Christensen noted, even industry analysts and experts cannot generally predict the demand (or even the likely customers) of disruptive innovation. So, quantifying and proving a merger's impact on dynamic innovation will be difficult—especially when the experts' prognosis is typically wrong.

Second, the CSI Antitrust framework is geared toward well-established products with a predictable, stable demand (like white bread). This static analysis of the market is often an unreliable indicator of the harm to disruptive innovation. There is often no predictable demand for disruptive innovations, no assurance that the product will disrupt the industry or even succeed, and uncertainty over which customers will use the technology and for what purpose.

To see why, consider the US and EU competition agencies' merger guidelines. If you read them, you will notice that they do not distinguish between app developers, platform operators, and toilet paper manufacturers. While the guidelines reference innovation, they don't explore the types and value of innovation and market conditions that foster the Tech Pirates. Instead, the guidelines primarily focus on price competition and assume a static equilibrium for most markets. When subject to market power or an outside force, such as entry, government regulation, new technology, or an energy crisis, this equilibrium is temporarily disrupted and ultimately rests at a new equilibrium.

However, *competitive* digital markets are not static equilibrium systems; instead, they are complex adaptive ecosystems. It is much harder to predict competitive outcomes and which Tech Pirates will succeed and fail in these dynamic markets. It means that "[f]or better or for worse, economic life is an adventure."[24] As competitive dynamics change in unforeseen ways, firms must continually accommodate and adjust to make the most of these changes. Those adjustments and accommodations, in turn, lead to further change by firms and public policies. Under a competitive evolutionary process, "chance plays a significant role" and "small, random (and therefore unpredictable) events may have severe long-run consequences."[25]

Although economic life is an adventure, it's not a roller coaster. Waking up tomorrow morning, we would not expect the price of our cloud computing services to have doubled overnight or billions of users switching away from the Tech Barons' products and services. But it is way harder to predict the extent of disruption by WhatsApp, Instagram, and many other nascent innovators before the Tech Barons acquired them. Since CSI Antitrust is limited to what's quantifiable—namely short-term pricing—not what's important—namely value-creating innovations—its predictive quality suffers. As courts demand more of CSI Antitrust, effective antitrust enforcement declines, as does its ability to protect value-creating innovation.

Antitrust's Focus on Narrowly Defined Markets, Not on Ecosystems

In any legal proceeding, the parties can rely on direct and circumstantial evidence. While we might think direct evidence is stronger (a videotape of the killing) than circumstantial evidence (a trail of blood leading to the defendant's home), that is not always the case.

Under CSI Antitrust, the courts typically require circumstantial evidence of market power (a high market share in an antitrust market), even when a plaintiff has strong direct evidence of monopoly power (such as the defendant coercing market participants to do things that they would not do in competitive markets). As one district court stated, "[c]entral to antitrust cases is the appropriate determination of the 'relevant market.'"[26]

To make matters worse, current antitrust focuses on very narrowly defined markets. This market definition exercise is ill-equipped to deal with platforms, much less with ecosystems, where Tech Barons affect the demand and supply of disruptive innovations. Divorced from disruptive innovation (and at times from business reality), the agencies' market definition test misses the bigger picture of ecosystems.

So, to prove that the Tech Baron is a monopoly, the plaintiff has to rely on a protracted process of defining a relevant antitrust market that primarily pits economic experts (often charging over $1,000 per hour) against one another. Why the economists? To define the antitrust market, one considers cross-elasticity of demand, which begins with the question of whether a hypothetical monopolist could profitably impose a small but significant and non-transitory increase in price (SSNIP), on the magnitude of 5 to 10 percent, for a specific product or service. If yes, say toilet paper, that is the relevant product market. If no, say premium diet orange soda, where would customers switch? Then the agency and court would reapply this SSNIP test to the larger product market. The test is repeated to determine the geographic market.

There are many problems with the SSNIP test. This analysis is workable only when demand is stable and predictable, markets are competitive, and with good data that is easy to obtain (like the retailer scan data in the white bread case). But one cannot apply this SSNIP test when the Tech Baron's product or service is free.[27] Nor can one easily apply the SSNIP test to multisided platforms.[28] Nor does the narrowly defined market correspond with the merger's impact on disruptive innovation.

Suppose, for example, Microsoft years ago sought to sustain its Windows monopoly for personal computers by acquiring the Android smartphone operating system (rather than allowing Google to acquire it). It is clearly anticompetitive when Microsoft acquires the nascent competitive threat to preserve its monopoly. But in applying the SSNIP test, one would conclude that the operating systems for personal computers and smartphones were not close substitutes and thus not in the same market. Because the merger would involve different product markets, it would unlikely garner antitrust scrutiny.[29] Nor was it foreseeable that we would spend more time on our smartphones. Nor could an agency predict how Android, under Google's control, along with Apple, would later dominate the smartphone ecosystem.

Likewise, under its current rules, Europe faces this same difficulty when the merging firms operate in separate but related markets.[30] As a result, the Tech Barons' anticompetitive acquisitions went unchallenged.

So, why define markets? One reason is that courts require it—even when there is direct evidence of monopoly power.

In Epic Games' case against Apple, the requirement for market definition took an illogical turn. There was ample direct evidence of Apple's monopoly power, including that (1) Apple's 30 percent commission on in-app purchases was divorced from its costs to run its App Store[31] or competition; (2) Apple's contract terms were standardized and non-negotiable (indeed Apple argued that its licensing agreement was not an agreement at all because "Apple unilaterally imposes it on developers"[32]); (3) competition never forced Apple to lower its commission rates or offer app developers better terms; and (4) both Apple's and Epic's economic experts agreed that "persistently high economic profit is suggestive of market power" and Apple's operating margins for its app store were staggering—over 75 percent for 2018 and 2019.[33] Moreover, the court found that Apple's restraints reduced competition and harmed innovation.[34]

And yet Epic's monopolization claims failed. Why? Because in the CSI Antitrust universe, Apple's market share of 57.2 percent was too low for monopoly power. Instead, for the court, Apple was "near the precipice of substantial market power, or monopoly power."[35] Ultimately, the court rejected every federal antitrust claim against Apple and upheld Apple's contracts of adhesion. The only relief for Epic, app developers, and consumers came under one state law (the California Unfair Competition Law, which is not saddled with CSI Antitrust's market definition fetish). How could the court lose sight of the forest because of the trees (devoting fifty-eight pages of factual and legal findings regarding the relevant antitrust market)? It is as if the judge is shown direct evidence of the crime (a videotape of the defendant killing the person), only to rule for the murderer because the government lacked circumstantial evidence.

Take, as another example, Facebook, and ask yourself, *Is it a monopoly?* Every policymaker and enforcer who examined the digital ecosystem concluded yes. Indeed, Facebook was not constrained by an advertiser boycott, the significant backlash from its multiple privacy violations, including Cambridge Analytica, or its harm, including to millions of teenagers' mental well-being. That demonstrates its monopoly power. Monopolies can do things (like imposing disadvantageous nonprice contractual terms on counterparties or revising contractual terms in their own favor) that firms without this power simply can't. But the absurdity of CSI Antitrust arose when a district court dismissed the FTC's and states' monopolization cases against Facebook. For one thing, the court found that the FTC did not sufficiently plead in its complaint that Facebook was a monopoly. The court was concerned, among other things, that the FTC's fifty-three-page complaint was "undoubtedly light on specific factual allegations regarding consumer-switching preferences."[36] It's hard to imagine how the FTC could quantify users' switching preferences for a free social network where no viable alternative exists. In particular, the court took issue with how the FTC calculated Facebook's market share. Quantifying Facebook's market share of personal social network market is problematic if the FTC cannot rely on

- revenues (as Facebook is ostensibly free for users),

- the percent of daily users or monthly users of personal social network services (which the court initially believed might overstate or understate the firm's market share depending on the various proportions of users who have accounts on multiple services, not to mention how often users visit each service and for how long), and

- the percentage of time users spent on Facebook versus other social media (since, as the court noted, the time spent on the platforms may not equal time spent on a personal social network if it offers multiple services).

Ultimately, the FTC filed a longer complaint that showed Facebook's commanding market share, using the same metrics that Facebook internally relied upon to measure itself against rivals. The court did not dismiss the FTC's amended complaint, but it did ominously warn how "the agency may well face a tall task down the road in *proving* its allegations."[37] What will happen if the FTC cannot prove Facebook's market share? It will probably lose. This is because the FTC's only recourse is to rely on direct evidence of Facebook's monopoly power, which the courts define as "the power to control prices or exclude competition."[38] Controlling prices is off the table for the Tech Baron's free services. As we saw, they harvest our data to better manipulate our behavior to get us to buy things we otherwise wouldn't have. But that's irrelevant under CSI Antitrust. But even if the Tech Baron charges a monopoly price (and reaps monopoly profits), that is insufficient. The courts under CSI Antitrust now require evidence that output also declined.[39] This makes no economic sense when a company can price discriminate. It is also impossible in the digital economy, where output is generally increasing across the board. So, the plaintiff must prove an impossible counterfactual, namely that output would have been even greater without the anticompetitive restraint.[40]

Consequently, no matter how egregious the anticompetitive behavior, so long as the Tech Barons aren't stupid enough to collude again[41] (which is the only legal area not captured by CSI Antitrust), they can often, under the prevailing interpretation of the law, avoid antitrust liability. Because CSI Antitrust focuses on narrowly defined markets (not ecosystems) and prices and output (not innovation), it is unsuitable for the multitrillion-dollar digital economy.

Antitrust Focuses on *Past*, Not Current or Future Anticompetitive Practices

Even when antitrust actions are successful, they rarely offer a timely remedy. Beyond large mergers (where the law often requires pre-merger review), antitrust enforcement is reactive. That is, a company engages in anticompetitive conduct, competition is reduced, the agency investigates, and then if sufficient evidence exists, the agency subsequently challenges the company for its past behavior. In complex cases, this process often takes years, if not decades—years of investigations, discovery, negotiations, decision making, litigation, and appeals. Unless subject to interim measures, the Tech Baron can continue its anticompetitive conduct until a final decision or a court orders it not to.

The result? *Even when the antitrust enforcers win, we still lose.* Antitrust relief is often too little and too late to restore competition in the digital economy, which, as we saw, is characterized by network effects and economies of scale. So, platforms have the incentive to elbow out rivals with anticompetitive practices. Once the markets tip in their favor, and as technology changes, the Tech Barons may no longer have to rely on these anticompetitive practices to maintain their power. Network effects now work in their favor. By the time they exhaust all other avenues and appeals, their dominance is secured. They pay the fine and agree to refrain from the past anticompetitive behavior.

For example, the US and EU antitrust cases against Microsoft spanned two decades. The relief, when it finally arrived, had mixed success. On the upside, the crackdown on Microsoft provided a competitive portal for the other companies to grow, just as the antitrust crackdown on then-monopoly IBM provided a competitive portal for PC operating systems, such as Microsoft. On the downside, Microsoft remains a Tech Baron, and its PC operating system, Windows, has mainly seen sustaining, incremental innovations rather than any dynamic disruptions.

Consider Apple, which told the maker of Fortnite in 2021 that its ability to release software on Apple platforms won't be reinstated until its litigation against the iPhone maker is resolved, which could take years.[42] Which app developer can afford to spend millions of dollars on antitrust litigation while being foreclosed from over one billion iPhone users?

Or consider the European Commission's Google Shopping investigation. Following numerous complaints, the commission opened its first monopolization investigation against Google in 2010. Due to several peculiarities, the investigation took years before concluding with a formal decision and remedy in 2017.[43] Following an action for annulment, the European General Court upheld the Commission's key findings in 2021. In early 2022, Google appealed this judgment to the European Court of Justice. Two other Google investigations in Europe were relatively swifter (each lasting around three years).[44] But Google appealed those two decisions as well, and no final opinions have been rendered. In the US, Google, as of 2021, was the subject of four governmental antitrust actions. Litigating these antitrust actions will likely drag on to the 2030s when wearables are predicted to replace smartphones.[45]

Antitrust's glacial reaction works in the Tech Baron's favor. (There is the possibility of "interim measures" in Europe and a preliminary injunction in the US where the agency can stop the anticompetitive practice while investigating. But that has been rarely employed in the digital economy.) In most cases, until a remedy is imposed, a Tech Baron can continue to consolidate its power and distort the innovation paths. Once levied, the remedy will rarely resurrect the pirates and their disruptive innovation. Their moment has passed. So, even if the Tech Barons eventually lose the antitrust battles, they still win.

Antitrust Focuses on What the Defendant Did, Not Why It Did It

Facebook repeatedly violated its users' privacy. For that, the FTC imposed a record fine of $5 billion. But a majority of FTC commissioners never considered why Facebook violated the FTC's earlier order and committed new privacy violations. As the two dissenting FTC commissioners observed, the FTC's settlement never addressed the root cause of Facebook's exploitative behavior.[46] Commissioner Rohit Chopra noted that "Facebook's violations were a direct result of the company's behavioral advertising business model," and the FTC's settlement did "little to change [Facebook's] business model or practices that led to the recidivism."[47]

It is only natural for antitrust enforcement to focus on the particular behavior of specific companies. But for the Tech Barons, their behavior is a symptom of their ecosystem's underlying value chain. Recall that Google's cofounders accurately perceived the risks of advertising. But they realized that if they did not increase revenues at the critical start-up phase, another search engine would. The value chain drives the competition, which drives the ensuing innovation.

So even if Facebook were broken up and displaced by TikTok, would we benefit? Yes, in some ways. But even if the antitrust enforcer topples a Tech Baron, it will not necessarily alter its value chain. If TikTok builds out its ecosystem on behavioral advertising, the toxic competition and toxic innovation will continue.

The Resulting Void

CSI Antitrust hamstrings enforcement in the digital economy. As Figure 9.1 illustrates, it focuses on narrowly defined markets when it should be considering ecosystems. It considers price and output when it should be considering innovation. It considers the effects of the restraint (increased price and reduced output), not why the Tech Baron behaves this way.

Figure 9.1

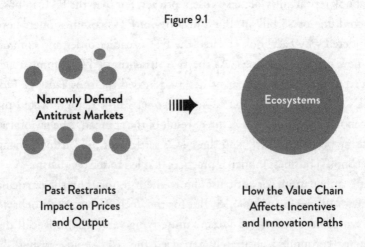

Narrowly Defined
Antitrust Markets

Ecosystems

Past Restraints
Impact on Prices
and Output

How the Value Chain
Affects Incentives
and Innovation Paths

We are left with a paradox. In the digital economy, what's quantifiable (market definition and the restraint's or merger's short-term impact on prices and output) is not what's essential (mergers' and conduct's impact on innovation, quality, or privacy). Occasionally the competition agencies raise innovation concerns (such as Visa's proposed acquisition of Plaid and Bayer's acquisition of Monsanto). But many agencies have been risk averse, unwilling to challenge the CSI Antitrust paradigm and risk losing in court. Even worse, under chapter 8's ideological platter, the competition agency would be perceived as chilling innovation. As the OECD observed in 2020, "Raising concerns over the [Tech Barons'] acquisition of start-ups with risky but potentially important innovative products would have been seen as speculative, prone to over-enforcement risk (and judicial challenge), and worse, might have projected an image of the agency as being a roadblock to innovation."[48] That has left, as the OECD noted, a "systematic bias against challenging mergers."[49]

Thus, agencies often focused on what they could—mainly prosecuting cartels (where CSI Antitrust does not apply), occasionally horizontal mergers that reduced the number of competitors from four to three or three to two, and where the agencies could prove the relevant market and quantify the anticompetitive effects.[50] Economics, rather than guiding enforcement, limits it to cases where with enough data (and a more compelling economic model than the defendant's), the court will be persuaded that prices will increase and output will decline.

Under CSI Antitrust, competition law drifts further from the *competition ideal*—the congressional belief, in line with democratic principles, in dispersing economic and political power from the hands of a few, to foster more opportunities to compete, improve, and win. The agencies no longer enforce a statute "designed to be a comprehensive charter of economic liberty aimed at preserving free and unfettered competition as the rule of trade."[51] Rather than dispersing private power to advance a range of economic and political interests,[52] the law, as now construed, allows it. Rather than treat corporate concentration as a threat to innovation, workers, consumers, businesses, and citizens, many agencies reluctantly accepted it.[53]

When competition agencies still raise innovation concerns, it's often as an afterthought in mergers to monopoly or when they have compelling evidence of higher prices and reduced output. At times, an agency has succeeded with claims that the merger would likely lessen innovation.[54] The agency may sometimes require remedies that address the merger's effects on research and development and innovation.[55] But often, innovation plays at best a secondary role, after price effects.

As the former chief economist of the European Commission Professor Tommaso Valletti noted, when the agency attempts to bring substantive considerations of innovation into the analysis, it often faces "an uphill battle." It is confronted with "an army of consultants." At a conference on "Declining Competition," Valletti opined that the leading corporations engage in a war of attrition.[56] Even when the agencies overcome these hurdles, they're often shut down by the courts' CSI Antitrust. As one district court held, the "DOJ has not proven that the Sabre-Farelogix merger *will* harm innovation."[57] But no one can prove that. The district court, in that case, discounted the expert economic testimony that "the merger involves 'taking an innovative firm that has been driving, driving ahead, creating the industry shakeup, and putting that under a firm that does not have the same incentive'" as "vague theories."[58] Ultimately, the parties abandoned that merger after the US appealed, and the appellate court vacated the lower court's decision. But the risk remains that other district courts will require proof that the merger *will* lessen innovation in some narrowly defined antitrust market divorced from reality.

Reflections

Of course, while we can criticize the Tech Barons for their anticompetitive conduct, we should also criticize the courts and our elected politicians who allowed antitrust to shrivel to the point of irrelevancy in the digital economy. The Tech Barons saw an opportunity in the legal void that CSI Antitrust produced.

Accordingly, Nancy Rose, head of MIT's Economics Department, commented on the need to overcome this CSI effect:

> The sense that if you cannot precisely quantify econometrically an effect, or predicted effect, to the fourth decimal place, it does not exist, and it's not relevant . . . is problematic for harms in areas of innovation . . .[59]

With the focus on the merger's impact on price, not innovation, in narrowly defined markets (not ecosystems), it becomes clear why none of the competition authorities challenged the Tech Barons' acquisitions of nascent threats. Existing antitrust theories of harm are ill-suited to address concerns over the Tech Barons' ecosystems.[60] So, under CSI Antitrust, there is an open season in acquiring or killing the Tech Pirates.

To be clear, the call for change should not be anchored in nostalgia of past antitrust policies when enforcement was more robust. Regardless of one's view on the success (or lack of it) of past enforcement policies, the key is in the understanding of the limitations of the present approach and the need to keep up with the digital economy. The consensus among policymakers is that something needs to be done. Andreas Mundt, the head of Germany's competition authority, noted in 2021 how the antitrust tools are outdated for the digital economy. He said it's akin to telling the enforcers to climb Mount Everest in leather boots and wool mittens, using hemp rope.

Enforcers are waging multiple campaigns against several Tech Barons and are scrutinizing their mergers. Still, they're using tools designed to deter yesteryear's monopolies, which mainly dominated markets (not interlocking digital platforms). Yesteryear's monopolies could not distort the supply and demand of disruptive innovations. They lacked the weapons of the current Tech Barons, including their nowcasting radar.

Unfortunately, despite their best intentions, the current enforcement actions against the Tech Barons (which will conclude long after this book is published) will likely offer incomplete relief (even if successful). Nor will the actions likely deter the Tech Barons or stem the toxic innovations. With all its imperfections, the current system gives Tech Barons time—years to kill the pirates and reorient the innovation paths to those inventions that reinforce their power.

To put it simply, antitrust enforcers lag the Tech Barons. The courts, in applying the antitrust laws, often lag the enforcers. (Some judges still blindly rely on theories of Chicago School adherents, like Robert Bork, about self-correcting markets and greater risks of false positives from governmental enforcement, without recognizing the different dynamics of digital markets.) As the economist John Maynard Keynes noted:

> The difficulty lies, not in the new ideas, but in escaping the old ones, which ramify, for those brought up as most of us have been, into every corner of our minds.

The good news is that most policymakers recognize the illogical outcomes under CSI Antitrust and the need for reform. After the judicial opinions in *Facebook* and *Apple*, the bipartisan condemnation by lawmakers was swift. Senior members of Congress, for example, noted "the dire need to modernize our antitrust laws to address anticompetitive mergers and abusive conduct in the digital economy."[61] "How a judge could look at the evidence and rule that Apple is not a monopoly defies logic," tweeted Representative Ken Buck, the top Republican member of the House Judiciary's antitrust panel and cosponsor of a legislative package aimed at reining in the Tech Barons.[62] Senator Blumenthal added that the *Apple* ruling is "insufficient and disappointing. It is now up to Congress to take meaningful action."[63]

Will their proposals rein in the Tech Barons? To answer that, we next need to consider an ancient Greek king and duck hunting.

CHAPTER 10

Pyrrhus, Ducks, and Proposed Reforms

PYRRHUS, THE KING OF Epirus in today's northern Greece, defeated the Romans in battle. But after one such victory, he remarked:

"Ne ego si iterum eodem modo vicero, sine ullo milite Epirum revertar."
  If I gain such a victory again from the Romans, then I must afterward return to Epirus without any soldier.

—CP. PAUL. DIAC, HIST., II, 16

Pyrrhus lost many men in his victories, and he could not replenish his fallen troops as quickly as the Romans could, who had far greater resources. From him, we get the term *Pyrrhic victories.*

So, who are the Romans in the current antitrust battles? One would think the U.S. Department of Justice, Federal Trade Commission, European Commission, and other leading agencies, but in reality, it is the Tech Barons.

As we saw in the last chapter, the CSI Antitrust legal framework constrains the agencies' ability to rein in the Tech Barons. Furthermore, the agencies cannot match the Tech Barons' resources in financing legions of outside economists and lawyers and affecting the public discussion through their lobbying efforts. The DOJ's Antitrust Division, for example, requested for 2021 a budget of $188.5 million for its 782 positions, including 390 attorneys.[1] If the Antitrust Division were a law firm, it wouldn't even crack the top one hundred based on the number of attorneys.[2] The FTC had fewer employees in 2021 (handling consumer protection, privacy, and competition issues) than during the Reagan administration.[3] In contrast, the Tech Barons have enlisted many of the top-tier law firms across the globe.

The result? A current legal and enforcement framework that insulates the Tech Barons. The war's outcome, as we saw, is determined well before the prosecution begins.

As this chapter explores, the proposed reforms are far superior to the current CSI Antitrust framework. We will benefit as a result—especially in limiting the Tech Barons' ability to acquire nascent competitive threats and removing some torpedoes from their arsenal. In returning to Figure 9.1 from the last chapter, the new proposals would advance the antitrust tools one step to better target platforms, as Figure 10.1 illustrates:

Figure 10.1

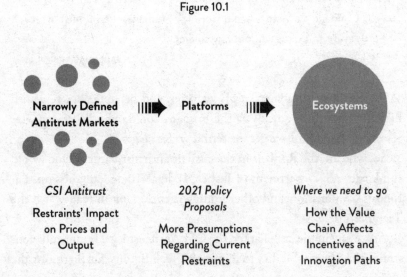

Narrowly Defined Antitrust Markets ⇛ Platforms ⇛ Ecosystems

CSI Antitrust	2021 Policy Proposals	Where we need to go
Restraints' Impact on Prices and Output	More Presumptions Regarding Current Restraints	How the Value Chain Affects Incentives and Innovation Paths

While an important step, the policy proposals, as we'll see, will not necessarily deter the Tech Barons or toxic innovation. As of 2022, policymakers are considering individual platforms when they should be thinking of ecosystems. Rather than considering the Tech Barons' likely future weapons, they focus on a potpourri of their past anticompetitive practices. And the fundamental belief is that the behavioral modifications will spur more competition and innovation.

Herein is the gravest error: many policymakers have not fully considered the prevailing ecosystems' value chain and thus do not appreciate the toxicity of competition and innovation. They focus on the symptoms yet often ignore the commercial incentives and their centrality in distorting innovation. Consequently, the proposed reforms, even *if* enacted, may offer little more than Pyrrhic victories. With the Tech Barons' lobbying their ideological platter, we will be preparing to fight old battles. At the same time, the Tech Barons have already marched on, conquering new ecosystems with new weapons.

"Your platforms are dangerous . . . and accountability is coming."

So said one senator after grilling a Facebook executive in 2021.[4] Let's start with the good news. There is widespread consensus that the light-touch antitrust policies of the past forty years have failed. Aware of the market power problem that extends far beyond Big Tech in the US and Europe, policymakers realize that "[f]orceful agency action is critical."[5] Indeed, in our discussions with policymakers, the focus is on what actions are needed to restore competition and promote innovation (rather than asking whether such steps are needed at all).

Legislative efforts are seeking to reenergize competition and innovation in the digital economy. In July 2021, the House Judiciary Committee, for example, voted in favor of a "historic package of bipartisan legislation" to address, among other things, Facebook's abusing "its monopoly power to buy or bury its competitive threats."[6] The six bills are:

1. *The Merger Filing Fee Modernization Act of 2021* (H.R. 3843), which would ensure that the US antitrust agencies "have the resources they need to enforce antitrust laws by increasing filing fees on the largest transactions while reducing filing fees on smaller transactions."[7] (The House Judiciary Committee approved this 29–12, with five Republicans voting in favor);

2. *The State Antitrust Enforcement Venue Act of 2021* (H.R. 3460), which would allow state attorneys general to bring antitrust cases in federal court without facing delays or higher costs due to the defendants' transferring these cases to different venues (approved 34–7, with fourteen Republicans voting in favor);

3. *The Augmenting Compatibility and Competition by Enabling Service Switching (ACCESS) Act of 2021* (H.R. 3849), which would give the FTC new authority and enforcement tools "to establish procompetitive rules for interoperability and data portability online"[8] (approved 25–19, with three Republicans voting in favor);

4. *The Platform Competition and Opportunity Act of 2021* (H.R. 3826), which would prohibit "the largest online platforms from engaging in mergers that would eliminate competitors, or potential competitors, or that would serve to enhance or reinforce monopoly power"[9] (approved 23–18–1, with three Republicans voting in favor);

5. *The American Choice and Innovation Online Act* (H.R. 3816), which would seek to restore competition online and ensure that digital markets are "fair and open by preventing dominant online platforms from using their market power to pick winners and losers, favor their own products, or otherwise distort the marketplace

through abusive conduct online"[10] (approved 24–20, with three Republicans voting in favor); and

6. *The Ending Platform Monopolies Act* (H.R. 3825), which would authorize the FTC and DOJ to take action to prevent "dominant online platforms from leveraging their monopoly power to distort or destroy competition in markets that rely on that platform."[11] Basically, the law would prevent dominant online platforms from operating and competing with other businesses and services on that platform.[12] (Approved 21–20, with two Republicans voting in favor.)

In addition to the six House bills, several senators have introduced legislation, including their version of the American Innovation and Choice Online Act, which, like the House bill, would crack down on the Tech Barons' self-preferencing, hindering interoperability, and tying services, and the Open App Markets Act, which, among other things, would allow users to install third-party app stores and obtain apps outside of Google's and Apple's app stores.

Europe's two key proposals—the Digital Markets Act and Digital Services Act—seek to remedy many of the shortcomings in EU competition law as applied to these Tech Barons. The acts would impose specific obligations for these powerful gatekeepers precisely because Europe's antitrust policies cannot address these "gatekeeper-related problems" effectively.[13] The proposals' objective "is to ensure a contestable and fair digital sector in general and core platform services in particular" and to promote, among other things, innovation in the digital sector.[14]

Change is also underway elsewhere. For example, to resolve Japan's concerns, Apple announced in 2021 that it would let developers of newspaper and media "reader" apps worldwide link to an external website to set up or manage an account.[15] South Korea, in 2021, banned major app stores operators—like Google and Apple—from requiring app developers to use only their payment systems for in-app purchases.

(This would allow developers and South Koreans to avoid the Tech Barons' hefty 30 percent commission on every transaction.)

Consequently, there is reason to be hopeful with so many policy proposals seeking to make antitrust more administrable, reinvigorate enforcement, and supplement it with regulatory tools to address the current market power problem.

These changes should help promote disruptive innovation in several ways.

First, while promoting innovation has always been a concern, there is a widespread belief that Tech Barons' unfair practices and lack of contestability within their ecosystems have led to less choice and innovation.[16] So, the aim is to replace the Tech Barons' unfair rules, which help entrench their power, with "fairer and more equitable conditions for all players in the digital sector," which "would allow them to take greater advantage of the growth potential of the platform economy."[17] The hope is that the new statutory obligations on the Tech Barons will loosen their grip and make the digital economy more contestable. Alternative platforms might then emerge that "could deliver high-quality, innovative products and services at affordable prices."[18] Innovation, especially among smaller businesses, could then flourish.[19]

Second is the shift away from the prevailing price-centric CSI Antitrust approach. The 2020 congressional report, for example, recommended that Congress "consider reasserting the original intent and broad goals of the antitrust laws, by clarifying that they are designed to protect not just consumers, but also workers, entrepreneurs, independent businesses, open markets, a fair economy, and democratic ideals."[20] The report recommends that Congress clarify that "market definition is not required for proving an antitrust violation, especially in the presence of direct evidence of market power." Policymakers across the Atlantic now recognize that *false negatives* (erroneous nonenforcement) are costlier than *false positives* (or erroneous enforcement) when it comes to conduct or mergers involving dominant firms.[21]

Third are calls for greater antitrust scrutiny of the Tech Barons' acquiring nascent competitive threats. Policymakers in the EU, US, and elsewhere have proposed:

- legislative changes to the standard for reviewing conglomerate transactions,[22]

- shifting or lessening the agency's burden of proof when challenging horizontal mergers,[23]

- invigorating vertical merger law,[24] and

- lowering the reporting thresholds for pre-merger review.[25]

So, depending on how rigorously the courts apply the presumption, these reforms can limit the Tech Barons' ability to acquire potential pirates.

A fourth improvement is to reduce the turnaround time for relief. Policymakers recognize that the legal system moves too slowly relative to the technological changes. Consequently, in 2021, Germany modernized its monopoly law by allowing its antitrust agency, the Bundeskartellamt, "to take even faster and more effective action" in the digital economy. The law prohibits the Tech Barons "from engaging in certain types of conduct much earlier," such as self-preferencing and denying rivals access to critical data. As Andreas Mundt, who heads the Bundeskartellamt, states, the law "shut[s] the stable door before the horse has bolted."[26] The law also enables the agency "to intervene in cases where a platform market threatens to 'tip' towards a large supplier."[27] So, rather than waiting for a particular platform market to tip to one or two of these Tech Barons, the Bundeskartellamt can intercede with interim measures (enjoining the Tech Baron's specific behavior while the antitrust agency investigates the conduct)[28] and market sector reviews.[29]

A fifth policy improvement is allowing the competition authorities to be more proactive than reactive. Currently, many agencies investigate only after receiving a credible complaint that a particular company

violated the antitrust law by engaging in specific anticompetitive conduct. The EU Commission has proposed preemptive market investigation tools that will allow it to proactively scrutinize markets and identify
and remedy problems that need addressing.[30] Some jurisdictions, like the
UK, already use similar instruments to investigate industries to ensure
their competitiveness. While the market investigation tool can be handy,
one criticism is that the investigations are lengthy, and thus ill-suited for
dynamic markets and complex remedies.

The sixth area of improvement is the proposed obligations and codes
of conduct for large platforms, including prohibiting some of the Tech
Barons' earlier anticompetitive tactics. The proposals would prevent the
Tech Barons from, among other things:

- using specific categories of data for their nowcasting radar to identify nascent competitive threats;[31]

- using defaults to favor their own technologies or using deception,
  manipulation, and dark patterns; [32]

- bundling services;[33]

- self-preferencing their products or services;[34] and

- killing Tech Pirates by reducing interoperability with their products[35]
  or hindering our ability to switch to the pirates' innovative products.[36]

Although European policymakers reached a provisional political
agreement on the Digital Markets Act in early 2022, neither Europe's
nor the US's policy proposals have been enacted as of the writing of this
book. The Tech Barons' trade, lobbying, and academic groups are already
pushing back. Using their resources and political power, they will likely
delay and dilute some of the proposals. While we may not see a complete legal transformation, we can nonetheless expect to witness change
in some key areas.

But let's suppose that the proposals are all implemented. Let's also assume that the competition agencies win all of their current cases against the Tech Barons, who are, after that, enjoined from engaging in the anticompetitive practices alleged in the complaints. Although a rather optimistic, and unlikely, outcome, let's suppose this will indeed happen. Will these changes significantly deter toxic innovation?

The changes will make it harder for the Tech Barons to kill off the Tech Pirates. We will likely see more competition and disruptive innovation. So, certainly an improvement over the current state of affairs. But the changes are unlikely to eliminate the toxic innovation. To see why, let's consider duck hunting.

Hunting Ducks

In hunting ducks, one needs to shoot where the duck is heading, not where it is now. Otherwise, the duck will be gone by the time the shot reaches its initial position. So, you calculate the duck's likely path and shoot ahead of it. If you practice enough, you can predict the flight path. But in following the duck's flight path, you can become fixated on calculating the proper lead. As one hunting blog post notes:

> if you try to compute the proper lead in your head each time you shoot, you'll get frustrated because each shot is different in terms of flight angle and speed. Some shots are going away, some are head-on and some are passing at 90 degrees. Some shots are at ducks zipping by at full speed, while others are at birds hovering over the decoys. If you must consciously think about how much lead to hold, you're probably going to miss.[37]

Why raise duck hunting when discussing the Tech Barons?

Of course, the aim isn't to kill the Tech Barons. Driving them out of business would chill innovation. Underlying all the policy proposals is the desire to avoid chilling value-creating innovation, including those from the Tech Barons.[38] Instead, the aim is to deter the Tech Barons' anticompetitive practices. With this in mind, the duck hunting analogy illustrates two potential pitfalls when proposing reforms in the digital economy.

First, one should not focus solely on past violations. Many of the specific obligations under the European and US proposals aim at the Tech Barons' past restraints. Policymakers and legislators need to consider that as technologies evolve, the Tech Barons may no longer require their earlier anticompetitive practices to maintain their power. Thus, the policy challenge is not cataloging earlier anticompetitive behavior but anticipating the Tech Barons' future anticompetitive tactics to colonize new platforms, expand their ecosystem, and eliminate Tech Pirates. The new policy tools must be specific enough to identify anticompetitive practices but sufficiently flexible to adjust to changing technologies and market realities.

Policymakers, however, are ill-equipped in accurately predicting the Tech Barons' future anticompetitive moves. So, they mostly shoot where the duck was, not where it is heading.

Consider, for example, the proposals to target the Tech Barons' self-preferencing. That made sense when Google overrode its search engine's "organic" algorithm to promote its comparison shopping tools on the first page and demote its rivals' services to the fourth page, which was online Siberia. In examining the difference between what its search algorithm would have recommended and the results Google actually suggested, the agency can prove that Google was self-preferencing. But search is already changing in several material ways, and proving self-preferencing will be far more complex. Search is becoming more personalized, so your results from the same query to the search engine might differ from my results. And how we search is changing from written to voice. As one pioneer in AI noted, with the advancements of natural language interfaces with our digital assistants, "computer keyboards will someday become museum pieces."[39] So, when you ask your digital assistant on your smartwatch or speakers a query, the assistant won't recite pages of search results. Instead, it will recommend one or two based on your preferences. As the nature of our search for information evolves, and because no two users will be alike, it will be harder to distinguish between personalization and discrimination. Thus, it will be a lot harder to prove that the Tech Baron engaged in self-preferencing. Enough said.

Second, a duck might not necessarily know it is being targeted. It doesn't know the hunter's shooting skills, and it doesn't take, as a result, avoidance measures. The duck may simply fly in the same trajectory. Contrast that with the Tech Barons, who know when their strategies are being targeted and have far more resources to outmaneuver the enforcers. One cannot underestimate the Tech Barons' agility to anticipate and offset new laws and regulations and the slow reactive nature of policymakers, enforcers, and regulators. As Andy Grove, former CEO of Intel, reportedly said:

> High tech runs three times faster than normal businesses. And the government runs three times slower than normal businesses. So we have a nine-times gap.[40]

In chapter 9, we saw how this gap widens as courts often run much slower than the agencies, resulting in CSI Antitrust undermining the agencies' ability to increase contestability in the digital economy. The proposed reforms can reduce this gap but will unlikely resolve the reactive nature of enforcement, which will always lag behind the market. So even when the law is updated to include the powerful platforms' current anticompetitive practices, there soon will be a regulatory gap.

Consequently, the current policy proposals have different shelf lives.

As the technology evolves, those policies that target specific anticompetitive practices by particular platforms (like a search engine's self-preferencing) will have the shortest shelf life.

Policies prohibiting the Tech Barons from hoarding critical inputs, such as personal data, will have a longer shelf life.[41] But they too will eventually be outdated. Currently, the Tech Barons' power is fueled in substantial part by the volume and variety of personal data that they quickly collect, which they use to train their algorithms, profile us for behavioral advertising, and manipulate our behavior. Stricter privacy regulations will likely clamp down on the personal data that the Tech Barons can freely collect. So, the barons consider how they can maintain their dominance under the new legal regime, or better yet, how they can use the privacy laws offensively to widen the competitive moat—consequently, the Tech Barons pivot.

By 2022, the Tech Barons had far more personal data about us than other companies did. As their competitive advantage in first-party data increased, they have become less reliant on third-party data, such as the data that other websites and apps collect about us. In contrast, smaller behavioral advertising rivals are far more dependent on cookies and other trackers, precisely because they collect far less first-party data about us. As a result, by 2022, the Tech Barons could afford to pivot from collecting a lot of third-party data about us when we visit third-party apps and websites to primarily collecting first-party data when we use their services. Thus, even though the technology had previously existed, Google and Apple in 2021 announced that we could finally limit third-party tracking. This move strengthened their position on account of other operators, as the Tech Barons continue to collect first-party data about us.

As the innovations become more intrusive, such as decoding our personality traits from the way we talk or move our mouse across the screen, future Tech Barons will require far less personal data about us. Think about it. Suppose Amazon's algorithms can accurately predict your emotional response to specific stimuli. In that case, it need not track right now whether you are highlighting this text (if you're reading this book on Kindle). Amazon can already predict what you will likely highlight. Indeed, its algorithms will have so many opportunities to perfect its profile of you that Amazon can give back some of your privacy, but not your autonomy.

As a result, the vices from behavioral advertising will continue. Only the means to predict and manipulate your emotions and thoughts will change. As our colleague Cecilia Rikap, who has been investigating the use of these new technologies, notes:

Decentralized learning is now used by the leading platforms. New technologies enable them to analyze data without the need to harvest it. So they may already have the capacity to bypass limitations on data harvesting. They are trying to do that. Text mining analysis suggests that this is the next frontier. Using transfer learning, the leading platforms may not need to fully rely on personal data. . . . In focusing on platforms and how restraints affect individuals, the regulators miss the overall picture, which is about the value that is being harvested from society.[42]

Policies that extend beyond specific past anticompetitive conduct will have a longer shelf life. One example is the Platform Competition and Opportunity Act of 2021, which would halt the Tech Barons' killer acquisitions, motivated by their ethos that "it is better to buy than compete." Mandating interoperability (if these obligations are tied to ecosystems and not particular platforms) will make it slightly harder to kill the Tech Pirates.

Finally, adaptive tools tailored to specific circumstances and different Tech Barons can have the longest shelf life. Noteworthy in this respect is the UK proposal for a pro-competition regime for digital markets. That regime will target firms with "strategic market status" and tailor a legally binding code for each. Rather than the one-off intervention (such as from a market investigation), the agency can update and fine-tune the code to effectively thwart new anticompetitive practices by the Tech Barons.[43]

Pyrrhic Victories

An astute reader (or avid historian of the Roosevelt-Taft-Wilson presidential debate over monopolies) might recognize that something is amiss. As we saw in chapter 1, the problem with the Tech Barons is their control over ecosystems, which gives them far more power than popular platforms or apps.

So rather than rely on regulating monopolies, why not break them up? Since they expanded their ecosystems through mergers and anti-competitive practices, they cannot claim they're natural monopolies. Moreover, in breaking them up, they will be less able to kill as many pirates and thus less likely to distort innovations paths. Across political lines, many Americans (65 percent) thought in 2021 that Big Tech's economic power was a problem facing the US economy, and many (59 percent) supported breaking up Big Tech.[44]

Indeed, we may see some structural remedies of Facebook and perhaps Google if the US agencies prevail in their antitrust cases.

Breaking up some of the Tech Barons' ecosystems could increase competition. Importantly, such remedy, if and when applied, will need to be carefully considered and designed. Its application and scope will depend on, among other things, the viability of behavioral remedies, the costs and inefficiencies associated with structural breakups, and the facts in each case. But for our discussion, the critical question is whether breaking up some of the Tech Barons will prevent the toxic competition and innovation, and the harmful spillover effects? Not necessarily.

This is a crucial point relevant beyond the Tech Barons' story. If companies, under the existing value chain, profit more from manipulating consumers, then increasing competition won't necessarily change these perverse incentives. In fact, at times, competition will make things worse. As our book *Competition Overdose* explores,[45] there are many instances of toxic competition. One example involves behavioral advertising. Its value chain—the cash generator—relies on manipulating our behavior. When it's more profitable to manipulate our behavior, even when it is toxic, no single company (even a Tech Baron) can stop the race to the bottom. The toxicity continues with or without the Tech Barons. In such cases, competition is about us but not *for* us. It brings out the worst in businesses as they compete to exploit us better. This toxic competition will promote innovations that extract or destroy value. No company can ignore the value chain, which takes a life of its own. If the incentives are misaligned, the creative energy within these markets will continue to explore how to better manipulate our behavior. As a result, toxic competition and innovation will continue when our policies disregard the offending value chain.

Ultimately none of the current policy proposals seek to align the eco-systems' value chains with society's interests. Neither fate nor the characteristics of the digital economy (such as network effects and economies of scale) drove the multiple decisions and actions that brought about the toxic innovations; instead, it was the incentives that the ecosystem promotes. So long as millions of apps and websites continue to rely on behavioral advertising, their incentives will not be aligned with our interests. Thus, even if enforcers break up the Tech Barons, we'll still have other platforms vying to manipulate our behavior.

The root of the problem will not always be the ecosystem per se, but its underlying value chain. To realign innovation with our societal interests, policymakers must target the source of the problem (the prevailing value chains that distort the market participants' incentives), not solely its symptoms.

Reflections

The Tech Barons recognize that the regulatory gap works in their favor. In early 2022 they still had the greatest latitude under the CSI Antitrust paradigm. The proposed reforms lead us in the right direction, but many will likely face significant resistance and amendments. The most onerous bill for the Tech Barons—the Ending Platform Monopolies Act (which would require structural separation)—squeaked out of the House Judiciary Committee on a one-vote margin (21–20). Some Tech Barons are already peddling their ideological platter to water down the proposals.

On the bright side, this is an excellent time for lobbyists. In the first six months of 2020 alone, Facebook, Amazon, Apple, and Google collectively spent over $20 million on lobbying.[46] As an indication of how much is at stake for the Tech Barons, Bloomberg reported how "the Computer Technology Association, an industry group, increased its spending on lobbying to $1.2 million in the second quarter, up 103.4% from the first quarter."[47]

As the United Nations Conference on Trade and Development observed:

> Global digital platforms take their earlier imperatives of expand, extract and enclose beyond national boundaries. As such, they have an interest in lobbying for international rules and regulations that allow and enable them to leverage their business models. Indeed, in the past few years, technology companies have replaced the financial sector as the biggest lobbyists, and major platforms have spent considerable resources in key locations.[48]

Another report observed how lobbyists "routinely plant questions for rivals at hearings, suggest bill text and seek exemptions to get out of regulation, much of it under the guise of helping Congress craft better policy."[49] Through lobbying and other means, the Tech Barons will strive to keep policymakers focused on past restraints, which by the time the proposals are enacted and enforced, will no longer be needed to maintain their power.

And so, the current policy proposals return us to Pyrrhus. The Tech Barons can afford to lose many battles. But they could ultimately win by wearing down the policymakers while keeping them focused on past anticompetitive practices.

As for Pyrrhus, the king died in 272 B.C. in the city of Argos, when a mother, watching her son battle the king from the roof of her house, grabbed a tile and threw it at Pyrrhus, breaking his neck. Another soldier then beheaded the unconscious king. There was nothing Homeric about the king's chaotic, disjointed death. But Pyrrhus ultimately represented "the last attempt of the Greeks to prevent the creation of the Roman Empire and to protect the 'free Greeks.'"[50] Granted, empires, like monopolies, do not last forever, but Rome survived in the West for more than seven hundred years after Pyrrhus's death.

So how can policymakers avoid the fate of Pyrrhus? Let's now consider a few measures.

CHAPTER 11

The Way Forward

ISRUPTIVE INNOVATION IS PATH-DEPENDENT. This means that current impediments to innovation affect the future levels, types, and value of innovation. It also means that the Tech Barons' current and past anticompetitive behavior will be felt for many years and that some potential innovations will be lost forever. Left to its own, the digital economy will advance the Tech Barons' narrow interests and gravitate further away from the public interest.

Something needs to be done, but the cost of regulatory failure is steep. If policymakers shoot wildly, innovation and competition can be harmed. On the other hand, while the regulators figure out where to aim, the Tech Barons will kill more pirates, distort innovation paths, and deliver innovation that increasingly extracts or destroys value, and this damage is not reversible.

So how do we get to where we need to be?

There is no silver bullet.

Policymakers must focus on the broader ecosystems, not just particular markets or platforms. They should move away from the narrow analysis, which undermines their ability to appreciate the true impact on innovation. In understanding how the value chains drive the Tech Barons' strategies, policymakers can realign the incentives of the underlying ecosystem to societal interests. This will involve recalibrating privacy, consumer protection, and competition policies, which are discussed elsewhere.[1]

To encourage innovations that actually and significantly benefit us, we suggest the following three interrelated principles that can help countries overhaul their policy switchboards:

Principle 1: Value—Consider the type of innovation and ask whether it creates, destroys, or extracts value.

As we have seen, innovation is neither inevitable nor invariably desirable. Since not all innovation increases value, policymakers and enforcers must inquire about the type of innovation (sustaining or disruptive) and whether it increases or reduces our well-being (that is, whether it destroys, extracts, or increases value).

Principle 2: Incentives—Ask who's designing the ecosystem and influencing the innovation paths, what are the ecosystem's value chains, and what incentives it fosters.

As we have seen, what's good for the Tech Baron is not necessarily what's good for us. And so, one must understand the incentives at play (that flow from the value chain) and ensure that these incentives align with our interests. Every ecosystem is regulated—whether by Tech Barons, informal norms, or laws, rules, and regulations. If policymakers assume that the marketplace is naturally self-regulating and that the market participants' incentives will always align with our interests, they are ill-informed.

Principle 3: Diversity—Promote an effective competitive process that enables disruption and innovation plurality and offers Tech Pirates a viable opportunity to prosper.

The diversity of innovation paths is crucial for future prosperity. We cannot predict who will emerge as the next Tech Pirate, given their high rate of failure and the evolutionary selection on which we rely to ensure that the right innovations prosper.[2] But we can hedge our bets by fostering a plurality of innovators and the ensuing collision of ideas from different fields.[3]

As we'll see, the Value, Incentives, and Diversity principles can inform policy choices on two complementary levels:

- First is the *Optimization Level*. Here our three principles can be used to improve the laws and enforcement policies to ensure that innovation serves society's interests, not those of the Tech Barons. This will help ensure that the incentives promoted by the ecosystem's value chain are aligned with our interests, the innovation adds (rather than extracts or destroys) value, and the competitive portals are open.

- Second is the *Innovation Support Level*. Here our three principles can inform how state aid, grants, tax breaks, and other supportive means can better sustain and promote Tech Pirates' disruptive innovation.

Armed with our three fundamental principles (Value, Incentives, Diversity) and our two levels of implementation (Optimization and Support), let's turn to the policy switchboard.

The Policy Switchboard

Many policy choices create incentives and disincentives that affect the nature and value of innovation. To the same extent, so does inaction. So, the challenge is striking the right balance to enable the benefits from the digital economy (including economies of scale) while promoting a diversity of value-creating innovation.

There is no single law (or set of financial incentives or penalties) that will fix the digital economy—quite the contrary. What's needed are multiple policies, each targeting different aspects of the digital economy.

Think of it as a policy switchboard packed with levers, each moving along a spectrum, and collectively these levers affect the supply and demand for different types of innovation.

Optimization policies include, among other things, competition laws, intellectual property laws, privacy and data protections laws, and other laws that influence the appropriation of knowledge and the commercialization and monetization of ideas. In the last chapter, we saw how policymakers are already considering how to recalibrate these levers to promote innovation, such as increasing interoperability, limiting the Tech Barons' ability to acquire nascent competitive threats, and requiring some structural separation (so that the Tech Barons cannot own a platform while competing with others on it).

Elsewhere on the policy switchboard are *innovation support policies*, such as providing resources, grants, loans, state guarantees, capital investment, and tax breaks; coordinating innovation efforts and technology transfers; and assisting in the technology's commercialization.[4]

Ideally one could calibrate which setting among the many levers would yield the optimal return of value-added innovation. Reality, as you would expect, is more complex. In a dynamic economy, policymakers must periodically adjust the levers to prevent the distortion of incentives and innovation. They must also add new levers to keep pace with new technologies (like the convergence of AI and neuroscience, or the building out of the metaverse). Policymakers will also need to radically alter other levers to address the changes in technology, business models, or prevailing ecosystems.

The challenge in promoting innovation becomes even more complicated when different enforcers and policymakers operate different levers, sometimes without coordinating with each other or fully appreciating the aggregated effect of the current policy choices and inaction.

Finally, the policy switchboard doesn't have a reset button. Given innovation's path dependency where past policy settings affect the future path of innovation, we cannot return to the early 2000s before the Tech

Barons took control. So, the error costs increase every year as we lose the innovations of would-be pirates, who could have provided the foundation for additional disruptive innovations.

So, how do we go about correcting the policy levers on the switchboard? While perfection is impossible, given the inherent regulatory gap, we can use the three guiding principles to improve the current policy settings (Figure 11.1).

Figure 11.1

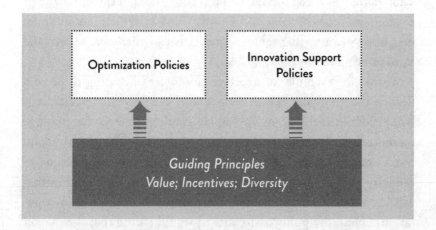

First, let's assess the policy switchboard's optimization policies using the Value, Incentives, and Diversity principles and then apply these three principles to potential innovation support policies.

Optimization Policies

Principle 1: Value

This is a legal blind spot. No agency or law today assesses an innovation's value. The mistaken belief is that the market determines the value, and any innovation with a positive price (or for which there is demand) adds value. As we saw, the market under the Tech Barons' control can produce many toxic innovations.

So, at a minimum, the laws should not incentivize (or foster) toxic innovation; instead, it must ensure the current and future innovations (and their implementation) serve our interests rather than those of a select few. To fill this void, at least one agency should be tasked with assessing the value of innovation. This does not mean a case-by-case assessment of whether a particular innovation creates, destroys, or extracts value (although those seeking IP protection should explain how their creation can promote value and identify the risks of their innovation in destroying or extracting value). Instead, that is where our second and third principles come into play.

Think, for example, of neuro-technologies, including those that decode our thoughts. These innovations can increase overall well-being, but the Tech Barons can implement them in ways that impinge on our privacy and autonomy and raise other significant ethical and moral concerns. Ideally, the policy switchboard would impose guard-rails to prevent the neuro-technologies from being used in areas that extract or destroy value (such as targeting and behavioral manipulation). Thus, the policy switchboard would ensure that the market participants' incentives are aligned with ours, and that these markets are contestable.

Even if the policy switchboard aligns incentives and deters most toxic innovations, the next challenge is balancing the value of the innovation with other important societal values. Competition and innovation do not trump everything else. For instance, how do we balance an increase in efficiency with the loss of human dignity? Automation with the loss of employment and increased inequality? Personalization with diminishing privacy? Centralized power with economies of scale? When assessing the value of innovation, we should remind ourselves that innovation, like competition, is not an end in itself. It serves a greater purpose.

On point are comments made by Europe's executive vice president and antitrust chief Margrethe Vestager, who noted how policies must ensure that future technology serves society and respects people's fundamental rights and freedoms:

> [T]echnology itself is just a tool. It doesn't have any purpose of its own. It's just a source of possibilities—a kind of power source, a bit like an electrical socket, that will run whatever we plug into it . . . if, as a society, we don't take control of the direction that digitisation takes, then others will do it for us. We'll leave the choices about technology's future—and the future of our society—in the hands of powerful governments and big tech companies. And we'll have no one to blame but ourselves, if their choices aren't the ones that we would have made.[5]

If nothing on the policy switchboard considers the value of the innovations, don't expect the Tech Barons to look out for our interests.

Principle 2: Incentives

The law should take into account incentives. Why? Some innovations might be inherently toxic (such as an addictive drug with no medicinal benefits). But for other innovations, it will depend on their use, who uses them, and their incentives. Monitoring their use will be unwieldy. An easier way to minimize these toxic applications is to ensure that incentives are aligned.

The law has already done this elsewhere through fiduciary duties. For example, to ensure that the agent's incentives are aligned with the principal's, the law imposes fiduciary duties so that the agent will further the principal's interests and not act contrary to those interests.

If the prevailing ecosystem's value chain incentivizes behavioral exploitation, then that is precisely how innovations will be engineered and deployed. So when the incentives are misaligned, laws can realign them. For instance, a law banning (or requiring users to opt into) behavioral advertising and personalized recommendations will remove a significant profit incentive to use innovations to manipulate our behavior.

The policy switchboard can also create positive incentives to promote value-enhancing innovation. Antitrust policies already promote positive-sum competition, enabling joint venturers to pool resources and labor to develop new products or technologies. Such cooperation can accelerate innovation and support its diffusion across industries. Being mindful of the incentives at play can help ensure innovation that serves unmet societal needs instead of devolving to zero-sum competition (where the aim is to extract value from customers, workers, or sellers).

Principle 3: Diversity

Our laws should promote diversity of innovation. Absent innovation diversity, disruption will simply fade away. Let's illustrate by looking at how diversity can guide our antitrust and patent policies.

One implication of the diversity principle is that the policy switchboard should not favor monopolies, seek to preserve them, or tolerate their anticompetitive abuses in the hopes that these national champions will provide technological change. Another insight is that policymakers cannot wait passively for the Schumpeterian creative destruction. Such passivity at times delays the Tech Pirates' arrival or postpones it indefinitely.

Under the diversity principle, antitrust policies should keep the competitive portals open. As we saw in the last chapter, policymakers are already seeking to encourage interoperability in the digital economy while prohibiting the Tech Barons' exclusionary strategies. The aim is to limit the Tech Barons' ability to shape the supply and demand of innovations so that consumers drive the selection process of the Tech Pirates. The diversity principle would also support policy measures that lower structural entry barriers, including outdated regulatory requirements. While mindful of the incentives at play, diversity would support efforts that open markets, platforms, and ecosystems.

The diversity principle can also help prevent the monopolization of knowledge by recalibrating intellectual property (IP) policies. The concern is that current IP policies inhibit, rather than promote, diversity in the context of large digital ecosystems. More often than not, patents, copyrights, and non-compete provisions are used strategically to increase barriers to entry or expansion, monopolize knowledge, and block its diffusion.[6] Without diving into the particularities of IP law, it is worth noting that the public policy behind the IP regime involves trade-offs, as the U.S. Supreme Court pointed out:

> The grant of a patent is the grant of a statutory monopoly.... Patents ... are meant to encourage invention by rewarding the inventor with the right, limited to a term of years fixed by the patent, to exclude others from the use of his invention. . . . But in rewarding useful invention, the rights and welfare of the community must be fairly dealt with and effectually guarded.[7]

The policy switchboard should protect and incentivize *useful* innovations while safeguarding the community's rights and welfare. The diversity principle can be used to consider the type and scope of innovation that can be protected, the duration of protection, the ease with which one may challenge a patent or other IP rights, and the remedy (fine, injunction, etc.).

Thus, in promoting diversity and aligning incentives, laws should weaken the Tech Baron's influence, and ensure that competition is healthy. Toxic innovations might still materialize, but regulators in assessing these innovations' value and risk can quickly intervene.

Innovation Support Policies

We need more Tech Pirates, and support policies can help achieve that. Besides changing the laws, our three principles can inform policies that promote innovation through, among other things, financial grants, tax breaks, loans, guarantees, and capital investments. Policies can also help with technology transfers, commercializing innovations, or providing the needed inputs. They can also increase the supply of innovative human capital, by, among other things, lowering the costs to educate and train workers (especially as automation will displace more jobs).[8]

To ensure that value-creating innovation is rewarded—in line with the public interest—the right mix of government-support policies is needed to create the conditions for growth. The Value, Incentives, and Diversity principles can help ensure that the public funds promote the right kind of innovation. To illustrate, let's consider two areas: *taxation, subsidies, and direct funding* and *investing in cities and regional industry clusters*.

Taxation, Subsidies, and Direct Funding

As we saw in chapter 8, the government can play a vital role in funding basic research that markets won't deliver (given the positive spillover effects). In addition, tax breaks, subsidies, and direct funding can enable innovators to establish themselves more easily, finance research and development, and access the market. These measures have been found to positively incentivize innovation, although they do not guarantee growth or value creation.[9] The challenge is to ensure that public funds and incentives are channeled effectively to those who create value and enhance innovation diversity. This is easier said than done. Among the challenges policymakers face are the abilities to effectively *identify* innovators who create value and foster growth, offer meaningful *support* that would help them bring the innovation to market, and do so without distorting competition, incentives, and innovation paths.

What are the risks in supporting particular Tech Pirates? Of a thousand potential Tech Pirates, we might expect only a few of them to deliver far more value than the others. The problem is that we can't predict which ones will actually disrupt markets.

Despite these limitations, the government can support diversity without betting on particular Tech Pirates. One way is in financing basic research that offers value. As we saw, market forces won't deliver where the social return from R&D investing is significantly greater than the Tech Pirate's private return (making it unprofitable for the firm to develop the innovation unless it receives public support).[10] In subsidizing research, the government can stimulate value-enhancing innovation free of adverse incentives. Tech Pirates can then incorporate this basic research for their disruptive innovation. So, the investment simultaneously helps Tech Pirates and promotes diversity.

Other policies may involve direct financial support. Here again, the three principles should guide public policy. We asked Romain Duval, assistant director at the International Monetary Fund, to elaborate on the challenges of channeling funds to promote the right kind of innovation. Duval confirmed that there is a growing recognition that subsidies and tax breaks should create a level playing field, but warned:

> Many times, the money is not going where it should be. We see that the smaller firms find it harder to get financing and that large incumbents are best positioned to make the most of the system. That weakens the effectiveness of R&D subsidies—most importantly, that of R&D tax credits, which primarily benefit incumbents. We need to rebalance the system and move away from the large firms and more towards smaller disruptive firms or potential entrants.[11]

İrem Güçeri, associate professor of economics and public policy at the Blavatnik School of Government, further elaborated on the challenges associated with optimizing public policies. Güçeri emphasized that while direct subsidies and tax incentives for R&D can be beneficial for different types of firms,

> the difficulty is to find a balance between incentivizing R&D and innovation that is most beneficial for the society as a whole and refraining from distorting the direction in which the market is evolving.
>
> Impact evaluation of policies in this area is complex; recent studies find that R&D subsidies and tax incentives are both useful in increasing R&D spending and innovation for the average firm, but we know that innovative firms are all very different from each other, there are outliers with disproportionately higher impact and the performance of the "average" firm does not necessarily give the policymakers a useful benchmark.

While the state has a central role in offering support, it is often challenging to identify those innovators who would benefit and deliver the most. Consequently, another way the diversity, incentive, and value principles can support value-creating innovations is through investment in cities and regional industry clusters.

Investing in Cities and Regional Industry Clusters

What makes cities so unique and relevant to value-enhancing innovation? Cities can play a far more significant role in promoting innovation than what they are currently given credit for. Geoffrey West, a senior fellow at the Los Alamos National Laboratory and author of the book *Scale*, arrived at a startling observation: innovation actually scales with cities, not companies.

When a city's population doubles (100 percent), the level of innovation increases 1.15 times (115 percent).[12] This adheres to a general rule that he found: around the world, cities generally follow the same power law behavior and scale nonlinearly. This has three important implications for our discussion.

First, cities are more efficient as they grow. When a city doubles in population, it does not require doubling the number of gas stations, banks, supermarkets, or infrastructure.[13] As the *Economist* noted, "Just as an elephant is a more efficient animal than a cat, big cities are more efficient than small ones. That is why people are drawn to them."[14]

A second implication is that as cities scale, we also get more innovation per capita. When a city's population doubles, we don't get double the patents, but instead 115 percent more patents. It also applies to wealth and wages, which increase by 115 percent (but note that many negatives also scale superlinearly). One possible reason is that when the city's population increases, its tempo (the rate and number of interactions among the citizens) and diversity increase, unleashing greater creativity and innovation.[15] Indeed, the business literature has recognized that "regional innovation clusters" offer fertile ground for accelerated innovation.[16]

Third, because cities, unlike companies, scale *super*linearly, they can continually grow in population, which potentially leads (absent physi-

cal space constraints) to open-ended growth—and thus to the possibility of open-ended growth in innovation. Just think of the population
trends from rural to urban and many cities' growing population over the
past seventy years. Delhi's population grew from about 1.4 million in
1950 to over 30 million by 2020. While some cities experience population declines (in particular St. Louis, Detroit, Cleveland, Buffalo, and
Pittsburgh, which all lost over half of their population since 1950[17]), it is
pretty hard for a city to die.

With this in mind, it becomes evident that growth in cities can often
yield significant growth in innovation. And yet many policymakers
underestimate the role of cities as innovation incubators.

Instead, policymakers typically overestimate the role of the dominant
firms in innovating (even as they pay lip service to the small businesses
that "are the backbone of our economy"). And yet, unlike cities, which
scale superlinearly as they grow, companies scale *sub*linearly as a function
of their size.[18] That means companies generally have a significant burst in
growth and innovations while young. Then they typically level off once
they get larger, until they decline and eventually die (bankruptcy, closed)
or are acquired.[19] Sublinearly scaling also means that if the company
doubles in size, the number of patents will not likely double, but will be
less, especially as the company ages.[20] So, while most cities become more
innovative and multidimensional as they grow in size (with a greater diversity of jobs and businesses), companies, in contrast, tend to become
more unidimensional and less innovative.[21]

When it comes to our three principles, cities and Tech Barons significantly diverge. Well-managed cities have no incentive to propagate toxic innovations or exclude Tech Pirates. The Tech Pirates often
are welcomed—as long as they serve the interests of the plurality of
the businesses and citizens. As cities become more multidimensional
as their population increases, diversity becomes second nature, and
greater opportunities exist for Tech Pirates.

In contrast, as the Tech Baron's ecosystem increases in size and continues to focus on its value chain, it becomes more unidimensional (the
technologies are mostly sustaining and support the value chain). While

agency problems exist in both cities (such as corrupt politicians excluding innovators in favor of family and friends' businesses) and Tech Barons (in excluding Tech Pirates to preserve their value chain), the former is an anomaly to good governance, while the latter is inherent to that ecosystem.

Thus, the policy switchboard must consider the role of cities and regional industry clusters in stimulating innovation. The policy switchboard should place greater weight on cities and regional industry clusters in deciding where and how to invest public funds. As Professor Richard Florida from the University of Toronto's School of Cities and the Rotman School of Management elaborates:

> Today, the city itself has replaced the industrial corporation as the key organizing unit or platform for innovation and entrepreneurial activity . . . It is not Google or Apple that are the critical dimensions of innovation it's the San Francisco Bay area that gave rise to them. Similarly, it's not Microsoft or Amazon but the greater Seattle area that's the important component, often hidden from view and out of the sight lines of policymakers. . . . If we want to promote diversity and economic dynamism, the key is to promote cities over firms. Cities are indeed the key platforms that will keep our economy dynamic and will mitigate the more monopolistic or anticompetitive tendencies of firms.[22]

But how can we optimize innovation through cities? Here our three principles can come into play.

For example, any city that primarily relies on a few companies or industries for economic growth is vulnerable to decline. Just consider the US cities whose population in 2010 declined by over 40 percent from their peak; many depended on a few firms or industries, such as Detroit, Scranton, and Gary, Indiana.[23] Likewise, as the business literature found, regional innovation clusters are more durable when they are diverse, as "diversity enables the cluster to adapt to changing conditions or to reinvent itself."[24]

Being mindful of the diversity principle can also yield informational benefits. Firms learn from their rivals, including mistakes, and mimic and improve upon their rivals' successes.[25] A positive correlation was found between industry variety and performance.[26] Similarly, the benefits from regional innovation clusters are tied to the firms' absorptive capacity: "the ability of a firm to identify, assimilate and exploit knowledge of the environment, as well as the ability to anticipate future technological advances."[27] With less diversity, there will be fewer opportunities for the firms to learn of the changing conditions and demands and respond thereto.

Policymakers must also better understand why some cities underperform or overperform relative to their population in the same country where the power laws apply. Size isn't everything. We already know that taller and bigger individuals can generally lift more weight than smaller, lighter individuals. Just compare Ted Arcidi, the record holder in the heavier weightlifting class (308 pounds). He can bench press far more (666 pounds) than the record holder in the lightest weight class (123 pounds), who can bench press 391 pounds. But once you factor in scale, you can estimate how much someone of that weight class should lift and whether the record holder underperforms or overperforms given that benchmark. The same applies to cities.

Policymakers should examine why some cities (like Corvallis, Oregon; Burlington, Vermont; San Jose, California; and Boise City, Idaho) outperform other similarly sized cities (in terms of the number of patents), and why other cities (like New York; Los Angeles; and Shreveport, Louisiana) underperform relative to their size. Undertaking this analysis may inform which policies should be calibrated to avoid the potential mistakes of the underperforming cities and to achieve the successes of the overachieving cities.

Last, the policy switchboard should erect guardrails to ensure that the valuable innovation in cities and regional industry clusters continues to serve the public interest. The three principles should be used to ensure that cities are not captured by a few powerful interest groups or firms and are not misled to adopt technologies against the public interest. For example, cities should be wary about entrusting a Tech Baron with the urban development of a smart city built "from the internet up."[28]

Post-pandemic, we may witness changes in urbanization as more start-ups decentralize or promote working remotely.[29] But cities and regional industry clusters will continue to play a central role. It is unlikely that the pandemic will reverse the century-long migration from rural areas to cities. Even if individuals work remotely, people will continue to migrate to cities, just perhaps not the same ones.[30]

In promoting diversity, value, and the right incentives, we can hedge our bets and increase the likelihood of the Tech Pirates' flourishing, knowing that some of their innovations will increase future prosperity.

Final Reflections

Each generation over the past two centuries has defied the predictions by the nineteenth-century economist Thomas Malthus. He feared that population growth rates would outstrip the food supply, resulting in a society that could not feed itself. What did Malthus famously underestimate? Innovation.

In the past, we avoided the Malthusian trap by promoting diversity and heterogeneity. History teaches us that plurality and openness are critical to such advancements. It also teaches us that absent the right conditions, a country's leadership in innovation and intellectual exploration may slowly fade away.[31]

Ultimately, as the population increases, the innovation cycles must also quicken to avoid the Malthusian trap. To address climate change and pandemics, just to name two pressing challenges, the innovation must come in months or years rather than decades. But these value-creating, paradigm-shifting innovations, while necessary for future prosperity (and to sustain humanity), are not inevitable. Similarly, in the digital economy, innovation is not assured, nor is the value it may deliver.

As the speed of innovation increases, so too the margin of error for our policies must decline. Recall the one in sixty rule mentioned at the start of this book. A slow boat has more time to correct its path than a jet. Today, in the digital economy, we are traveling at supersonic speed in a questionable direction.

The three fundamental principles—Value, Incentives, and Diversity—can help guide us and ensure the innovations deliver their promise. Think, for example, of the significant advancements in artificial intelligence and the many benefits they herald in computing, banking, automation, health, risk management, services, and other facets of our life. Alongside these benefits, there are also costs and risks—to social and economic equality, privacy, social cohesion, and political stability. To capture the benefits of innovation, while taking stock of the collateral effects, we should always ask, at a minimum, the following three questions:

Does the innovation create, destroy, or extract value—and if it creates value, who's getting the value?
If the answer is that you need not worry since the innovation must have value (otherwise, no one would be using it or buying it), and there is no other evidence that it increases (or will likely increase) overall well-being, then you know that you have (or likely will have) a problem.

What laws are in place to ensure that the incentives of those employing the innovation are aligned with the public interest?
If the answer is that you should not bother yourself with unnecessary queries and that competition will always align incentives, then you know that you have (or likely will have) a problem.

Finally, who are we counting on for advancing new disruptive technologies?
If the answer is the Tech Barons or a few national champions, you know you have a problem. You can be confident that the Tech Pirates and innovation diversity have left the building, and you can expect more toxic innovations. But if you are told, "We don't exactly know

*who will deliver, but we are hedging our bets by opening the competi-
tive portals and optimizing innovation diversity," and the number of
startups is indeed increasing, then you have less to fear.*

Betting on the entrenched Tech Barons, whose incentives are not necessarily aligned with ours, to provide the paradigm-shifting innovation
is a terrible bet. Their value chain helps us understand an underlying
contributor to the populism and fear-mongering that are destabilizing
democratic institutions today: it is the instinctive understanding, on the
part of the public, that our smart gadgets and smart cities might not, in
the end, actually save us. They might even do us harm. This is not surprising because they are not ultimately designed for our benefit. Instead,
they are designed to exploit us, and those who are most vulnerable to
exploitation—the economically and culturally marginal and at-risk segments of our population—will be the ones to suffer most.

The current incentives and policies have put the digital economy on
the wrong trajectory. Instead of improving our standard of living, the
technological advances may prolong (and in some countries worsen) the
already significant wealth inequality, reduce our autonomy and well-
being, and destabilize democracies. And we can't expect this trajectory
to self-correct. We need to fundamentally overhaul our policy switchboard. We should be betting on and investing in Tech Pirates, cities and
regional industry clusters, and, more generally, in diversity. We can, and
should, expect more, but only if we demand it.

Acknowledgments

WE BEGAN DEVELOPING OUR thesis in late 2017 after the European Commission approached us about researching competition and innovation in the digital economy. We benefited from the many subsequent exchanges with policymakers, enforcers, economists, lawyers, and scholars in Europe, Australia, Japan, India, South Korea, and North and South America, and with those working in the tech industry. We are grateful to their taking the time to discuss our ideas and help develop them. We were also fortunate to present parts of this book to competition agencies and policymakers, who enriched our discussion accordingly. We also thank the readers of *Competition Overdose* who reached out to us with useful insights on toxic competition and its impact on innovation.

For their help, support, and feedback at various stages of this project, special thanks are due to Pascal G. Bouvier, Federico Diez, Romain Duval, Richard Florida, Ori Gal, Robert Johnson, Alex Kacelnik, Barry Lynn, Eamonn Molloy, Casey Oppenheim, Pinar Ozcan Van Rens, Cecilia Rikap, Daniel Schwarz, Moshe Shahaf, and Amedee Von Moltke. Of course, all opinions and errors are ours.

Maurice would like to thank the University of Tennessee College of Law for its summer research grants.

Thanks are also due to our agent, Trena Keating, for her guidance and outstanding support. We are grateful to Hollis Heimbouch at Harper-Collins for her enthusiasm and insights, and Wendy Wong for shepherding this book through the publication process.

Finally, we thank our families for all of their support—before, during, and after the completion of this book.

Notes

Introduction

1. Marco Iansiti and Karim R. Lakhani, *Competing in the Age of AI* (Boston, MA: Harvard Business Review Press, 2020).
2. Erik Brynjolfsson and Andrew McAfee, "The Business of Artificial Intelligence," in Thomas Davenport et al., *Artificial Intelligence: The Insights You Need from Harvard Business Review* (Boston, MA: Harvard Business Review Press, 2019).
3. Timothy B. Lee, "Tesla Is Now Worth More Than Ford and GM—Combined," Ars Technica (January 13, 2020), https://arstechnica.com/cars/2020/01/teslas-stock-just -blew-past-500-for-a-new-record/.

Chapter 1: The Rise of the Big-Tech Barons

1. Alphabet Inc. (GOOG) Q2 2019 Results—Earnings Call Transcript (July 25, 2019), https://seekingalpha.com/article/4277828-alphabet-inc-goog-q2-2019-results -earnings-call-transcript.
2. Tomás Dias Sant´Ana et al., "The Structure of an Innovation Ecosystem: Foundations for Future Research," 58(12) *Management Decision* (2020): 2725–42, https://doi.org /10.1108/md-03-2019-0383 (noting how "the importance of building an ecosystem has gained prominence in both the strategy and practice of organizations").
3. Edward Curry, "The Big Data Value Chain: Definitions, Concepts, and Theoretical Approaches," in José María Cavanillas, Edward Curry, and Wolfgang Wahlster, *New Horizons for a Data-Driven Economy: A Roadmap for Usage and Exploitation of Big Data in Europe* (Cham: Springer, 2016): 33 (noting definitions and how within a healthy business ecosystem companies can work together in a complex business web where they can easily exchange and share vital resources).

4. Michael G. Jacobides, Carmelo Cennamo, and Annabelle Gawer, "Distinguishing between Platforms and Ecosystems: Complementarities, Value Creation and Coordination Mechanisms," Working Paper (2020), https://8dc2143b-87ef-4888-82ec-3db9521c8f92 .filesusr.com/ugd/0b15b1_7e0678d2815541bb920c77ec41e4d305.pdf; James F. Moore, "Predators and Prey: A New Ecology of Competition," *Harvard Business Review* (May–June 1993), https://hbr.org/1993/05/predators-and-prey-a-new-ecology-of -competition; Michael A. Cusumano, Annabelle Gawer, and David B. Yoffie, *The Business of Platforms: Strategy in the Age of Digital Competition, Innovation, and Power* (New York: Harper Business, 2019).

5. *Epic Games v. Apple*, 4:20-cv-05640-YGR, slip op. at 58 (N.D. Cal. September 10, 2021).

6. The key themes below are discussed in greater detail in Ariel Ezrachi and Maurice E. Stucke, *Virtual Competition: The Promise and Perils of the Algorithm-Driven Economy* (Cambridge, MA: Harvard University Press, 2019); Ariel Ezrachi and Maurice E. Stucke, "Digitalisation and Its Impact on Innovation," Report Prepared for the European Commission DG Research & Innovation (2018).

7. OECD, "Data-Driven Innovation for Growth and Well-Being: Interim Synthesis Report" (2014): 29, http://www.oecd.org/sti/inno/data-driven-innovation-interim -synthesis.pdf. Also see: Carl Shapiro and Hal R. Varian, *Information Rules: A Strategic Guide to the Network Economy* (Boston, MA: Harvard Business School Press, 2005).

8. "Five Tech Giants Just Keep Growing," *Wall Street Journal* (May 1, 2021), https:// www.wsj.com/articles/five-tech-giants-just-keep-growing-11619841644.

9. Kashmir Hill, "I Tried to Live without the Tech Giants. It Was Impossible," *New York Times* (July 31, 2020), https://www.nytimes.com/2020/07/31/technology/blocking -the-tech-giants.html.

10. Karen Weise and Michael Corkery, "People Now Spend More at Amazon Than at Walmart," *New York Times* (August 17, 2021), https://www.nytimes.com/2021/08 /17/technology/amazon-walmart.html.

11. *Riley v. California*, 573 U.S. 373, 395, 134 S. Ct. 2473, 2490, 189 L. Ed. 2d 430 (2014) (citing Harris Interactive, 2013 Mobile Consumer Habits Study [June 2013]). It is "no exaggeration to say that many of the more than 90% of American adults who own a cell phone keep on their person a digital record of nearly every aspect of their lives—from the mundane to the intimate."

12. Samantha Subin, "Facebook's Outage Has People Rethinking How They Make Money Online," CNBC (October 9, 2021).

13. See, e.g., United States Congress, House of Representatives Report "Investigation of Competition in Digital Markets—Majority Staff Report and Recommendations" (2020): 175 (hereafter "House Report") (noting that Google's profit margins were "greater than 20% for nine out of the last 10 years [2011–2020], close to three times larger than the average for a U.S. firm").

14. Australian Competition & Consumer Commission (ACCC), "Digital Platforms Inquiry—Final Report" (2019): 7 (based on the share price for Alphabet and Facebook on June 20, 2019).

15. Joseph A. Schumpeter, *Capitalism Socialism and Democracy* (New York: Harper & Brothers, 1942).

16. *United States v. Microsoft*, 253 F.3d 34, 49–50 (D.C. Cir. 2001).

17. Ibid.

18. Ibid. (quoting Howard A. Shelanski and J. Gregory Sidak, "Antitrust Divestiture in Network Industries," 68(1) *University of Chicago Law Review* (2001): 1, 11–12).

19. Testimony of Mark Zuckerberg, Facebook, Inc., before the United States House of Representatives, Committee on the Judiciary Subcommittee on Antitrust, Commercial, and Administrative Law (July 29, 2020), https://docs.house.gov/meetings/JU/JU05/20200729/110883/HHRG-116-JU05-Wstate-ZuckerbergM-20200729.pdf.

20. Statement by Jeffrey P. Bezos, Founder and Chief Executive Officer, Amazon, before the U.S. House of Representatives, Committee on the Judiciary, Subcommittee on Antitrust, Commercial, and Administrative Law (July 29, 2020), https://docs.house.gov/meetings/JU/JU05/20200729/110883/HHRG-116-JU05-Wstate-BezosJ-20200729.pdf.

21. Also note writing by John Kenneth Galbraith, *American Capitalism: The Concept of Countervailing Power* (Boston: Houghton Mifflin Company, 1952).

22. C. Scott Hemphill, "Disruptive Incumbents: Platform Competition in an Age of Machine Learning," 119(7) *Columbia Law Review* (2019): 1973, 1990 (noting how "Schumpeter and others have argued that monopoly is also a potent platform for further innovation"). Joseph A. Schumpeter in *Capitalism, Socialism, and Democracy* argued that innovators require the means to "safeguard" investment through "insuring or hedging" (88), and that monopoly is valuable as protection "against temporary disorganization of the market." This point is echoed in Peter Thiel with Blake Masters, *Zero to One: Notes on Startups, or How to Build the Future* (London: Virgin Books, 2015): 33 ("The promise of years or even decades of monopoly profits provides a powerful incentive to innovate."). The U.S. Supreme Court, for example, surmised that monopoly prices "is an important element of the free-market system. The opportunity to charge monopoly prices—at least for a short period—is what attracts 'business acumen' in the first place; it induces risk taking that produces innovation and economic growth." *Verizon Communications Inc. v. Law Offices of Curtis V. Trinko, LLP*, 540 U.S. 398, 407, 124 S. Ct. 872, 879, 157 L. Ed. 2d 823 (2004).

23. Kenneth. J. Arrow, "Economic Welfare and the Allocation of Resources for Invention," in Richard R. Nelson, *The Rate and Direction of Inventive Activity: Economic and Social Factors* (Princeton, NJ: Princeton University Press, 1982).

24. Statement of Tim Cook, Apple, Inc., before the U.S. House of Representatives, Committee on the Judiciary, Subcommittee on Antitrust, Commercial, and Administrative Law, 3 (July 29, 2020), https://docs.house.gov/meetings/JU/JU05/20200729/110883/HHRG-116-JU05-Wstate-CookT-20200729.pdf.

25. Testimony of Mark Zuckerberg.

26. Ibid.

27. Ibid.

28. Written Testimony of Sundar Pichai, Chief Executive Officer, Alphabet Inc., before the United States House of Representatives, Committee on the Judiciary Subcommittee on Antitrust, Commercial, and Administrative Law (July 29, 2020): 3, https://docs .house.gov/meetings/JU/JU05/20200729/110883/HHRG-116-JU05-Wstate -PichaiS-20200729.pdf.

29. "The Global Innovation 1000 Study—Investigating Trends at the World's 1000 Largest Corporate R&D Spenders," https://www.strategyand.pwc.com/gx/en/insights /innovation1000.html.

30. "List of Countries by GDP," Statistics Times, https://statisticstimes.com/economy /countries-by-gdp.php.

31. Andrew Sather, "R&D Spending as a Percentage of Revenue by Industry," March 8, 2021, https://einvestingforbeginners.com/rd-spending-as-a-percentage-of-revenue-by industry/.

32. Testimony of Mark Zuckerberg.

33. Ibid.

34. Written Testimony of Sundar Pichai.

35. Ibid.

36. Statement of Tim Cook.

37. "Amazon 2020 Annual Report," https://s2.q4cdn.com/299287126/files/doc_financials /2021/ar/Amazon-2020-Annual-Report.pdf.

38. Larry Downes and Paul Nunes, *Big Bang Disruption: Business Survival in the Age of Constant Innovation* (London: Portfolio Penguin, 2015).

39. Michael G. Jacobides, "Designing Digital Ecosystems," in Michael G. Jacobides, Arun Sundararajan, and Marshall Van Alstyne, *Platforms and Ecosystems: Enabling the Digital Economy* (World Economic Forum, Briefing Paper, 2019): 13–18, https:// www3.weforum.org/docs/WEF_Digital_Platforms_and_Ecosystems_2019.pdf.

40. "Coral reef," Wikipedia, accessed July 14, 2021, https://en.wikipedia.org/wiki/Coral _reef#cite.

41. Testimony of Mark Zuckerberg.

42. Statement of Nate Sutton, Associate General Counsel, Competition, Amazon.com, Inc., before the United States House of Representatives Committee on the Judiciary Subcommittee on Antitrust, Commercial and Administrative Law (July 16, 2019), https://docs.house.gov/meetings/JU/JU05/20190716/109793/HHRG-116-JU05 -Wstate-SuttonN-20190716.pdf.

43. Written Testimony of Sundar Pichai.

44. Ibid.

45. Written Testimony of Adam Cohen, Director, Economic Policy, Google LLC, before the United States House of Representatives Committee on the Judiciary Subcommittee on Antitrust, Commercial and Administrative Law, "Online Platforms and Market Power, Part 2: Innovation and Entrepreneurship" (July 16, 2019), https:// docs.house.gov/meetings/JU/JU05/20190716/109793/HHRG-116-JU05-Wstate -CohenA-20190716.pdf.

46. "Microsoft Annual Report 2020," https://www.microsoft.com/investor/reports/ar20 /index.html.
47. Ibid.

Chapter 2: The Tech Pirates

1. Sarah Todd, "The Steve Jobs Speech That Made Silicon Valley Obsessed with Pirates," *Quartz* (October 22, 2019), https://qz.com/1719898/steve-jobs-speech-that-made -silicon-valley-obsessed-with-pirates/.
2. Andy Hertzfeld, "Pirate Flag" (August 1983), https://www.folklore.org/StoryView.py ?story=Pirate_Flag.txt.
3. For a personal account of the entrepreneur spirit, see: Jim McKelvey, *The Innovation Stack* (New York: Portfolio/Penguin, 2020).
4. Video: "The Real Story behind Apple's Famous '1984' Super Bowl Ad," Bloomberg (December 3, 2014), https://www.youtube.com/watch?v=PsjMmAqmblQ.
5. Steven Si and Hui Chen, "A Literature Review of Disruptive Innovation: What It Is, How It Works and Where It Goes," 56(4) *Journal of Engineering and Technology Management* (2020).
6. Clayton M. Christensen, *The Innovator's Dilemma—When New Technologies Cause Great Firms to Fail* (Boston, MA: Harvard Business Review Press, 2016). Also see: Rajesh K. Chandy and Gerard J. Tellis, "The Incumbent's Curse? Incumbency, Size, and Radical Product Innovation," 64(3) *Journal of Marketing* (2000); Birgitta Sandberg and Leena Aarikka-Stenroos, "What Makes It So Difficult? A Systematic Review on Barriers to Radical Innovation," 43(8) *Industrial Marketing Management* (2014): 1293–1305.
7. Clayton M. Christensen, *The Innovator's Dilemma*, xviii (noting that all sustaining technologies "improve the performance of established products, along the dimensions of performance that mainstream customers in major markets have historically valued").
8. Ibid., 14.
9. Ibid., xviii.
10. Ibid., xx.
11. Christian Hopp et al., "Disruptive Innovation: Conceptual Foundations, Empirical Evidence, and Research Opportunities in the Digital Age," 35(3) *Journal of Product Innovation Management* (2018): 446–57 (surveying literature); Carlos Tadao Kawamoto and Renata Giovinazzo Spers, "A Systematic Review of the Debate and the Researchers of Disruptive Innovation," 14(1) *Journal of Technology Management and Innovation* (April 2019): 73–82; Jill Lepore, "The Disruption Machine: What the Gospel of Innovation Gets Wrong," *New Yorker* (June 16, 2014), https://www .newyorker.com/magazine/2014/06/23/the-disruption-machine.
12. Carlos Tadao Kawamoto and Renata Giovinazzo Spers, "A Systematic Review" (noting that for Christensen disruptive innovations "either create new markets, bring new attractiveness to nonconsumers, or offer more convenience, at lower prices, to lower-income consumers in an existing market" and that these innovations for nonconsumers

bring new consumers to the market, previously untapped due to lack of ability to consume or enjoy the good [or service] or insufficient resources); Jonathan C. Ho, "Disruptive Innovation from the Perspective of Innovation Diffusion Theory," *Technology Analysis & Strategic Management* (2021), DOI: 10.1080/09537325.2021.1901873.

13. "A Third Way to Innovation—Questions for David Robertson, Interview by Karen Christensen," Rotman Management (Winter 2018), https://www.rotman.utoronto.ca /Connect/Rotman-MAG/IdeaExchange/Page1/Winter2018-David-Robertson (discussing a Third Way of innovation where (1) a set of complementary innovations around a core product make the product more appealing or valuable; (2) the complementary innovations operate together and with the key product as a system to carry out a single strategy or purpose—what Robertson calls the promise to the user; and (4) the complementary innovations—even those delivered by outside partners— are closely and centrally managed by the owner of the key product); Steven Si and Hui Chen, "A Literature Review," 101568 (synthesizing the literature in describing disruptive innovation as: an innovation process in which technologies, products, or services are initially inferior than those provided by incumbents in the attributes that mainstream consumers value, but these technologies, products, or services can attract and satisfy the consumers in low-end or new markets with advantages in performance attributes [such as being cheap, simple, or convenient] that these consumers value but which at the same time are neglected by mainstream markets. Over time, through incremental improvement of technology or process, a disruptive innovation gradually satisfies the needs of mainstream consumers, so as to attain certain market share from or even replace incumbents in mainstream markets); Clifford Maxwell and Scott Duke Kominers, "What Makes an Online Marketplace Disruptive?," *Harvard Business Review* (May 24, 2021) (noting how disruptive innovations bring nonproducers and nonconsumers together—disruptive marketplaces make good on famed Silicon Valley investor Bill Gurley's observation that internet marketplaces "literally create 'money out of nowhere'" because "in connecting economic traders that would otherwise not be connected, they unlock economic wealth that otherwise would not exist"); more generally, see Joshua Gans, *The Disruption Dilemma* (Cambridge, MA: MIT Press, 2016) (who explores demand and supply side disruption and notes that disruption occurs when "successful firms fail because they continue to make the choices that drove their success"). Neele Petzold, Lina Landinez, and Thomas Baake, "Disruptive Innovation from a Process View: A Systematic Literature Review," 28(2) *Creativity and Innovation Management* (2019): 157–74.

14. For the different taxonomies of innovation, see Claudia S. L. Dias and João J. Ferreira, "What We (Do Not) Know about Research in the Strategic Management of Technological Innovation?," 21(3) *Innovation: Organization & Management* (2019): 398–420, DOI: 10.1080/14479338.2019.1569464; Delio Ignacio Castaneda and Sergio Cuellar, "Knowledge Sharing and Innovation: A Systematic Review," 27(3) *Knowledge & Process Management* (2020): 159–73, https://onlinelibrary.wiley.com/doi/epdf /10.1002/kpm.1637; Adrian Kovacs et al., "Radical, Disruptive, Discontinuous and

Breakthrough Innovation: More of the Same?," *Academy of Management Annual Meeting Proceedings* (2019): 14866, DOI: 10.5465/AMBPP.2019.272; Steven Si and Hui Chen, "A Literature Review," 101568.

15. Steven Si and Hui Chen, "A Literature Review," 101568 (noting that "disruptive innovation usually adopts a completely different business model that must not only be sustainable from an economic perspective, but also be consistent with existing market realities, customer expectations, and competitive pressures" and how this "requires a new approach to convert value into profits, especially in terms of revenue and pricing structure").

16. Our definition, in focusing on the value chain of an ecosystem or a dominant firm, differs from Michael Porter's definition of value chain analysis and its purpose. See: Michael Porter, "The Value Chain and Competitive Advantage," in David Barnes, *Understanding Business: Processes* (London: Routledge in association with the Open University, 2001): 50. Porter uses the concept to disaggregate the firm "into strategically relevant activities in order to understand the behavior of costs and the existing and potential sources of differentiation." For the application of value chain to big data ecosystems, see: Edward Curry, "The Big Data Value Chain: Definitions, Concepts, and Theoretical," 29, 30–33 (defining the Big Data Value Chains as the information flow within a big data system as a series of steps needed to generate value and useful insights from data, which includes data acquisition, data analysis, data curation, data storage, and data usage).

17. See, e.g., *Epic Games v. Apple*, slip op. at 32 (noting that in Apple's fiscal year 2019, 83 percent of apps with at least one download on its App Store were free to consumers).

18. Ibid., 43. As the court found, over 80 percent of all Apple consumer accounts generated virtually no revenue, as 80 percent of all apps on the App Store were free. Slip op. at 1. On a revenue basis, gaming apps accounted for approximately 70 percent of all Apple's App Store revenues. This 70 percent of revenue was generated by less than 10 percent of all App Store consumers. These gaming-app consumers were primarily making in-app purchases, which was the focus of Epic Games' antitrust claims.

19. Ibid., 28 (noting how the "creation, constant update, and modernization of the SDKs and APIs was not insignificant. To protect its system, Apple built tools, kits, and interfaces that would allow other developers to build native apps. Epic Games did not introduce any evidence to rebut Apple's claim that in those initial years, the engineering work was novel, sophisticated, time-consuming and expensive. These tools simplified and accelerated the development process of native apps."). On the other hand, the evidence in that trial "established that a significant portion of the App Store revenue is built upon long-term relationships between developers and consumers independent of Apple." For example, during a 2019–2020 presentation, Apple recognized that "in any given month, 41% of [Apple's] monthly billings are generated from apps that were downloaded more than 180 days prior," as contrasted to 31 percent for apps downloaded between 30 and 180 days prior and to 28 percent for apps downloaded less than 30 days prior. As Apple conceded at trial, "This engagement is almost completely

driven by [App Store] developers, and the App Store does not participate in a meaningful way." Ibid.

20. Over half of Apple's App Store billings (53.7 percent) came from less than .5 percent of all Apple accounts in the third quarter of 2017. *Epic Games v. Apple*, slip op. at 43.

21. Google and Apple, with some minor exceptions, collect a 30 percent commission on every purchase made through their app stores, whether an initial download or an in-app purchase.

22. Ibid.

23. Kristina Rakic, "Breakthrough and Disruptive Innovation: A Theoretical Reflection," 15(4) *Journal of Technology Management & Innovation* (2020); Adrian Kovacs et al., "Radical, Disruptive, Discontinuous and Breakthrough Innovation"; Birgitta Sandberg and Leena Aarikka-Stenroos, "What Makes It So Difficult?," 1293–1305; Joseph Bower and Clayton Christensen, "Disruptive Technologies: Catching the Wave," *Harvard Business Review* (January–February 1995): 43–53, https://hbr.org/1995/01/disruptive-technologies-catching-the-wave.

24. Anuraag Singh, Giorgio Triulzi, and Christopher L. Magee, "Technological Improvement Rate Predictions for All Technologies: Use of Patent Data and an Extended Domain Description," 50(9) *Research Policy* (2021), https://doi.org/10.1016/j.respol.2021.104294; Alison Gopnik, "Innovation Relies on Imitation: A New Study of Computer Coders Shows That the Best Problem-Solvers Learn from the Efforts of Their Peers," *Wall Street Journal* (October 1, 2020), https://www.wsj.com/articles/innovation-relies-on-imitation-11601571842 (discussing study involving coding contestants, where the researchers found that pragmatists who flexibly switched back and forth between copying and substantially altering and improving the code were by far the most likely to receive higher scores than the "copiers" who consistently imitated the successful solutions, making only the smallest changes, and the "mavericks" who "didn't copy the entries that were already out there but tried something new, more like the stereotypical lone genius").

25. Steven Johnson, *Where Good Ideas Come From: The Natural History of Innovation* (London: Penguin, 2010).

26. Anuraag Singh, Giorgio Triulzi, and Christopher L. Magee, "Technological Improvement Rate Predictions for All Technologies" (finding that while different technologies all improve exponentially, they do so at different rates); Clayton M. Christensen, *The Innovator's Dilemma*, 113, 166–68.

27. Jim McKelvey, "Good Entrepreneurs Don't Set Out to Disrupt," *Harvard Business Review* (2020).

28. Clayton M. Christensen, *The Innovator's Dilemma*, 178–79, 182 (discussing the need for agnostic marketing where no one knows whether, how, or in what quantities a disruptive product can or will be used before they experience using it).

29. Steven Johnson, *Where Good Ideas Come From*, 52.

30. For a review of various internal and external barriers, see: Helen T. Wagner et al., "Path Dependent Constraints on Innovation Programmes in Production and Op-

erations Management," 49(11) *International Journal of Production Research* (2011): 3069–85; Pablo D'Estea et al., "What Hampers Innovation? Revealed Barriers versus Deterring Barriers," 41(2) *Research Policy* (2012): 482–88; John Baldwin and Zhengxi Lin, "Impediments to Advanced Technology Adoption for Canadian Manufacturers," 31(1) *Research Policy* (2002): 1–18; Werner Hölzl and Jürgen Janger, "Innovation Barriers across Firms and Countries," WIFO Working Papers, No. 426, Austrian Institute of Economic Research (WIFO), Vienna, 2012, https://www.econstor.eu/bitstream /10419/128992/1/wp_426.pdf; Birgitta Sandberg and Leena Aarikka-Stenroos, "What Makes It So Difficult?"

31. Geoffrey A. Moore, *Escape Velocity: Free Your Company's Future from the Pull of the Past* (New York: HarperCollins, 2011): 31.

32. See generally: W. Chan Kim and Renée Mauborgne, *Blue Ocean Strategy: How to Create Uncontested Market Space and Make the Competition Irrelevant* (Boston, MA: Harvard Business Review Press, 2015).

33. Geoffrey A. Moore, *Escape Velocity*, 85.

34. Ufuk Akcigit and William R. Kerr, "Growth through Heterogeneous Innovations," NBER Working Paper 16443, 126(4) *Journal of Political Economy* (August 2018), http://www.nber.org/papers/w16443; Birgitta Sandberg and Leena Aarikka-Stenroos, "What Makes It So Difficult?"; Arthur Fishman, Hadas Don-Yehiya, and Amnon Schreiber, "Too Big to Succeed or Too Big to Fail?," 51 *Small Business Economics* (2018): 811–22, https://doi.org/10.1007/s11187-017-9968-1 (citing literature that larger incumbent firms tend to pursue relatively more incremental and relatively more process innovation than smaller firms, which tend to pursue more radical innovation).

35. *Epic Games v. Apple*, slip op. at 102.

36. X, accessed January 4, 2022, https://x.company.

37. Steven Johnson, *Where Good Ideas Come From*, 46 (discussing neural networks).

38. For illustration, see for example: Hakan Ener et al., "'Digital Colonization' of Highly Regulated Industries: An Analysis of Big Tech Platforms' Entry into Healthcare and Education," *California Management Review* (2021).

39. Delio Ignacio Castaneda and Sergio Cuellar, "Knowledge Sharing and Innovation: A Systematic Review" 27(3) *Knowledge & Process Management* (2020) 159–173, https://onlinelibrary.wiley.com/doi/epdf/10.1002/kpm.1637.

40. See the OECD definition in the Oslo Manual: "An innovation is the implementation of a new or significantly improved product (good or service), or process, a new marketing method, or a new organizational method in business practices, workplace organization or external relations," OECD/Eurostat. *Oslo Manual: Guidelines for Collecting and Interpreting Innovation Data*, 3rd Edition (Paris: OECD Publishing, 2005): 46, para 146, http://dx.doi.org/10.1787/9789264013100-en; also see: Fred Gault, *Defining and Measuring Innovation in All Sectors of the Economy: Policy Relevance*, OECD Blue Sky Forum III, Ghent, Belgium, September 19–21, 2016; Fred Gault, "Defining and Measuring Innovation in All Sectors of the Economy," 47(3) *Research Policy* (2018): 617–22.

41. The positive definition of innovation suggests that any negative change should not be seen as innovation but as an external negative change. We find this normative assumption to create a false expectation that any investment in research and development would increase welfare. As we illustrate later, this is not necessarily the case. Note in this respect the OECD comment that accepts alternative change—*new* or *improved*—to substantiate innovation. "The minimum requirement for an innovation is that the product, process, marketing method or organizational method must be new (or significantly improved) to the firm." Oslo Manual, at para 148.

42. On the possible adverse effects of competition, see our work on competition overdose: Maurice E. Stucke and Ariel Ezrachi, *Competition Overdose: How Free Market Mythology Transformed Us from Citizen Kings to Market Servants* (New York: Harper Business, 2020).

43. Christian Nielsen and Henrik Dane-Nielsen, "Value Creation in Business Models Is Based on Intellectual Capital—and Only Intellectual Capital!," 7(2) *Journal of Business Models* (2019): 64–81.

44. "Value," *Merriam-Webster*, accessed January 4, 2022, https://www.merriam-webster.com /dictionary/value.

45. In this respect we narrow the definitions of Mariana Mazzucato, who defined value creation as the ways in which different types of resources are established to produce new goods and services, and value extraction as activities focused on moving around resources to gain disproportionately from the ensuring trade. Mariana Mazzucato, *The Value of Everything: Making and Taking in the Global Economy* (New York: Public Affairs, 2020): 6.

46. OECD, "Measuring Well-being and Progress: Well-being Research," accessed January 4, 2022, https://www.oecd.org/statistics/measuring-well-being-and-progress.htm.

47. James F. Moore, "Predators and Prey: A New Ecology of Competition," 71(3) *Harvard Business Review* (1993): 75–86; Annabelle Gawer and Michael A. Cusumano, "Industry Platforms and Ecosystem Innovation," 31(3) *Journal of Product Innovation Management* (2014): 417–33; Carmelo Cennamo, Annabelle Gawer, and Michael G. Jacobides, "Towards a Theory of Ecosystems," 39(8) *Strategic Management Journal* (2018): 2255–76.

48. Airbnb, Inc. Form 10-K for the fiscal year ended December 31, 2020, 4, https:// d18rn0p25nwr6d.cloudfront.net/CIK-0001559720/84dcc076-235d-4520-805c -0e64b6fe8c40.pdf.

49. Nitin Nohria and Hemant Taneja, "A New Model to Spark Innovation Inside Big Companies," *Harvard Business Review* (May 12, 2021) (noting that "an internal start-up that reaches $100 million in annual revenue [a remarkable feat for a start-up that can earn it a stratospheric valuation] will have delivered just one percent in incremental growth for a $10 billion company").

50. W. Chan Kim and Renée Mauborgne, *Blue Ocean Strategy*.

51. Aashish Pahwa, "The History of WhatsApp," Feedough (September 8, 2021), https:// www.feedough.com/history-of-whatsapp/.

52. FTC Complaint. *FTC v. Facebook, Inc.*, No. 1:20-cv-03590 (D.D.C. December 9, 2020), para. 17.
53. Ibid., para. 18.
54. FTC Substitute Amended Complaint. *FTC v. Facebook, Inc.*, No. 1:20-cv-03590 (D.D.C. September 8, 2021) para. 108.
55. Ibid., para. 110.
56. Ibid., para. 111.
57. Ibid., para. 113.
58. Ibid., para. 122.
59. Ibid., para. 126.

Chapter 3: Disrupting Disruptive Innovation

1. Christian Hopp et al., "Disruptive Innovation," 446–57.
2. Maurice E. Stucke and Allen P. Grunes, *Big Data and Competition Policy* (Oxford: Oxford University Press, 2016): 285–87.
3. Deepa Seetharaman and Betsy Morris, "Facebook's Onavo Gives Social-Media Firm Inside Peek at Rivals' Users," *Wall Street Journal* (August 13, 2017), https://www .wsj.com/articles/facebooks-onavo-gives-social-media-firm-inside-peek-at-rivals -users-1502622003.
4. Multi-State Complaint, *State of New York et al v. Facebook Inc.*, No. 1:20-cv-03589 (D.D.C. December 9, 2020) para. 147; Eve Smith, "The Techlash against Amazon, Facebook and Google—and What They Can Do," *Economist* (January 20, 2018), https://www.economist.com/news/briefing/21735026-which-antitrust-remedies -welcome-which-fight-techlash-against-amazon-facebook-and (noting how this nowcasting radar "helped [Facebook] spot several potential threats, including Instagram, a photo app, which it bought in 2012; WhatsApp, a messaging service, for which it paid a stunning $22bn in 2014; and tbh, a social-polling app, which it acquired last year [2017]. When Snapchat rebuffed it in 2013, it responded by cloning the app's most successful features.").
5. The European Commission raised concerns as to the legality of it using non-public independent seller data to benefit its own online retail business: https://ec.europa.eu /commission/presscorner/detail/en/ip_20_2077. In the US, the Congressional Antitrust Subcommittee noted, similarly, how Amazon would use its nowcasting radar to "(1) copy the product to create a competing private-label product; or (2) identify and source the product directly from the manufacturer to free ride off the seller's efforts, and then cut that seller out of the equation," House Report, 275 (internal footnotes omitted). Amazon claims that "it has no incentive to abuse sellers' trust because third-party sales make up nearly 60% of its sales and Amazon's first-party sales are relatively small," House Report, 275. But as Congress learned, "Amazon admitted that by percentage of sales—a more telling measure—Amazon's first-party sales are significant and growing in a number of categories." Congress in 2020 estimated that Amazon may, in fact, "overtake its third-party sellers in several categories as its first-party business continues to grow," House Report, 276.

6. House Report, 275 (internal footnotes omitted).

7. "How to Submit Your App to the App Store and Get It Approved," *FarShore* (March 9, 2017), https://www.farshore.com/blog/submit-app-to-app-store-get-approved/.

8. Kif Leswing, "Apple Says It Rejected Almost 1 Million New Apps in 2020 and Explains Common Reasons Why," CNBC (May 11, 2021), https://www.msn.com/en-us/news/technology/apple-says-it-rejected-almost-1-million-new-apps-in-2020-and-explains-common-reasons-why/ar-BB1gCnpx.

9. Ibid.

10. "Number of iPhone Users in the United States from 2012 to 2022," Statista (March 1, 2021), https://www.statista.com/statistics/232790/forecast-of-apple-users-in-the-us/.

11. *Epic Games v. Apple*, No. 4:20-CV-05640-YGR, 2020 WL 5993222, *17 (N.D. Cal. Oct. 9, 2020).

12. "Android—Statistics & Facts," Statista, accessed January 4, 2022, https://www.statista.com/topics/876/android/.

13. Disconnect, Inc. Complaint of Disconnect, Inc., Regarding Google's Infringement of Article 102 TFEU through Bundling into the Android Platform and the Related Exclusion of Competing Privacy and Security Technology, Case COMP/40099 June 2015), para. 18.

14. Ibid., para. 38.

15. Julie Bort, "Why Google Banned a Privacy Tool Called 'Disconnect Mobile' from the Android App Store," *Business Insider* (August 28, 2014).

16. Ibid.

17. Reed Albergotti, Alistair Barr, and Elizabeth Dwoskin, "Why Some Privacy Apps Get Blocked from the Android Play Store," *Wall Street Journal* (August 28, 2014).

18. Ibid.

19. Ibid.

20. Michael Muchmore, "Google Chrome's Sham 'Do Not Track' Feature," *PC Magazine* (May 16, 2014), https://in.pcmag.com/browsers/58948/google-chromes-sham-do-not-track-feature.

21. House Report, 385.

22. Multi-State Complaint, *Utah et al. v. Google LLC*, para. 116.

23. Ibid.

24. Ibid., para. 125.

25. Bruce Sterling, "Dead Media Beat: Mapquest," *Wired* (October 9, 2019), https://www.wired.com/beyond-the-beyond/2019/10/dead-media-beat-mapquest/.

26. Facebook 2020 10-K, 17.

27. "What Does Facebook Platform Mean?," Techopedia, accessed January 4, 2022, https://www.techopedia.com/definition/27916/facebook-platform.

28. House Report, 166.

29. House Report, 166–67.

30. House Report, 167.

31. Ibid.

32. House Report, 169.

33. House Report, 143.

34. "Number of Monthly Active Facebook Users Worldwide as of 2nd Quarter 2012," Statista (November 1, 2021), https://www.statista.com/statistics/264810/number-of -monthly-active-facebook-users-worldwide/.

35. Olivia Solon, "As Tech Companies Get Richer, Is It 'Game Over' for Startups?," *Guardian* (October 20, 2017), https://www.theguardian.com/technology/2017/oct/20/tech -startups-facebook-amazon-google-apple; Betsy Morris and Deepa Seetharaman, "The New Copycats: How Facebook Squashes Competition from Startups," *Wall Street Journal* (August 9, 2017), https://www.wsj.com/articles/the-new-copycats -how-facebook-squashes-competition-from-startups-1502293444.

36. Jason Del Rey, "Amazon Invested Millions in the Startup Nucleus—Then Cloned Its Product for the New Echo—Another Cautionary Tale for Would-be Amazon Partners," Vox (May 10, 2017), https://www.vox.com/2017/5/10/15602814/amazon -invested-startup-nucleus-cloned-alexa-echo-show-voice-control-touchscreen-video.

37. Ibid.

38. Olivia Solon, "As Tech Companies Get Richer."

39. Dana Mattioli and Cara Lombardo, "Amazon Met with Startups about Investing, Then Launched Competing Products—Some Companies Regret Sharing Information with Tech Giant and Its Alexa Fund," *Wall Street Journal* (July 23, 2020), https://www.wsj .com/articles/amazon-tech-startup-echo-bezos-alexa-investment-fund-11595520249.

40. Ibid.

41. Ibid.

42. "iPhone (1st Generation)—Full Phone Information," Igotoffer Apple, accessed January 4, 2022, https://igotoffer.com/apple/iphone-1st-generation.

43. Shanhong Liu, "Global Market Share Held by Operating Systems for Desktop PCs, from January 2013 to June 2021," Statista (September 10, 2021), https://www.statista. com/statistics/218089/global-market-share-of-windows-7/.

44. S. O'Dea, "Mobile Operating Systems' Market Share Worldwide from January 2012 to June 2021," Statista (June 29, 2021), https://www.statista.com/statistics/272698 /global-market-share-held-by-mobile-operating-systems-since-2009/.

45. Karolina Safarzyńska and Jeroen C. J. M. van den Bergh, "Evolutionary Models in Economics: A Survey of Methods and Building Blocks," 20(3) *Journal of Evolutionary Economics* (2010): 329–73, DOI: 10.1007/s00191-009-0153-9.

Chapter 4: Distorting the Demand for Innovation

1. Peter Berthold et al., "Rapid Microevolution of Migratory Behaviour in a Wild Bird Species," 360 *Nature* (1992): 668–70, https://www.nature.com/articles/360668a0; Darren E. Irwin, "Speciation: New Migratory Direction Provides Route toward Divergence," 19(24) *Current Biology* (2009): R1111–13, https://www.sciencedirect.com /science/article/pii/S0960982209019848; Sue Anne Zollinger, "Blackcaps Change Their Migration Patterns . . . But Why?," Indiana Public Radio (September 23, 2009),

https://indianapublicmedia.org/amomentofscience/blackcaps-change-migration
-patternsbut.php.

2. Everett M. Rogers, *Diffusion of Innovations* (New York: Free Press, 2003). Classical
theory on diffusion of innovation holds that "the very early adopter group consists of
novelty seekers who are innovative and have financial resources to take risks on new
ideas." Jonathan C. Ho, "Disruptive Innovation from the Perspective of Innovation
Diffusion Theory," *Technology Analysis & Strategic Management* (March 17, 2021),
DOI: 10.1080/09537325.2021.1901873. For our purposes, the Tech Barons' use of
friction and retention can distort adoption by both high-end and low-end disruption.

3. Geoffrey A. Moore, *Escape Velocity*, 49.

4. "Discover What Google Assistant Is," accessed January 4, 2022, https://assistant
.google.com.

5. Case AT.39740, *Google Search (Shopping)* European Commission (June 27, 2017).
Upheld by the European General Court in Case T-612/17 *Google and Alphabet v.
Commission (Google Shopping)* (November 10, 2021). In January 2022, Google ap-
pealed the judgment of the General Court. Case C-48/22P *Google and Alphabet v
Commission* (Google Shopping). Appeal pending.

6. Press Release (EU Commission): "Antitrust: Commission Fines Google €2.42 Billion
for Abusing Dominance as Search Engine by Giving Illegal Advantage to Own Comparison Shopping Service" (June 27, 2017), https://ec.europa.eu/commission/presscorner
/detail/en/IP_17_1784.

7. Case AT.39740, *Google Search (Shopping)*, para 460.

8. Ibid., para 345.

9. Ibid., para 596. Other platforms are concerned about similar behavior happening to
them. For example, a significant amount of traffic is directed to Expedia's travel websites through participation in pay-per-click and display advertising campaigns on
search engines. Expedia warns its investors of the risk that the leading search engines
"offering comprehensive travel planning, shopping or booking capabilities, or increasingly refer those leads directly to suppliers or other favored partners." This could
increase the cost of traffic directed to Expedia's websites and harm its business. "Expedia 2017 Annual Report," 10, https://annualreport.stocklight.com/NASDAQ
/EXPE/17588959.pdf.

10. Case AT.39740 *Google Search (Shopping)*, para 595.

11. Ibid., para 656.

12. Multi-State Complaint, *Utah et al. v. Google LLC*, No. 3:21-cv-05227 (N.D. Cal. July
7, 2021), para. 108.

13. House Report, 382–83.

14. Johan Moreno, "Google Estimated to Be Paying $15 Billion to Remain Default
Search Engine on Safari," *Forbes* (August 27, 2021), https://www.forbes.com/sites
/johanmoreno/2021/08/27/google-estimated-to-be-paying-15-billion-to-remain
-default-search-engine-on-safari/; Chance Miller, "Analysts: Google to Pay Apple
$15 Billion to Remain Default Safari Search Engine in 2021" (August 25, 2021),

https://9to5mac.com/2021/08/25/analysts-google-to-pay-apple-15-billion-to
-remain-default-safari-search-engine-in-2021/.

15. StatCounter, "Search Engine Market Share Worldwide, Jan. 2009–Aug 2021," https://
gs.statcounter.com/search-engine-market-share#monthly-200901-202108.

16. Multi-State Complaint, *Utah et al. v. Google LLC*, paras. 121 and 124 (alleging that
Google's MADAs require OEMs to (1) preinstall and place the Google Play Store icon
on the home screen of Android devices, and that no competing app store be any more
prominent and (2) preinstall a suite of Google proprietary apps, to make it impossible
to delete or remove many of these Google apps, and to provide all of them preferential
placement on device home screens or the very next screen).

17. House Report, 215.

18. Ibid.

19. Multi-State Complaint, *Utah et al. v. Google LLC*, para. 124.

20. Case AT.40099, *Google Android*.

21. Everett Rogers, 177.

22. Ibid., 203.

23. Multi-State Complaint, *Utah et al. v. Google LLC*, para. 19.

24. Ibid., para. 77.

25. State AG Android Complaint para 89 (alleging that "[h]aving recognized that
sideloading constitutes a competitive risk to its business, Google has been waging
<redacted> by degrading the consumer experience. To do this, Google embeds
its generally misleading warnings and hurdles to sideloading into the Google-
certified Android OS"). As the states allege in their complaint, Google's repre-
sentations "would lead users to believe Google when it displays warnings that the
apps or app stores they are attempting to sideload are 'unknown,' harmful, and
could damage their devices. Despite its claims of Android's superior security, Google purposefully deceives users by presenting warnings that falsely describe highly
popular apps from well-known developers as an 'unknown app,' which gives the
user the false or misleading impression that apps and app stores downloaded from
any source other than the Play Store are PHAs or that they are otherwise harmful";
Ibid., para. 230.

26. Jamie Luguri and Lior Jacob Strahilevitz, "Shining a Light on Dark Patterns," 13(1)
Journal of Legal Analysis (March 23, 2021): 43; Nir Eyal with Ryan Hoover, *Hooked:
How to Build Habit-Forming Products* (New York: Penguin, 2019); Karen Yeung,
"'Hypernudge': Big Data as a Mode of Regulation by Design," 20(1), *Information,
Communication & Society* (2017): 118, 121; Daniel Susser, Beate Roessler, and Helen
Nissenbaum, "Technology, Autonomy and Manipulation," 8(2) *Internet Policy Review*
(June 30, 2019): 1, 3; Byung-Kwan Lee and Wei-Na Lee, "The Effect of Information
Overload on Consumer Choice Quality in an On-Line Environment," 21(3) *Psychol-
ogy and Marketing* (February 12, 2004): 159; "Dark Patterns," accessed January 4,
2022, https://www.darkpatterns.org/types-of-dark-pattern.

27. Natasha Lomas, "Aptoide, a Play Store Rival, Cries Antitrust Foul over Google

Hiding Its App," Tech Crunch (June 4, 2019), https://techcrunch.com/2019/06/04/aptoide-a-play-store-rival-cries-antitrust-foul-over-google-hiding-its-app/.

28. Ibid.

29. Ibid.

30. Multi-State Complaint, *Utah et al. v. Google LLC*, para. 92.

31. Facebook, "What Is the Face Recognition Setting on Facebook and How Does It Work?," accessed January 4, 2022, https://www.facebook.com/help/122175507864081?ref=learn_more.

32. April Glaser, "Facebook's Face-ID Database Could Be the Biggest in the World. Yes, It Should Worry Us," *Slate* (July 9, 2019), https://slate.com/technology/2019/07/facebook-facial-recognition-ice-bad.html.

33. "Amazon's Friction-Killing Tactics to Make Products More Seamless," *First Round Review*, https://review.firstround.com/amazons-friction-killing-tactics-to-make-products-more-seamless.

34. House Report, 104.

35. House Report, 53.

36. L. Ceci, "Leading Google Apps in the Google Play Store in June 2021, by Downloads (in Millions)," Statista (December 7, 2021), https://www.statista.com/statistics/248959/top-global-google-app-downloads-google-play/.

37. Venkatesh Abhay, "Google Is Trying to Dissuade Edge Users from Using Chrome Extensions," Neowin (February 21, 2020), https://www.neowin.net/news/google-is-trying-to-persuade-edge-users-from-using-chrome-extensions/ (discussing the clash between Microsoft and Google over Microsoft's Edge browser).

38. GlobalWebIndex Report, "The State of Mobile Ad-Blocking in 2017" (Q2 2017), http://insight.globalwebindex.net/hubfs/The-State-of-Mobile-Ad-blocking-in-2017.pdf.

39. Ibid.

40. Ibid. Of US respondents who have not blocked ads on a mobile, more than six in ten said that they did not know that it was possible to block ads via their smartphone.

41. Wladimir Palant, "Adblock Plus for Android Removed from Google Play Store," *Adblock Plus* (March 14, 2013), https://adblockplus.org/blog/adblock-plus-for-android-removed-from-google-play-store.

42. Lara O'Reilly, "Ad Blocker Usage Is Up 30%—and a Popular Method Publishers Use to Thwart It Isn't Working," *Business Insider* (January 31, 2017), http://www.businessinsider.com/pagefair-2017-ad-blocking-report-2017-1.

43. Kif Leswing, "Battle of the Ad Blockers: iOS vs. Android," *Fortune* (September 22, 2015), http://fortune.com/2015/09/22/ad-block-ios-android/.

44. GlobalWebIndex Report, 131.

45. Ibid.

46. Tom Warren, "Google's Chrome Ad Blocking Arrives Today and This Is How It Works," *Verge* (February 14, 2018), https://www.theverge.com/2018/2/14/17011266/google-chrome-ad-blocker-features. Samsung in 2016 introduced ad-blocking technology

for its version of the Android phone. Sarah Perez, "Following Apple's Move, Samsung Rolls Out Ad Blocking to Android Devices," *Tech Crunch* (February 1, 2016), https://techcrunch.com/2016/02/01/following-apples-move-samsung-rolls-out-ad-blocking-to-android-devices/.

47. Dieter Bohn, "Google Delays Blocking Third-party Cookies in Chrome until 2023," *Verge* (June 24, 2021), https://www.theverge.com/2021/6/24/22547339/google-chrome-cookiepocalypse-delayed-2023.

48. See, e.g., AGCOM, "Average Monthly Time Spent Per User on Leading Online Platforms in Italy in March 2021 (in Minutes)," Statista (July 12, 2021), https://www-statista-com.utk.idm.oclc.org/statistics/1068649/italy-monthly-time-spent-on-leading-websites/; Ofcom, "Leading Internet Properties Ranked by Time Spent in the United Kingdom (UK) as of September 2019 (in Minutes)," Statista (June 24, 2020), https://www-statista-com.utk.idm.oclc.org/statistics/272879/leading-internet-properties-in-the-uk-by-time-spent/; Verto Analytics, "Most Popular Digital Brands in the United States from May to July 2017, Ranked by Monthly User Engagement (in Hours.Minutes)," Statista (August 18, 2017).

49. "Largest Companies by Market Cap," accessed January 4, 2022, https://companiesmarketcap.com.

50. WordStream, "A Google Projects Resting Ground: The Google Graveyard," accessed January 4, 2022, https://www.wordstream.com/articles/retired-google-projects.

51. Shoshana Zuboff, *The Age of Surveillance Capitalism: The Fight for a Human Future at the New Frontier of Power* (London: Profile Books, 2019): 139.

52. Steve Jobs quote, https://www.inc.com/jason-aten/this-was-steve-jobs-most-controversial-legacy-it-was-also-his-most-brilliant.html.

53. Press Release (EU Commission): "Antitrust: Commission Sends Statement of Objections to Google on Android Operating System and Applications" (April 20, 2016), http://europa.eu/rapid/press-release_IP-16-1492_en.htm.

Chapter 5: Distortions beyond the Tech Barons' Ecosystems

1. Biz Carson, "DOJ Lawyers Ask Startup Investors about Big Tech's 'Kill Zones'—As the DOJ Worries That Big Tech Is Squashing Smaller Startups, the Feds Ask VCs for Their Thoughts," *Protocol* (February 12, 2020), https://www.protocol.com/doj-antitrust-venture-capital-workshop.

2. An OECD Report on "Start-ups, Killer Acquisitions and Merger Control" cites economic research that considers the effects of acquisitions on VC investments. "For example, Zingales et al. (2019) model investment incentives and show that nascent acquisitions lead to reduced incentives to invest in start-ups. This effect occurs because the prospect of acquisition discourages early adoption of nascent products, and hence makes entry difficult, thereby making them less attractive investments. The authors follow this by identifying a decline in venture capital funding for starts-ups in the 'same space' as the companies acquired by Google and Facebook. Similarly, Singer (2019) cites analysis showing that VC funding for start-ups in the same category as Google

(internet software), Facebook (social platform software) and Amazon (internet retail) have each declined dramatically in recent years." OECD, "Start-ups, Killer Acquisitions and Merger Control—Background Note" (June 10, 2020): 32, https://one .oecd.org/document/DAF/COMP(2020)5/en/pdf (citing Sai Krishna Kamepalli, Raghuram G. Rajan, and Luigi Zingales, "Kill Zone," Stigler Center, New Working Paper Series No. 39, November 2019) (no citation was given for the Singer paper).

3. Bureau of Labor Statistics, "Survival Rate of Businesses Established in 1994 and 2000 in the United States," Statista (July 10, 2012).

4. Clayton M. Christensen, *The Innovator's Dilemma*, 179; Mariana Mazzucato, *The Value of Everything*, 193.

5. See, e.g., NVCA, "Value of Venture Capital Investment Deals in the United States 2020, by Stage (in Billion U.S. Dollars)," Statista (March 30, 2021) (noting that in 2020, US companies in their later stage acquired the largest value of venture capital investment deals: companies during their late stage acquired VC investments worth $110.3 billion; companies in their early stage acquired VC investments worth $43.6 billion, and those in their angel and seed stage acquired investments worth $10.4 billion); KPMG, "Median Deal Size of Venture Capital-Backed Companies in the United States from 2010 to 2020, by Stage (in Million U.S. Dollars)," Statista (January 20, 2021) (showing that the median deal size for companies in their angel/seed stage grew from $.5 million in 2010 to $1.3 billion in 2020, whereas it grew from $6 billion to $10 billion for later stage companies over that period).

6. Antitrust Division of the United States Department of Justice, Public Workshop on Venture Capital and Antitrust (February 12, 2020): 30, https://www.justice.gov/atr /page/file/1255851/download.

7. Sai Krishna Kamepalli, Raghuram Rajan, and Luigi Zingales, "Kill Zone," Becker Friedman Inst. Working Paper No. 2020–19 (March 17, 2020), https://ssrn.com /abstract=3555915.

8. Asher Schechter, "Google and Facebook's 'Kill Zone': 'We've Taken the Focus Off of Rewarding Genius and Innovation to Rewarding Capital and Scale,'" Pro Market (May 25, 2018), https://promarket.org/2018/05/25/google-facebooks-kill-zone -weve-taken-focus-off-rewarding-genius-innovation-rewarding-capital-scale/.

9. Submission by Paul Arnold to the United States House of Representatives, Committee on the Judiciary Subcommittee on Antitrust, Commercial, and Administrative Law (September 3, 2020): 48.

10. Olivia Solon, "As Tech Companies Get Richer."

11. "Stigler Committee on Digital Platforms, Final Report," Subcommittee on Market Structure and Antitrust, 77 (incorporating comments by Ian Hathaway who critiques a report commissioned by Facebook to explore the impact on investment). See: http://www.ianhathaway.org/blog/2018/10/12/platform-giants-and-venture-backed -startups.

12. Ibid.

13. Congressional Research Service, "Mergers and Acquisitions in Digital Markets" (March 30, 2021): 1 (noting how Facebook acquired at least 63 companies, Alphabet at least 260, Amazon at least 100, Apple at least 120, and Microsoft at least 167); House Report, 392.

14. Jason Furman et al., "Independent Report of the UK Digital Competition Expert Panel 'Unlocking Digital Competition'" (March 13, 2019): para 3.44.

15. "Non-HSR Reported Acquisitions by Select Technology Platforms, 2010–2019: An FTC Study" (September 15, 2021), https://www.ftc.gov/reports/non-hsr-reported -acquisitions-select-technology-platforms-2010-2019-ftc-study.

16. Press Release (US FTC): "FTC Staff Presents Report on Nearly a Decade of Unre-ported Acquisitions by the Biggest Technology Companies" (September 15, 2021), https://www.ftc.gov/news-events/press-releases/2021/09/ftc-report-on-unreported -acquisitions-by-biggest-tech-companies.

17. Axel Gautier and Joe Lamesch, "Mergers in the Digital Economy," CESifo Working Paper Series 8056 (2020), https://ideas.repec.org/p/ces/ceswps/_8056.html.

18. See, for example, presentation by Uber to the UK Expert Panel, para 3.40.

19. Oliver Latham, Isabel Tecu, and Nitika Bagaria, "Beyond Killer Acquisitions: Are There More Common Potential Competition Issues in Tech Deals and How Can These Be Assessed?," *Competition Policy International—Antitrust Chronicle* (May 2020), https://www.competitionpolicyinternational.com/beyond-killer-acquisitions-are -there-more-common-potential-competition-issues-in-tech-deals-and-how-can-these -be-assessed/#_edn1.

20. One can draw a distinction between the theories of harm applicable to "killer acquisitions" and "acquisitions of nascent competitors." See: OECD, *Start-ups, Killer Acquisitions and Merger Control*; Colleen Cunningham, Florian Ederer, and Song Ma, "Killer Ac-quisitions," 129(3) *Journal of Political Economy* (2021): 649.

21. FTC Amended Complaint, *FTC v. Facebook, Inc.*, No.1:20-cv-03590-JEB (D.D.C. August 19, 2021), para. 1.

22. Ibid., para. 58.

23. Brian Fung, "Congress Grilled the CEOs of Amazon, Apple, Facebook and Google. Here Are the Big Takeaways," CNN Business (July 30, 2020), https://edition .cnn.com/2020/07/29/tech/tech-antitrust-hearing-ceos/index.html; Casey Newton and Nilay Patel, "'Instagram Can Hurt Us': Mark Zuckerberg Emails Outline Plan to Neutralize Competitors," *Verge* (July 29, 2020), https://www.theverge.com/2020/7/29 /21345723/facebook-instagram-documents-emails-mark-zuckerberg-kevin-systrom -hearing.

24. FTC Amended Complaint, *FTC v. Facebook, Inc.*, para. 81.

25. Ibid., para. 95.

26. Ibid., para. 7.

27. Ibid., para. 91.

28. "Instagram Founder Feared Zuckerberg Would Go into 'Destroy Mode' over Facebook

Sale, Says U.S. Rep. Jayapal," CNBC (July 29, 2020), https://www.cnbc.com/video /2020/07/29/instagram-founder-feared-zuckerberg-would-go-into-adestroy-modea -if-he-didnat-sell-to-facebook-says-u-s-rep-jayapal.html.

29. FTC Amended Complaint, *FTC v. Facebook, Inc.*

30. Ibid., para. 102.

31. Ibid.

32. House Report, 394.

33. Dara Kerr, "Google Reveals It Spent $966 Million in Waze Acquisition," CNET (July 25, 2013), https://www.cnet.com/news/google-reveals-it-spent-966-million-in -waze-acquisition/.

34. Noam Bardin, "Why Did I Leave Google or, Why Did I Stay So Long?," PayGo (February 17, 2021), https://paygo.media/p/25171.

35. Suzanne Rowan Kelleher, "Did Google Just Deliver a Death Blow to Waze?," *Forbes* (October 21, 2019), https://www.forbes.com/sites/suzannerowankelleher /2019/10/21/did-google-just-deliver-a-death-blow-to-waze/?sh=72ca5a8718c4.

36. Noam Bardin, "Why Did I Leave."

37. Ufuk Akcigit et al., "Rising Corporate Market Power: Emerging Policy Issues," International Monetary Fund (March 15, 2021), https://www.imf.org/en/Publications /Staff-Discussion-Notes/Issues/2021/03/10/Rising-Corporate-Market-Power -Emerging-Policy-Issues-48619. See also: Ioannis Kokkoris and Tommaso Valletti, "Innovation Considerations in Horizontal Merger Control," 16(2) *Journal of Competition Law & Economics* (2020): 220, https://academic.oup.com/jcle/article-abstract /16/2/220/5820042.

38. Sai Krishna Kamepalli, Raghuram Rajan, and Luigi Zingales, 5. See also Cristina Caffarra, Gregory Crawford, and Tommaso Valletti, "'How Tech Rolls': Potential Competition and 'Reverse' Killer Acquisitions," VOXEU (May 11, 2020), https://voxeu .org/content/how-tech-rolls-potential-competition-and-reverse-killer-acquisitions. For an opposite argument, see: Simon Bishop and Stephen Lewis, "How Merger Control Rolls: A Response to Caffarra, Crawford and Valletti" (December 2020), https:// www.rbbecon.com/how-merger-control-rolls-a-response-to-caffarra-crawford-and -valletti/.

39. James F. Moore, "Predators and Prey: A New Ecology of Competition," 71(3) *Harvard Business Review* (1993): 75, https://hbr.org/1993/05/predators-and-prey-a-new -ecology-of-competition.

40. Mariana Mazzucato, *The Value of Everything*, 194.

41. Press Release (EU Commission): "Antitrust: Commission Sends Statement of Objections to Apple on App Store Rules for Music Streaming Providers" (April 30, 2021), https://ec.europa.eu/commission/presscorner/detail/en/ip_21_2061.

42. Android Open Source Project, "Android Unites the World! Use the Open Source Android Operating System to Power Your Device," accessed January 4, 2022, https:// source.android.com.

43. Multi-State Complaint, *Utah et al. v. Google LLC*, No. 3:21-cv-05227 (N.D. Cal.

July 7, 2021), para. 103 (alleging that Google forces app developers, as a condition of appearing in the Google Play Store, to sign a non-negotiable Developer Distribution Agreement, which prohibits developers from using "Google Play to distribute or make available any Product that has a purpose that facilitates the distribution of software applications and games for use on Android devices outside of Google Play"). As the states further alleged in their complaint, "This requirement unreasonably raises the cost of customer acquisition for the competing app distribution channels, as they cannot reach consumers through widely used forms of advertising that are uniquely effective in reaching users who are immediately prepared to acquire an app but instead must find alternative means of advertising to reach users."

44. Multi-State Complaint, *Utah et al. v. Google LLC*, para. 107.

45. Complaint filed in *United States v. Google*, No. 1:20-cv-03010 (D.D.C. October 20, 2020).

46. FTC Opposition to Motion to Dismiss, 5, in *FTC v. Facebook*, No.1:20-cv-03590-JEB (D.D.C. July 4, 2021).

47. Ibid.

48. Ibid.

49. Delio Ignacio Castaneda and Sergio Cuellar, "Knowledge Sharing and Innovation: A Systematic Review," 159–73.

50. Anuraag Singh, Giorgio Triulzi, and Christopher L. Magee, "Technological Improvement Rate Predictions for All Technologies: Use of Patent Data and an Extended Domain Description," 50(9) *Research Policy* (2021): 104294, ISSN 0048-7333, https://doi.org/10.1016/j.respol.2021.104294 (citing some of the literature of how technologies have extensive interaction with one another [spillover] in that technological ideas can be used for various purposes and that prior technological and scientific ideas are at the root of even the most novel technologies).

51. Matthew C. Le Merle and Alison Davis, *Corporate Innovation in the Fifth Era: Lessons from Alphabet/Google, Amazon, Apple, Facebook* (Corte Madera, CA: Cartwright Publishing, 2017): 171.

52. Ibid., 182.

53. On absorption capacity, see: Wesley M. Cohen and Daniel A. Levinthal, "Absorptive Capacity: A New Perspective on Learning and Innovation," 35(1) *Administrative Science Quarterly* (1990): 128–52; Tengjian Zou, Gokhan Ertug, and Gerard George, "The Capacity to Innovate: A Meta-Analysis of Absorptive Capacity," 20(2) *Innovation: Organization & Management* (2018): 87, 121. On innovation clusters, see: Xavier Ferras-Hernandez and Petra A. Nylund, "Clusters as Innovation Engines: The Accelerating Strengths of Proximity," 16(1) *European Management Review* (2019): 37.

54. Cecilia Rikap and Bengt-Åke Lundvall, "Big Tech, Knowledge Predation and the Implications for Development," *Innovation and Development* (2020) DOI: 10.1080/2157930X.2020.1855825.

55. Ibid., 2, 6.

56. Michele Boldrin and David K. Levine, "2003 Lawrence R. Klein Lecture—The Case

against Intellectual Monopoly," 45(2) *International Economic Review* (2004): 327–50; Ugo Pagano, "The Crisis of Intellectual Monopoly Capitalism," 38(6) *Cambridge Journal of Economics* (2014): 1409–129; Cédric Durand and William Milberg, "Intellectual Monopoly in Global Value Chains," 27(2) *Review of International Political Economy* (2020): 404–29.

57. Terrence J. Sejnowski, *The Deep Learning Revolution* (Cambridge, MA: MIT Press, 2018): 193.

58. Joseph A. Schumpeter, *Capitalism, Socialism and Democracy.* For criticism, note, for example: Michele Boldrin and David K. Levine, "2003 Lawrence R. Klein Lecture."

59. On the value of open innovation, see: Henry Chesbrough, *Open Innovation Results: Going Beyond the Hype and Getting Down to Business* (Oxford, UK: Oxford University Press, 2019).

60. Wesley M. Cohen and Daniel A. Levinthal, "Absorptive Capacity."

61. *United States v. Google.*

62. "Sonos Unveils Next Generation Beam with Support for Dolby Atmos and New Audio Formats," Yahoo! Finance (September 14, 2021), https://finance.yahoo.com /news/sonos-unveils-next-generation-beam-130000678.html.

63. House Report, 50 (statement of Patrick Spence, CEO, Sonos, Inc.).

Chapter 6: Toxic Innovation Galore

1. When discussing technology based on patent applications, it should be noted that not all patents have been transformed into products and services. Some of the technologies may have been developed, but not necessarily implemented. Still, they offer a valuable indication as to the assets a company is trying to secure and the direction in which its technology is heading. See comments by Jason M. Schultz, a law professor at New York University, cited in: Sahil Chinoy, "What 7 Creepy Patents Reveal about Facebook," *New York Times* (June 21, 2018), https://www.nytimes.com/interactive /2018/06/21/opinion/sunday/facebook-patents-privacy.html.

2. Even when healthy, this competition can occur: (1) on various dimensions (such as price, quality, service, variety, innovation); (2) operating at different levels of efficiency; (3) with different levels of product differentiation, entry barriers, and transparency; (4) at different stages of the product life cycle; and (5) with different demands for technological innovation.

3. Joseph E. Stiglitz, *Freefall: America, Free Markets, and the Sinking of the World Economy* (New York: W.W. Norton, 2010): 5, 80.

4. Gillian Tett, *Fool's Gold: How the Bold Dream of a Small Tribe at J.P. Morgan Was Corrupted by Wall Street Greed and Unleashed a Catastrophe* (London: Abacus, 2009).

5. Sergey Brin and Lawrence Page, "The Anatomy of a Large-Scale Hypertextual Web Search Engine," 30(1-7) Computer Networks and ISDN Systems (1998): 107–17, https://snap.stanford.edu/class/cs224w-readings/Brin98Anatomy.pdf.

6. Tracy Samantha Schmidt, "Inside the Backlash Against Facebook," *Time* (September 6, 2006), http://content.time.com/time/nation/article/0,8599,1532225,00.html.

7.   Antone Gonsalves, "Facebook Founder Apologizes in Privacy Flap; Users Given More Control—Founder Mark Zuckerberg Says the Social Networking Site 'Really Messed This One Up,'" InformationWeek (September 8, 2006), https://www.informationweek .com/facebook-founder-apologizes-in-privacy-flap-users-given-more-control/d/d -id/1046840?piddl_msgorder=asc.

8.   Jennifer Shore and Jill Steinman, "Did You Really Agree to That? The Evolution of Facebook's Privacy Policy," *Technology Science* (August 10, 2015), https://techscience .org/a/2015081102/.

9.   "Facebook's Average Revenue per User as of 4th Quarter 2020, by Region (in U.S. Dollars)," Statista (January 28, 2021), accessed May 5, 2021, https://www.statista.com /statistics/251328/facebooks-average-revenue-per-user-by-region/.

10.   In a 2018 survey, for example, nearly 42 percent said they would be willing to spend only between \$1 and \$5 per month for an ad-free Facebook, about 25 percent said they'd pay between \$6 and \$10, 22 percent were willing to pay between \$11 and \$15, and only about 12 percent were willing to pay more than \$15 per month. See: Rani Molla, "How Much Would You Pay for Facebook Without Ads?," Vox Recode (April 11, 2018), https://www.vox.com/2018/4/11/17225328/facebook-ads-free -paid-service-mark-zuckerberg.

11.   Douglas MacMillan, "Tech's 'Dirty Secret': The App Developers Sifting Through Your Gmail—Software Developers Scan Hundreds of Millions of Emails of Users Who Sign Up for Email-Based Services," *Wall Street Journal* (July 2, 2018), https:// www.wsj.com/articles/techs-dirty-secret-the-app-developers-sifting-through-your -gmail-1530544442; Laura Tucker, "Fears Confirmed: Third-Party App Developers Can Access Your Gmail," MakeTechEasier (July 3, 2018), https://www.maketecheasier .com/third-party-app-developers-access-gmail-emails/; Andrew Braun, "Which Email Providers Are Scanning Your Emails?," MakeTechEasier (September 24, 2018), https://www.maketecheasier.com/which-email-providers-scanning-emails/.

12.   Ibid.

13.   For example, one patent ("Correlating media consumption data with user profiles") explores such use to identify which television shows you may watch. See: Sahil Chinoy, "What 7 Creepy Patents Reveal about Facebook." Also note: Press Release (US FTC): "FTC Issues Warning Letters to App Developers Using 'Silverpush' Code: Letters Warn Companies of Privacy Risks in Audio Monitoring Technology" (March 17, 2016), https://www.ftc.gov/system/files/attachments/press-releases/ftc-issues-warning -letters-app-developers-using-silverpush-code/160317samplesilverpushltr .pdf.

14.   For example: U.S. patent 10192546, "Pre-wakeword speech processing" (Amazon Technologies, Inc.); U.S. patent 10714081, "Dynamic voice assistant interaction" (Amazon Technologies, Inc.); U.S. patent 10692506, "Keyword determinations from conversational data" (Amazon Technologies, Inc.); "Truth, Trust and the Future of Commerce," Sparks & Honey Report (June 2018).

15.   Sam Biddle, "Facebook Uses Artificial Intelligence to Predict Your Future Actions for

Advertisers, Says Confidential Document," *The Intercept* (April 13, 2018), https://theintercept.com/2018/04/13/facebook-advertising-data-artificial-intelligence-ai/.

16. Oleksii M. Skriabin et al., "Neurotechnologies in the Advertising Industry: Legal and Ethical Aspects," 17(2) *Innovative Marketing* (2021): 189–201, https://www.businessperspectives.org/index.php/journals/innovative-marketing/issue-382/neurotechnologies-in-the-advertising-industry-legal-and-ethical-aspects.

17. Sophie Kleber, "Three Ways AI Is Getting More Emotional," in Thomas Davenport et al., *Artificial Intelligence: The Insights You Need from Harvard Business Review* (Boston, MA: Harvard Business Review Press, 2019), 137.

18. Ibid.

19. Erik Brynjolfsson and Andrew McAfee, "The Business of Artificial Intelligence," 10, 23 (noting how the software companies like Affectiva are using AI-based vision systems to recognize emotions such as joy, surprise, and anger in focus groups).

20. Oleksii Skriabin et al., "Neurotechnologies in the Advertising Industry."

21. This was the "first experimental evidence for massive-scale emotional contagion via social networks." Adam D. I. Kramer, Jamie E. Guillory, and Jeffrey T. Hancock, "Experimental Evidence of Massive-Scale Emotional Contagion through Social Networks," 24 *PNAS* (2014): 111, https://www.pnas.org/content/111/24/8788.

22. Ibid ("a larger percentage of words in the users' status updates were negative and a smaller percentage were positive").

23. Daniel Ringbeck, Dominic Seeberger, and Arnd Huchzermeier, "Toward Personalized Online Shopping: Predicting Personality Traits Based on Online Shopping Behavior," SSRN (June 24, 2019), http://dx.doi.org/10.2139/ssrn.3406297. The study first gathered the self-reported personality traits of participants in the experiment via an online survey and in the following track their browsing behavior when shopping within a realistic online shop for books, which was set up for this study. That online shop contains about 120 books from four different categories: fiction, nonfiction, romance, and textbooks. The study then employed Google Analytics trackers to record every browsing action taken by consumers in the shop at the most granular level. We find that consumers' browsing behavior data is sufficient for us to predict their personality traits with the aid of a machine learning classification algorithm.

24. Ibid. Consumers with high NFA "buy products to explore them"; "buy more impulsively and value products for the feelings they produce"; "take more risks, switch brands more often, enjoy exploring new products, and seek more information before purchasing"; and react more favorably to violent, sexual, and fear-provoking content.

25. Ibid., 19 ("Openness [O] and Extraversion [E] stand out as individual personality traits that can be predicted with high accuracy based on a short observation time: after only 10 seconds, the algorithm's predictive accuracy regarding O and E is 0.70 and 0.72 respectively.")

26. As the study's authors noted, "additional product views would result in even more revealing data on customer behavior and hence should further improve predictive performance."

27. U.S. patent application 20210035298, "Utilization of luminance changes to determine user characteristics" (Apple); "Apple Glass Will Analyze Users' Eyes to Track User Attention," Beebom (February 7, 2021), https://beebom.com/apple-glass-will-analyze-users-eyes-and-adjust-the-display/.

28. U.S. patent application 20200358627, "Meeting insight computing system" (Microsoft).

29. U.S. patent application 20150356180, "Inferring relationship statuses of users of a social networking system" (Facebook)"; U.S. patent application 20150039524, "Detecting and responding to sentiment-based communications about a business on a social networking system" (Facebook).

30. U.S. patent application 9740752B2, "Determining user personality characteristics from social networking system communications and characteristics" (Facebook).

31. Ibid.

32. "Patently Creepy: Facebook's Plan to 'Read Emotions' through Your Smartphone," RT (June 8, 2017), https://www.rt.com/viral/391420-facebook-patent-emotions-camera/.

33. U.S. patent application 20120143693, "Targeting advertisements based on emotion" (Microsoft).

34. U.S. patent 10762429, "Emotional/cognitive state presentation" (Microsoft).

35. Ibid.

36. U.S. patent application 20170140049, "Web search based on browsing history and emotional state" (IBM); Sidney Fussell, "Alexa Wants to Know How You're Feeling Today," *Atlantic* (October 12, 2018), https://www.theatlantic.com/technology/archive/2018/10/alexa-emotion-detection-ai-surveillance/572884/.

37. Sidney Fussell, "Alexa Wants to Know."

38. Didem Kaya Bayram and Furkan Akyurek, "How Our Voices Could Turn into a Weapon of Mass, Hyper-Targeted Advertising," TRT World (July 12, 2018), https://www.trtworld.com/life/how-our-voices-could-turn-into-a-weapon-of-mass-hyper-targeted-advertising-18681.

39. U.S. patent application 20150242679A1, "Techniques for emotion detection and content delivery" (Facebook).

40. Didem Kaya Bayram and Furkan Akyurek, "How Our Voices Could Turn."

41. "AI Can Predict Whether Your Relationship Will Last Based on How You Speak to Your Partner," The Conversation (September 29, 2017), https://theconversation.com/ai-can-predict-whether-your-relationship-will-last-based-on-how-you-speak-to-your-partner-81420.

42. Terrence J. Sejnowski, *The Deep Learning Revolution*, 181.

43. Ibid.

44. Sophie Kleber, "Three Ways," 138.

45. Terrence J. Sejnowski, *The Deep Learning Revolution*, 182.

46. See for example range of related patents: U.S. patent application 9235849B2, "Generating user information for use in targeted advertising" (Google); U.S. patent application 20110010239, "Model-based advertisement optimization" (Yahoo); U.S. patent application 9672525B2, "Identifying related information given content and/or presenting

related information in association with content-related advertisements" (Google); U.S. patent application 20050021397, "Content-targeted advertising using collected user behavior data" (Google).

47. Sophie Kleber, "Three Ways," 142.

48. Oleksii Skriabin et al., "Neurotechnologies in the Advertising Industry."

49. Robin Marks, "'Neuroprosthesis' Restores Words to Man with Paralysis— Technology Could Lead to More Natural Communication for People Who Have Suffered Speech Loss," University of California San Francisco, https://www.ucsf.edu /news/2021/07/420946/neuroprosthesis-restores-words-man-paralysis.

50. Ibid.

51. "Imagining a New Interface: Hands-free Communication without Saying a Word," Tech@ Facebook, https://tech.fb.com/imagining-a-new-interface-hands-free-communication -without-saying-a-word/.

52. "Virtual Reality," Facebook Engineering, https://engineering.fb.com/category/virtual -reality/.

53. "Facebook, Inc. (FB), Second Quarter 2021 Results Conference Call" (July 28, 2021), https://s21.q4cdn.com/399680738/files/doc_financials/2021/q2/FB-Q2-2021 -Earnings-Call-Transcript.pdf.

54. Ibid.

55. *Epic Games v. Apple*, slip. op., 20.

56. Ibid., 20, n. 132.

57. Justin Scheck, Newley Purnell, and Jeff Horwitz, "Facebook Employees Flag Drug Cartels and Human Traffickers. The Company's Response Is Weak, Documents Show," *Wall Street Journal* (September 16, 2021), https://www.wsj.com/articles/facebook -drug-cartels-human-traffickers-response-is-weak-documents-11631812953?mod =article_inline.

58. Ibid.

59. Ibid.

60. Ibid.

61. Ibid.

62. Ibid.

63. Video: "Big Data, Big Questions: Implications for Competition and Consumers" Subcommittee on Competition Policy, Antitrust, and Consumer Rights Hearing (September 21, 2021), Sen. Lee at 1:38, https://www.judiciary.senate.gov/meetings /big-data-big-questions-implications-for-competition-and-consumers.

64. Georgia Wells, Jeff Horwitz, and Deepa Seetharaman, "Facebook Knows Instagram Is Toxic for Teen Girls, Company Documents Show," *Wall Street Journal* (September 14, 2021), https://www.wsj.com/articles/facebook-knows-instagram-is-toxic-for-teen-girls -company-documents-show-11631620739?mod=article_inline.

65. Ibid.

66. Ibid.

67. Ibid.

68. Royal Society for Public Health (RSPH), "Instagram Ranked Worst for Young People's Mental Health" (May 19, 2017), https://www.rsph.org.uk/about-us/news /instagram-ranked-worst-for-young-people-s-mental-health.html (finding young people themselves say four of the five most used social media platforms actually make their feelings of anxiety worse, noting the "growing evidence linking social media use and depression in young people, with studies showing that increased use is associated with significantly increased odds of depression").

69. Georgia Wells, Jeff Horwitz, and Deepa Seetharaman, "Facebook Knows Instagram Is Toxic."

70. Ibid.

71. Ibid. (noting how Facebook, among other things, used focus groups, online surveys, and diary studies in 2019 and 2020, and large-scale surveys of tens of thousands of people in 2021 that paired user responses with Facebook's own data about how much time users spent on Instagram and what they saw there).

72. Ibid.

73. Ibid.

74. Ibid., showing image of Teen Mental Health Deep Dive, Instagram slide presentation, *Wall Street Journal*, 2019.

75. Ibid.

76. Georgia Wells and Jeff Horwitz, "Facebook's Effort to Attract Preteens Goes Beyond Instagram Kids, Documents Show," *Wall Street Journal* (September 28, 2021), https:// www.wsj.com/articles/facebook-instagram-kids-tweens-attract-11632849667.

77. Ibid.

78. Ibid.

79. Video: "Big Data," Sen. Lee at 1:37.

80. Ibid. at 2:03–2:04.

81. Ibid. at 2:03.

82. For the impact of smartphones on children, see: Jean M. Twenge, *iGen: Why Today's Super-Connected Kids Are Growing Up Less Rebellious, More Tolerant, Less Happy— and Completely Unprepared for Adulthood—and What That Means for the Rest of Us* (New York: Atria Books, 2017).

83. Damjan Jugovic Spajic, "How Much Time Does the Average Person Spend on Their Phone?," KomandoTech (February 11, 2020), https://kommandotech.com/statistics/ how-much-time-does-the-average-person-spend-on-their-phone/.

84. The *Diagnostic and Statistical Manual of Mental Disorders (DSM–5)* defines and classifies mental disorders in order to improve diagnoses, treatment, and research: https:// www.psychiatry.org/psychiatrists/practice/dsm.

85. Daria J. Kuss and Mark D. Griffiths, "Social Networking Sites and Addiction: Ten Lessons Learned," 14(3) *International Journal of Environmental Research and Public Health* (2017): 311, https://www.ncbi.nlm.nih.gov/pmc/articles/PMC5369147/.

86. Gustavo Ferreira Veiga et al., "Emerging Adults and Facebook Use: The Validation of the Bergen Facebook Addiction Scale (BFAS)," 17 *International Journal of Mental*

Health and Addiction (2018): 279; Julia Brailovskaia and Jürgen Margraf, "Facebook Addiction Disorder (FAD) among German Students—A Longitudinal Approach," *PLoS One* (December 14, 2017), https://doi.org/10.1371/journal.pone.0189719 (noting how Facebook use is very attractive for narcissists, and could make them especially vulnerable to Facebook addiction disorder).

87. Cecilie Schou Andreassen and Ståle Pallesen, "Social Network Site Addiction—an Overview," 20(25) *Current Pharmaceutical Design* (2014): 4053, https://pubmed.ncbi.nlm.nih.gov/24001298/; Julia Brailovskaia and Jürgen Margraf, "Facebook Addiction Disorder (FAD)" (defining Facebook addiction disorder through six typical characteristics of addiction disorders: "salience [e.g., permanent thinking of Facebook use], tolerance [e.g., requiring increasing time on Facebook to achieve previous positive using effect], mood modification [e.g., mood improvement by Facebook use], relapse [reverting to earlier use pattern after ineffective attempts to reduce Facebook use], withdrawal symptoms [e.g., becoming nervous without possibility to use Facebook], and conflict (e.g., interpersonal problems caused by intensive Facebook use]").

88. Haley Sweetland Edwards, "The Masters of Mind Control," 191(15) *Time International* (April 2018), 30.

89. Anna Lembke, "Digital Addictions Are Drowning Us in Dopamine," *Wall Street Journal* (August 13, 2021), https://www.wsj.com/articles/digital-addictions-are-drowning-us-in-dopamine-11628861572.

90. "Tristan Harris," accessed January 4, 2022, https://www.tristanharris.com; Haley Sweetland Edwards, "The Masters of Mind Control."

91. Roger McNamee, "I Mentored Mark Zuckerberg. I Loved Facebook. But I Can't Stay Silent about What's Happening," *Time* (January 17, 2019), http://time.com/5505441/mark-zuckerberg-mentor-facebook-downfall/.

92. Ibid.

93. Ibid. ("Every action a user took gave Facebook a better understanding of that user—and of that user's friends—enabling the company to make tiny 'improvements' in the user experience every day, which is to say it got better at manipulating the attention of users."); Roger McNamee, *Zucked: Waking Up to the Facebook Catastrophe* (New York: Penguin Press, 2019): 9, 62–63, 98–101.

94. Roger McNamee, *Zucked*, 103.

95. Comments made by Sandy Parakilas in an interview to BBC panorama. For the article and video: Hilary Andersson, "Social Media Apps Are 'Deliberately' Addictive to Users," BBC Panorama (July 4, 2018), https://www.bbc.co.uk/news/technology-44640959.

96. Evan Osnos, "Can Mark Zuckerberg Fix Facebook Before It Breaks Democracy?," *New Yorker* (September 10, 2018), https://www.newyorker.com/magazine/2018/09/17/can-mark-zuckerberg-fix-facebook-before-it-breaks-democracy.

97. Video: "Facebook Admits They Intentionally Made Us Addicted," *Viral Nation*, https://www.viralnation.com/blog/facebook-execs-admit-to-intentionally-making-us-addicted/.

98. Thuy Ong, "Sean Parker on Facebook: 'God Only Knows What It's Doing to Our Children's Brains,'" Verge (November 9, 2017), https://www.theverge.com/2017/11/9/16627724/sean-parker-facebook-childrens-brains-feedback-loop.

99. "Smartphones—The Dark Side," BBC Panorama, available online: https://www.bbc.co.uk/programmes/b0b9dzb6.

100. Hilary Andersson, "Social Media Apps."

101. "Facebook, Inc. (FB), Second Quarter 2021 Results Conference Call."

102. Ibid.

Chapter 7: Ripple Effects

1. Video: Interview with Chamath Palihapitiya, founder and CEO Social Capital, "Money as an Instrument of Change," https://www.youtube.com/watch?v=PMotykw0SIk&t=1281s, at minute 21.

2. Jeff Horwitz and Deepa Seetharaman, "Facebook Executives Shut Down Efforts to Make the Site Less Divisive," *Wall Street Journal* (May 26, 2020), https://www.wsj.com/articles/facebook-knows-it-encourages-division-top-executives-nixed-solutions-11590507499; Keach Hagey and Jeff Horwitz, "Facebook Tried to Make Its Platform a Healthier Place. It Got Angrier Instead," *Wall Street Journal* (September 15, 2021), https://www.wsj.com/articles/facebook-algorithm-change-zuckerberg-11631654215?mod=article_inline.

3. Ibid.

4. Luke Darby, "Facebook Knows It's Engineered to 'Exploit the Human Brain's Attraction to Divisiveness,'" *GQ* (May 27, 2020), https://www.gq.com/story/facebook-spare-the-share.

5. Andre Ye, "The Algorithm Worth Billions: How YouTube's Addictive Video Recommender Works," FAUN (May 11, 2020), https://faun.pub/the-algorithm-worth-billions-how-youtubes-addictive-video-recommender-works-d75646dac6a3.

6. Ibid.

7. Karen Hao, "YouTube Is Experimenting with Ways to Make Its Algorithm Even More Addictive," *MIT Technology Review* (September 27, 2019), https://www.technologyreview.com/2019/09/27/132829/youtube-algorithm-gets-more-addictive/; Jonas Kaiser and Adrian Rauchfleisch, "Unite the Right? How YouTube's Recommendation Algorithm Connects the U.S. Far-Right," *Medium* (April 11, 2018), https://medium.com/@MediaManipulation/unite-the-right-how-youtubes-recommendation-algorithm-connects-the-u-s-far-right-9f1387ccfabd.

8. Rana Foroohar, *Don't Be Evil: The Case against Big Tech* (London: Penguin, 2019), 53.

9. Keach Hagey and Jeff Horwitz, "Facebook Tried."

10. Karen Hao, "The Facebook Whistleblower Says Its Algorithms Are Dangerous. Here's Why," *MIT Technology Review* (October 5, 2021), https://www.technologyreview.com/2021/10/05/1036519/facebook-whistleblower-frances-haugen-algorithms/.

11. Brian Dean, "How Many People Use YouTube in 2021?," Backlink, accessed January 4, 2022, https://backlinko.com/youtube-users#daily-active-users; "Number of Daily

Active Facebook Users Worldwide as of 3rd Quarter 2021 (in Millions)," Statista (January 28, 2022), https://www.statista.com/statistics/346167/facebook-global-dau/.

12. Newley Purnell and Jeff Horwitz, "Facebook Services Are Used to Spread Religious Hatred in India, Internal Documents Show," *Wall Street Journal* (October 23, 2021), https://www.wsj.com/articles/facebook-services-are-used-to-spread-religious-hatred-in-india-internal-documents-show-11635016354.

13. Evan Osnos, "Can Mark Zuckerberg Fix Facebook before It Breaks Democracy?"

14. Dissenting Statement of Commissioner Rohit Chopra, *In re Facebook, Inc.*, Commission File No. 1823109 (July 24, 2019).

15. Nathan Grayson, "As Streamers Spread Dangerous Conspiracy Theories, Twitch Does Little to Stop Them," Kotaku (May 29, 2020), https://kotaku.com/as-streamers-spread-dangerous-conspiracy-theories-twit-1843684035; Patricia Hernandez, "Twitch Removes PogChamp Emote after Star Encourages 'Further Violence' at Capitol Hill," Polygon (January 6, 2021), https://www.polygon.com/2021/1/6/22218059/pogchamp-twitch-removed-emote-ryan-gootecks-gutierrez-trump-capitol-hill; Daniel Avelar, "WhatsApp Fake News during Brazil Election 'Favoured Bolsonaro,'" *Guardian* (October 30, 2019), https://www.theguardian.com/world/2019/oct/30/whatsapp-fake-news-brazil-election-favoured-jair-bolsonaro-analysis-suggests.

16. Institute of Strategic Dialogue, "Recommended Reading: Amazon's Algorithms, Conspiracy Theories and Extremist Literature" (April 2021): 8, https://www.isdglobal.org/wp-content/uploads/2021/04/Amazon-1.pdf.

17. Yaël Eisenstat, "How to Hold Social Media Accountable for Undermining Democracy," *Harvard Business Review* (January 11, 2021), https://hbr.org/2021/01/how-to-hold-social-media-accountable-for-undermining-democracy.

18. Keach Hagey and Jeff Horwitz, "Facebook Tried."

19. Peter Dizikes, "Study: On Twitter, False News Travels Faster Than True Stories," MIT News Office (March 8, 2018), https://news.mit.edu/2018/study-twitter-false-news-travels-faster-true-stories-0308.

20. Keach Hagey and Jeff Horwitz, "Facebook Tried." (One proposed change was to take away the boost the algorithm gave to content most likely to be reshared by long chains of users. "Mark doesn't think we could go broad" with the change, wrote the Facebook team leader to colleagues after the meeting. Mr. Zuckerberg said he was open to testing the approach, she said, but "We wouldn't launch if there was a material tradeoff with MSI [meaningful social interactions] impact.")

21. Republican Staff Report, "Reining in Big Tech's Censorship of Conservatives" (October 6, 2020), https://republicans-judiciary.house.gov/wp-content/uploads/2020/10/2020-10-06-Reining-in-Big-Techs-Censorship-of-Conservatives.pdf.

22. Keach Hagey and Jeff Horwitz, "Facebook's Internal Chat Boards Show Politics Often at Center of Decision Making," *Wall Street Journal* (October 24, 2021), https://www.wsj.com/articles/facebook-politics-decision-making-documents-11635100195.

23. FTC Complaint, *In the Matter of Aleksandr Kogan (Chief Executive Officer of Cam-*

bridge Analytica), para. 8, https://www.ftc.gov/system/files/documents/cases/182_3106 _and_182_3107_complaint.pdf.

24. Fed. Trade Comm'n, Press Release: "FTC Sues Cambridge Analytica, Settles with Former CEO and App Developer" (July 24, 2019), https://www.ftc.gov/news-events /press-releases/2019/07/ftc-sues-cambridge-analytica-settles-former-ceo-app-developer.

25. Video: Chanel 4 News, "Cambridge Analytica Uncovered: Secret Filming Reveals Election Tricks," https://www.youtube.com/watch?v=mpbeOCKZFfQ.

26. Ibid.

27. Dan Patterson, "Cambridge Analytica: 'We Know What You Want before You Want It,'" TechRepublic (August 10, 2016), https://www.techrepublic.com/article/we -know-what-you-want-before-you-want-it/.

28. See, for example: Josh Dawsey, "Russian-Funded Facebook Ads Backed Stein, Sanders and Trump," *Politico* (September 26, 2017), https://www.politico.com/story/2017/09/26 /facebook-russia-trump-sanders-stein-243172; "How the Facebook Ads That Targeted Voters Centered on Black American Culture: Voter Suppression Was the End Game," Stop Online Violence Against Women, https://stoponlinevaw.com/wp-content /uploads/2018/10/Black-ID-Target-by-Russia-Report-SOVAW.pdf.

29. Evan Osnos, "Can Mark Zuckerberg Fix Facebook before It Breaks Democracy?"

30. "Why We're Concerned about Profiling and Micro-Targeting in Elections," Privacy International (April 30, 2020), https://privacyinternational.org/news-analysis/3735 /why-were-concerned-about-profiling-and-micro-targeting-elections.

31. Jamie Bartlett, *The People vs. Tech: How the Internet Is Killing Democracy (and How We Save It)* (London: Ebury Press, 2018): 81.

32. Ibid., 89.

33. Rana Foroohar, *Don't Be Evil*.

34. Jessica Dawson, "Microtargeting as Information Warfare," 6(1) *Cyber Defense Review* (2021): 63.

35. Keach Hagey and Jeff Horwitz, "Facebook Tried to Make Its Platform a Healthier Place."

36. Ibid.

37. Ibid.

38. Facebook for Business, "About Ads about Social Issues, Elections or Politics," accessed January 4, 2022, https://www.facebook.com/business/help/167836590566506 ?id=288762101909005.

39. The OECD, for example, noted that small and medium-sized enterprises (SMEs) that are regarded as key engine for innovation account on average "for over 90% of the innovative firms" and "incur between 20% and 60% of business expenditures on product or process innovation." "OECD SME and Entrepreneurship Outlook 2019," https://www.oecd-ilibrary.org/sites/34907e9c-en/1/2/2/6/index.html?itemId=/content /publication/34907e9c-en&_csp_=97b1ca7ff34abaf04c3b6ec7089258c9&itemIGO =oecd&itemContentType=book.

40. Economic Innovation Group, "Dynamism in Retreat," https://eig.org/dynamism.

41. "In 1982, young firms [those five years old or younger] accounted for about half of all firms, and one-fifth of total employment," observed Jason Furman, chairman, Council of Economic Advisers. But by 2013, these figures fell "to about one-third of firms and one-tenth of total employment." Speech: Jason Furman, chairman, Council of Economic Advisers, "Beyond Antitrust: The Role of Competition Policy in Promoting Inclusive Growth," Searle Center Conference on Antitrust Economics and Competition Policy, Chicago, IL (September 16, 2016). Also note: Jonathan B. Baker, "Market Power in the U.S. Economy Today," Washington Center for Equitable Growth (March 2017), http://equitablegrowth.org/research-analysis/market-power-in-the-u-s-economy-today/.

42. Leigh Buchanan, "American Entrepreneurship Is Actually Vanishing. Here's Why," Inc., https://www.inc.com/magazine/201505/leigh-buchanan/the-vanishing-startups-in-decline.html.

43. House Report, 47 (citing John Haltiwanger et al., "Declining Business Dynamism in the U.S. High-Technology Sector").

44. IMF Staff Discussion Note, "Rising Corporate Market Power: Emerging Policy Issues" (March 2021), https://www.vbb.com/media/Insights_Articles/SDNEA202101.pdf.

45. Insights based on: Ufuk Akcigit and Sina T. Ates, "Ten Facts on Declining Business Dynamism and Lessons from Endogenous Growth Theory," NBER Working Paper 25755 (April 2019); Ufuk Akcigit and Sina T. Ates, "What Happened to U.S. Business Dynamism?," NBER Working Paper 25756 (May 2019).

46. *Verizon Communications Inc. v. Law Offices of Curtis V. Trinko, LLP*, 540 U.S. 398, 407 (2004).

47. House Report, 47.

48. Commission Staff Working Document, "Impact Assessment Report—Accompanying the Document Proposal for a Regulation of the European Parliament and of the Council on Contestable and Fair Markets in the Digital Sector (Digital Markets Act)," COM (2020): 842 final, at point 92.

49. Federico J. Díez, Daniel Leigh, and Suchanan Tambunlertchai, "Global Market Power and Its Macroeconomic Implications," IMF Working Paper WP/18/137 (June 2018), https://www.imf.org/en/Publications/WP/Issues/2018/06/15/Global-Market-Power-and-its-Macroeconomic-Implications-45975; Gustavo Grullon, Yelena Larkin, and Roni Michaely, "Are US Industries Becoming More Concentrated?," 23(4) *Review of Finance* (2019): 697, https://academic.oup.com/rof/article/23/4/697/5477414?login=true; Germán Gutiérrez and Thomas Philippon, "Declining Competition and Investment in the U.S," NBER Working Paper No. 23583 (July 2017), https://www.nber.org/papers/w23583. The paper used a mixture of firm- and industry-level data to test the implications of higher US and foreign competition on both leader and industry investment. To test the idea that firms that do not face the threat of entry have less incentive to invest and innovate, the study used Chinese import exposure. Industries "most affected by Chinese competition saw a decline in the number of domestic firms,

but at the same time, leaders in these industries increased investment the most." Firms "in industries with higher excess entry in the 1990's invested more in the 2000's, after controlling for firm fundamentals."

50. Philippe Aghion et al., "Competition and Innovation: An Inverted-U Relationship," 120 *Quarterly Journal of Economics* (2005): 720, 701–28, https://www.ucl.ac.uk /~uctp39a/ABBGH_QJE_2005.pdf; Philippe Aghion, Ufuk Akcigit, and Peter Howitt, "The Schumpeterian Growth Paradigm," 7 *Annual Review of Economics* (2015): 557–75, https://www.annualreviews.org/doi/abs/10.1146/annurev-economics-080614 -115412; Kenneth. J. Arrow, "Economic Welfare and the Allocation of Resources for Invention," in Richard Nelson, *The Rate and Direction of Inventive Activity: Economic and Social Factors Princeton* (Princeton, NJ: Princeton University Press, 1982); Morton I. Kamien and Nancy L. Schwartz, "On the Degree of Rivalry for Maximum Innovative Activity," 90 *Quarterly Journal of Economics* (1976): 245–60.

51. Keach Hagey and Tripp Mickle, "Google Charges Over Twice Its Rivals in Ad Fees, Suit Shows," *Wall Street Journal* (October 22, 2021), https://www.wsj.com/articles /google-charges-more-than-twice-its-rivals-in-ad-deals-wins-80-of-its-own-auctions -court-documents-say-11634912297.

52. Stacy Mitchell and Olivia LaVecchia, "Amazon's Stranglehold," Institute for Local Self-Reliance (November 2016), https://ilsr.org/wp-content/uploads/2020/04/ILSR _AmazonReport_final.pdf.

53. Alphabet 2020, 10-K, 17.

54. Dan Milmo, "Facebook Whistleblower Accuses Firm of Serially Misleading over Safety," *Guardian* (October 5, 2021), https://www.theguardian.com/technology /2021/oct/05/facebook-whistleblower-accuses-firm-of-serially-misleading-over -safety; Dan Milmo, "Five Questions in Westminster for Facebook Whistleblower Frances Haugen," *Guardian* (October 25, 2021), https://www.theguardian.com /technology/2021/oct/25/five-questions-in-westminster-for-facebook-whistleblower -frances-haugen.

55. Video: "Tristan Harris—Facebook's Danger to Society" (October 6, 2021), https:// www.youtube.com/watch?v=qMcyuiMEEXs.

56. Craig Timberg, "New Whistleblower Claims Facebook Allowed Hate, Illegal Activity to Go Unchecked," *Washington Post* (October 22, 2021), https://www.washingtonpost .com/technology/2021/10/22/facebook-new-whistleblower-complaint/.

Chapter 8: The Innovation Narrative

1. "Why Americans Don't Fully Trust Many Who Hold Positions of Power and Responsibility," Pew Research Center (September 19, 2019), https://www.people -press.org/2019/09/19/why-americans-dont-fully-trust-many-who-hold-positions -of-power-and-responsibility/.

2. Alice Dechêne, Christoph Stahl, and Jochim Hansen, "The Truth about the Truth: A Meta-Analytic Review of the Truth Effect," 14(2) *Personality and Social Psychology Review* (December 18, 2009): 238, https://journals.sagepub.com/doi

/abs/10.1177/1088868309352251; *Walker, Jr. v. Gill*, No. 2162016CV00316, 2018 WL 3326517, at *8 (N.H. Super. April 12, 2018) (providing the historical context of the phrase "If you repeat a lie often enough, people will believe it, and you will even come to believe it yourself" to the Publications Relating to Various Aspects of Communism [1946]; United States Congress, House Committee on Un-American Activities, Issues 1–15, 19).

3. Tom Stafford, "How Liars Create the 'Illusion of Truth,'" *BBC—Future* (October 26, 2016), https://www.bbc.com/future/article/20161026-how-liars-create-the-illusion-of-truth.

4. *Williamson v. United States*, 512 U.S. 594, 599–600, 114 S. Ct. 2431, 2435, 129 L. Ed. 2d 476 (1994) (observing "One of the most effective ways to lie is to mix false-hood with truth, especially truth that seems particularly persuasive because of its self-inculpatory nature").

5. *Epic Games v. Apple*, 2020 WL 7012286 (N.D. Cal.).

6. For some of these other app stores, see: "Ultimate Mobile App Stores List (2021)," BuildFire, https://buildfire.com/mobile-app-stores-list/.

7. Hila Lifshitz-Assaf and Frank Nagle, "The Digital Economy Runs on Open Source. Here's How to Protect It," *Harvard Business Review* (September 2, 2021), https://hbr.org/2021/09/the-digital-economy-runs-on-open-source-heres-how-to-protect-it.

8. Ibid. (Noting how Amazon took a version of Elasticsearch that Elastic had made open source, repackaged it, and sold it to their customers under nearly the same name. Elastic argued that essentially Amazon took free code that created value for the whole community and walled it off so that they were the only ones who could capture value from it.)

9. Tim Wu, "Bell Labs and Centralized Innovation," 54(5) *Communications of the ACM* (May 2011): 31–33.

10. Ibid.

11. Press Release (European Commission): "Antitrust: Commission Sends Statement of Objections to Apple on App Store Rules for Music Streaming Providers."

12. Dan Gallagher, "Apple Has Two Trillion Reasons to Fight for the App Store," *Wall Street Journal* (May 3, 2021), https://www.wsj.com/articles/apple-has-two-trillion-reasons-to-fight-for-the-app-store-11620039781.

13. *Epic Games v. Apple*, slip op. at 41.

14. Press Release (European Commission): "Antitrust: Commission Sends Statement of Objections."

15. John Stuart Mill, *On Liberty* (New York: Sterling Publishing, 2004): 121.

16. John Van Reenen, "Can Innovation Policy Restore Inclusive Prosperity in America?," Aspen Economic Strategy Group (November 21, 2019): 121, https://www.economicstrategygroup.org/publication/can-innovation-policy-restore-inclusive-prosperity-in-america/.

17. Ibid.

18. Ibid., 119.

19. See, e.g., Ekaterina Turkina, Boris Oreshkin, and Raja Kali, "Regional Innovation Clusters and Firm Innovation Performance: An Interactionist Approach," 53(8) *Regional Studies* (March 2019): 1193, https://www.tandfonline.com/doi/abs/10.1080 /00343404.2019.1566697.

20. Abby Monteil, "50 Inventions You Might Not Know Were Funded by the US Government," Stacker (December 9, 2020), https://stacker.com/stories/5483/50-inventions -you-might-not-know-were-funded-us-government.

21. Mariana Mazzucato, *The Value of Everything*, 196.

22. Ibid., 191.

23. Ibid.

24. John Stuart Mill, *On Liberty*, 123.

25. Ibid.

26. Thomas Philippon, *The Great Reversal—How America Gave Up on Free Markets* (Cambridge, MA: Harvard University Press, 2019): 256.

27. Alphabet 2020 10-K, 39; Microsoft 2021 10-K, 42.

28. Facebook 2020 10-K, 64 ("Research and development expenses consist primarily of salaries and benefits, share-based compensation, and facilities-related costs for employees on our engineering and technical teams who are responsible for building new products as well as improving existing products.") and 65 (of the $18.447 billion in R&D expenses for 2020, $4.918 billion was for share-based compensation expenses).

29. Apple 2018 10-K, 38 ($2.668 billion of $14.236 billion in R&D expenses).

30. Annex A, available online: https://www.mauricestucke.com/chart.

31. Anuraag Singh, Giorgio Triulzi, and Christopher L. Magee, "Technological Improvement Rate Predictions for All Technologies: Use of Patent Data and an Extended Domain Description," 50(9) *Research Policy* (2021): 104294 (finding from its dataset contains all patents issued by USPTO from 1976 to 2015 for which valid U.S. Patent Classification system and International Patent Classification).

32. Jonathan B. Baker, *The Antitrust Paradigm: Restoring a Competitive Economy* (Cambridge, MA: Harvard University Press, 2019): 167 (noting that "when the dominant firm views R&D rivalry as a strategic complement it will have a postmerger incentive to channel the acquired firm's R&D capabilities into developing complementary products for those of the dominant firm rather than substitute products. As a result, buyers will have fewer substitutes to choose from, and the merged firm's products will face less competition.").

33. Speech: Margrethe Vestager at OECD's conference on competition and the digital economy (June 3, 2019), https://ec.europa.eu/commission/commissioners/2014-2019 /vestager/announcements/competition-and-digital-economy_en.

34. Ibid.

35. *Epic Games v. Apple*, No. 4:20-cv-05640-YGR, Slip op., 1 (N.D. Cal September 10, 2021).

36. Alphabet 2020 10-K, 7.

37. Facebook 2020 10-K, 7.

38. David S. Evans, "Why the Dynamics of Competition for Online Platforms Leads to Sleepless Nights but Not Sleepy Monopolies," SSRN (July 25, 2017), http://dx.doi.org/10.2139/ssrn.3009438.

39. Holman W. Jenkins, "Google and the Search for the Future—The Web Icon's CEO on the Mobile Computing Revolution, the Future of Newspapers, and Privacy in the Digital Age," *Wall Street Journal* (August 14, 2010), https://www.wsj.com/articles/SB10001424052748704901104575423294099527212.

40. Apple 2020 10-K, 7.

41. *United States v. E. I. du Pont de Nemours & Co.*, 351 U.S. 377, 420, 76 S. Ct. 994, 1020, 100 L. Ed. 1264 (1956) (Warren, C.J., dissenting).

42. Geoffrey West, *Scale: The Universal Laws of Growth, Innovation, Sustainability, and the Pace of Life in Organisms, Cities, Economies, and Companies* (London: Penguin Press, 2018): 402.

43. Michael A. Cusumano, Annabelle Gawer, and David B. Yoffie, *The Business of Platforms: Strategy in the Age of Digital Competition, Innovation, and Power* (New York: HarperCollins, 2019), 108.

44. "Desktop Operating System Market Share Worldwide, 2009–2021," Statcounter—Global Stats, accessed January 4, 2022, https://gs.statcounter.com/os-market-share/desktop/worldwide/#yearly-2009-2021.

45. "Largest Companies by Market Cap," accessed January 4, 2022, https://companiesmarketcap.com.

46. *Verizon Commc'ns Inc. v. Law Offices of Curtis V. Trinko, LLP*, 540 U.S. 398, 407, 124 S. Ct. 872, 879, 157 L. Ed. 2d 823 (2004); Giulo Federico, "Horizontal Mergers, Innovation and the Competitive Process," 8(10) *Journal of European Competition Law & Practice* (2017), 668.

47. *Verizon v. Trinko.*

48. Facebook, Inc.'s Motion to Dismiss FTC's Complaint, filed in *FTC v. Facebook Inc.*, No. 1:20-cv-03590-JEB (D.D.C. October 3, 2021), 23 (quoting dicta to successfully dismiss the FTC's monopolization complaint).

49. Computer & Communications Industry Association (CCIA) White Paper, "National Security Issues Posed by House Antitrust Bills" (2021), https://www.ccianet.org/wp-content/uploads/2021/09/CCIA-KS-NatSec-White-Paper.pdf.

50. Jonathan B. Baker, *The Antitrust Paradigm*, 172 (noting the economic argument for patents is "the ability of patent holders to exclude others allows them to earn a greater profit by appropriating a larger share of social gains from their innovations, a prospect that provides would-be innovators with incentives for R&D investment").

51. Kenneth. J. Arrow, "Economic Welfare and the Allocation of Resources for Invention," in Richard R. Nelson, *The Rate and Direction of Inventive Activity: Economic and Social Factors* (Princeton, NJ: Princeton University Press, 1982): 609–26.

52. Consider discussion in chapters 1 and 2, and note: Frank Crowley and Declan Jordan, "Does More Competition Increase Business-Level Innovation? Evidence from Domestically Focused Firms in Emerging Economies," 26(5) *Economics of Innovation and*

New Technology (2017): 38–49, https://www.tandfonline.com/doi/abs/10.1080/104 38599.2016.1233627; Richard Blundell, Rachel Griffith, and John van Reenen, "Market Share, Market Value and Innovation in a Panel of British Manufacturing Firms," 66(3) *Review of Economic Studies* (1999): 529–54, https://academic.oup.com/restud /article-abstract/66/3/529/1575508.

53. Jonathan B. Baker, *The Antitrust Paradigm*, 27–28.

54. High levels of competition can decrease the rate of innovation (the bottom of the inverted U), a decrease in competition (from an initial high position) increases the rate of creation, but then innovation declines as competition lessens to the point of monopoly; Philippe Aghion, et al., "Competition and Innovation: An Inverted-U Relationship," 120(2) *Quarterly Journal of Economics* (2005): 720, 701–28, https://www .ucl.ac.uk/~uctp39a/ABBGH_QJE_2005.pdf (suggesting that competition may increase the incremental profit from innovating [the "escape-competition effect"] but may also reduce innovation incentives for laggards [the "Schumpeterian effect"]). See also: Philippe Aghion, Ufuk Akcigit, and Peter Howitt, "The Schumpeterian Growth Paradigm," 7 *Annual Review of Economics* (2015): 557–75; and more generally, Morton I. Kamien and Nancy L. Schwartz, "On the Degree of Rivalry for Maximum Innovative Activity," 90 *Quarterly Journal of Economics* (1976): 245.

55. See, e.g., Jonathan B. Baker, *The Antitrust Paradigm*, 28 (noting that the earlier inverted U studies "were not reliable because they did not successfully control for differences in technological opportunity across industries").

56. Mitsuru Igami and Kosuke Uetake, "Mergers, Innovation, and Entry-Exit Dynamics: Consolidation of the Hard Disk Drive Industry, 1996–2016," 87(6) *Review of Economic Studies* (2020): 2672–702, https://academic.oup.com/restud/article -abstract/87/6/2672/5568308.

57. Jonathan B. Baker, *The Antitrust Paradigm*, 28.

58. Arora Ashish et al., "The Changing Structure of American Innovation: Some Cautionary Remarks for Economic Growth," NBER Working Paper 25893 (May 2019).

59. Video: "Declining Competition: A Transatlantic Challenge," https://vimeo.com /523765033#t=21m23s.

60. The reality is that for Tencent, the world's largest video game company by revenue, minors account for a small percentage of its revenues. Most revenues come from adults.

61. On the competition between Tech Barons, across industries, see: Nicolas Petit, "Technology Giants, the Moligopoly Hypothesis and Holistic Competition: A Primer," *SSRN* (2016), http://dx.doi.org/10.2139/ssrn.2856502; Nicolas Petit, *Big Tech and the Digital Economy: The Moligopoly Scenario* (Oxford: Oxford University Press, 2020).

62. Facebook, Inc. (FB), "First Quarter 2021 Results Conference Call" (April 28, 2021).

63. Allison Prang, "Mark Zuckerberg's Net Worth Drops by $31 Billion. He's Now the 10th Richest Person in the World," *Wall Street Journal* (Feb. 4, 2022).

64. Likewise, Google announced allowing its leading browser Chrome to remove support for third-party cookies. David Temkin, "Google Charts a Course towards a More

Privacy-First Web," blog.google (March 3, 2021), https://blog.google/products/ads
-commerce/a-more-privacy-first-web/; Chetna Bindra, "Building a Privacy-First Future
for Web Advertising," blog.google (January 25, 2021), https://blog.google/products
/ads-commerce/2021-01-privacy-sandbox/.

65. "Tech Competition: The Rules of the Tech Game Are Changing," *Economist* (February 27, 2021).

66. Note the OECD event on "Competition Economics of Digital Ecosystems," with contributions from Professors Amelia Fletcher, Marc Bourreau, Daniel A. Crane, Georgios Petropoulos, Nicolas Petit, and David J. Teece. Available online: https://www.oecd.org/daf/competition/competition-economics-of-digital-ecosystems.htm.

67. Lance Whitney, "Apple, Google, Others Settle Antipoaching Lawsuit for $415 Million," CNET (September 3, 2015), https://www.cnet.com/news/apple-google-others-settle-anti-poaching-lawsuit-for-415-million/.

68. Daisuke Wakabayashi and Jack Nicas, "Apple, Google and a Deal That Controls the Internet," *New York Times* (October 25, 2020), https://www.nytimes.com/2020/10/25/technology/apple-google-search-antitrust.html.

69. Australian Competition and Consumer Commission (ACCC) "Digital Platforms Inquiry—Final Report" (July 26, 2019): 10, 30 (recommending changes to search engine and internet browser defaults so that Google provides Australian users of Android devices with the same options being rolled out to existing Android users in Europe: the ability to choose their default search engine and default internet browser from a number of options); UK Competition and Markets Authority (CMA) "Online Platforms and Digital Advertising Market Study—Final Report" (July 1, 2020), para. 89 and para. 3,106 (finding that in 2019, Google paid Apple £1.2 billion for default positions in the UK alone, which represented over 17 percent of Google's total annual search revenues in the UK).

70. Apple 2019 Form 10-K.

71. Bennett Cyphers, "Google's FloC Is a Terrible Idea," Electronic Frontier Foundation (March 3, 2021), https://www.eff.org/deeplinks/2021/03/googles-floc-terrible-idea; Eerke Boitn, "Google's Scrapping Third-Party Cookies—but Invasive Targeted Advertising Will Live On," *The Conversation* (March 8, 2021), https://theconversation.com/googles-scrapping-third-party-cookies-but-invasive-targeted-advertising-will-live-on-156530.

72. Laurie Clarke, Oscar Williams, and Katharine Swindells, "How Google Quietly Funds Europe's Leading Tech Policy Institutes," *New Statesman* (July 30, 2021), https://www.newstatesman.com/science-tech/big-tech/2021/07/how-google-quietly-funds-europe-s-leading-tech-policy-institutes; Brody Mullins and Jack Nicas, "Paying Professors: Inside Google's Academic Influence Campaign," *Wall Street Journal* (July 14, 2017), https://www.wsj.com/articles/paying-professors-inside-googles-academic-influence-campaign-1499785286.

73. "Big Tech's Backdoor to the FTC," Tech Transparency Project (March 2021): 8, https://www.techtransparencyproject.org/sites/default/files/Big-Techs-Backdoor-to-the-FTC_031221.pdf.

74. Ibid.

75. Ibid.

76. David McLaughlin, "One Tech-Funded University Helped Shape FTC's Hands-off Approach," *Bloomberg Businessweek* (March 12, 2021), https://www.bloomberg.com /news/articles/2021-03-12/how-george-mason-university-shaped-ftc-s-hands-off -approach-to-tech.

77. Daisuke Wakabayashi, "Big Tech Funds a Think Tank Pushing for Fewer Rules. For Big Tech," *New York Times* (July 24, 2020), https://www.nytimes.com/2020/07/24 /technology/global-antitrust-institute-google-amazon-qualcomm.html.

78. "Proposals to Address Gatekeeper Power and Lower Barriers to Entry Online," Subcommittee on Antitrust, Commercial, and Administrative Law Hearing (February 25, 2021), https://judiciary.house.gov/calendar/eventsingle.aspx?EventID=4382.

79. Ibid.

80. "Report: Google Academics Inc.," Tech Transparency Project (July 11, 2017), https:// www.techtransparencyproject.org/articles/google-academics-inc.

81. Daisuke Wakabayashi, "Big Tech Funds a Think Tank."

Chapter 9: Current Antitrust Enforcement

1. Statement by Jeffrey P. Bezos, founder and chief executive officer, Amazon before the U.S. House of Representatives, Committee on the Judiciary, Subcommittee on Antitrust, Commercial, and Administrative Law (July 29, 2020), https://docs .house.gov/meetings/JU/JU05/20200729/110883/HHRG-116-JU05-Wstate -BezosJ-20200729.pdf.

2. Testimony of Mark Zuckerberg, Facebook, Inc., before the United States House of Representatives, Committee on the Judiciary, Subcommittee on Antitrust, Commercial, and Administrative Law (July 29, 2020), https://docs.house.gov/meetings/JU /JU05/20200729/110883/HHRG-116-JU05-Wstate-ZuckerbergM-20200729.pdf.

3. OECD Policy Roundtable, "Competition, Patents and Innovation 2006," https:// www.oecd.org/daf/competition/39888509.pdf.

4. U.S. Department of Justice and the Federal Trade Commission, "Horizontal Merger Guidelines" (August 19, 2010) § 6.4; see also: EU Guidelines on the assessment of horizontal mergers OJ (2004) C 31/5, 8. ("Effective competition brings benefits to consumers, such as low prices, high quality products, a wide selection of goods and services, and innovation.")

5. "Start-ups, Killer Acquisitions and Merger Control—Note by the United States," OECD DAF/COMP/WD(2020)23 (June 11, 2020), https://www.justice.gov/atr /page/file/1316551/download.

6. U.S. Department of Justice and the Federal Trade Commission, "Horizontal Merger Guidelines" (August 19, 2010): 2 ("enhanced market power can also be manifested in non-price terms and conditions that adversely affect customers, including reduced product quality, reduced product variety, reduced service, or diminished innovation. Such non-price effects may coexist with price effects, or can arise in their absence.

When the Agencies investigate whether a merger may lead to a substantial lessening of non-price competition, they employ an approach analogous to that used to evaluate price competition."); EC Guidelines on the Assessment of Horizontal Mergers under the Council Regulation on the control of concentrations between undertakings, 2004/C 31/03, para 8 (likewise noting that "effective competition brings benefits to consumers, such as low prices, high quality products, a wide selection of goods and services, and innovation").

7. US Horizontal Merger Guidelines, § 6.4.

8. FTC Complaint, *FTC v. Facebook, Inc.*, No. 1:20-cv-03590 (D.D.C. December 9, 2020), para. 72.

9. "Start-ups, Killer Acquisitions and Merger Control—Note by the United States," para. 43.

10. "Unlocking Digital Competition: Report of the UK Digital Competition Expert Panel" (March 2019), para. 3.43 (noting that "there have been no false positives in mergers involving the major digital platforms, for the simple reason that all of them have been permitted").

11. "Start-ups, Killer Acquisitions and Merger Control—Note by the United States," OECD DAF/COMP/WD(2020)23, para 14 (June 11, 2020), https://www.justice .gov/atr/page/file/1316551/download.

12. See, e.g., *Google/ITA*. *Google/Fitbit*. *Microsoft/LinkedIn*.

13. Jonathan B. Baker, *The Antitrust Paradigm*, 151 (noting how enforcement agencies identify innovation issues in one-third of their merger challenges, almost always along with other concerns not involving innovation, and that mergers taking place in R&D-intensive industries are almost always flagged for innovation concerns, but that these statistics overstate the extent of enforcement attention. Half the time innovation comes up, the agencies simply mention innovation without elaboration. And while the agencies have lately shown interest in innovation issues, the courts have not yet grappled with the mechanisms by which mergers can harm innovation.).

14. OECD Background Note: "Start-ups, Killer Acquisitions and Merger Control" (2020): 16, www.oecd.org/daf/competition/start-ups-killer-acquisitions-and-merger-control-2020.pdf, citing Axel Gautier and Joe Lamesch, "Mergers in the Digital Economy," CESifo Working Paper No. 8056 (2020), https://ssrn.com/abstract=3529012.

15. Section 7 of the Clayton Act prohibits an acquisition "where in any line of commerce or in any activity affecting commerce in any section of the country, the effect of such acquisition may be substantially to lessen competition," 15 U.S.C. § 18. The term "may be" in the statute requires only "an appreciable danger" of harm to competition, *United States v. H&R Block, Inc.*, 833 F. Supp. 2d 36, 49 (D.D.C. 2011) (quotation omitted).

16. *United States v. Energy Solutions*, 265 F. Supp. 3d 415, 436 (D. Del. 2017).

17. David I. Gelfand, "Preserving Competition the Only Solution, Evolve," Speech, Loyola 2015 Antitrust Colloquium (April 24, 2015), https://www.justice.gov/atr /file/518896/download; Video: "Declining Competition: A Transatlantic Challenge" (March 15, 2021), https://vimeo.com/523765033#t=21m23s%20(at%201:34).

18. *U.S. v. Kimberly-Clark Corp. and Scott Paper*, Civil No.: 3:95 CV 3055-P (December 12, 1995), https://www.justice.gov/atr/case-document/complaint-141.

19. Speech: Charles E. Biggio, "Merger Enforcement at the Antitrust Division," Before the Antitrust Law Committee, Chicago Bar Association (May 15, 1996), https://www .justice.gov/atr/speech/merger-enforcement-antitrust-division.

20. Speech: Constance K. Robinson, "Quantifying Unilateral Effects in Investigations and Cases," Before the George Mason Law Review Symposium, Antitrust in the Information Revolution: New Economic Approaches for Analyzing Antitrust Issues (October 11, 1996), https://www.justice.gov/atr/speech/quantifying-unilateral-effects -investigations-and-cases.

21. Speech: Charles A. James, "Rediscovering Coordinated Effects," American Bar Association Annual Meeting, Section of Antitrust Law (August 13, 2002): 7–8, http://www .justice.gov/atr/public/speeches/200124.pdf (noting "one interesting side-effect of the 1992 Guidelines has been the emergence of unilateral effects as the predominant theory of economic harm pursued in government merger investigations and challenges."); Malcolm B. Coate, "The Merger Review Process at the Federal Trade Commission from 1989 to 2016," SSRN (February 28, 2018), https://ssrn.com/abstract=2955987 (identifying for FTC mergers a trend toward unilateral effects analysis).

22. Malcolm B. Coate, "The Merger Review Process," 6.

23. Ibid., 18.

24. Richard R. Nelson and Sidney G. Winter, *An Evolutionary Theory of Economic Change* (Cambridge, MA: Harvard University Press, 1985): 370.

25. Bart Verspagen, "The Use of Modelling Tools for Policy in Evolutionary Environments," in Albert Faber et al., *Environmental Policy and Modelling in Evolutionary Economics* (2006): 6.

26. *Epic Games v. Apple*, No. 4:20-cv-05640-YGR, Slip op., 1 (N.D. Cal September 10, 2021).

27. Instead the agencies must use other non-price factors, which the European Commission and Bundeskartellamt have done in their cases against the Tech Barons. Likewise the district court agreed with the FTC that it "must plead specific facts regarding the price or non-price terms under which [personal social network]—service users would switch (if ever) to alternatives. Instead, *at this stage* the FTC may permissibly plead that certain 'factors' of both the service at issue and its potential substitutes—e.g., their 'price, use[,] and qualities'—render them not 'reasonably interchangeable' in the eyes of users." *FTC v. Facebook*, Case No. 1:20-cv-03590-JEB, slip op. at 24 (D.D.C. June 28, 2021) (emphasis added). It remains to be seen whether the district court will require proof of cross-elasticity of demand at the summary judgment or trial stage.

28. *Epic Games v. Apple*, 56–57.

29. OECD Background Note: "Start-ups, Killer Acquisitions and Merger Control," 10.

30. Jacques Crémer, Yves-Alexandre de Montjoye, and Heike Schweitzer, "Competition Policy for the digital Era—Final Report," European Commission (2019): 116–17 (suggesting that "there exists a gap in currently accepted theories of harm," the result

of which is that such transactions may go unchallenged despite early elimination of potential competitive threats).

31. *Epic Games v. Apple*, 35.

32. Ibid., 141.

33. Ibid., 41, 93.

34. Ibid., 100–4, 118.

35. Ibid., 139.

36. *FTC v. Facebook, Inc.*, No. 1:20-cv-03590 (D.D.C. June 28, 2021), *12.

37. *FTC v. Facebook, Inc.*, No. CV 20-3590 (JEB), 2022 WL 103308, at *1 (D.D.C. Jan. 11, 2022).

38. *United States v. Grinnell Corp.*, 384 U.S. 563, 571, 86 S. Ct. 1698, 1704, 16 L. Ed. 2d 778 (1966).

39. *Epic Games v. Apple*, 137 (noting that "Epic Games failed to produce evidence that this rate [of 30% which the court agreed was supra-competitive] has had any impact on the output of mobile gaming transactions.")

40. "Unfortunately, what is needed is a comparison of output in a 'but-for' world without the challenged restrictions. Such comparison is not in the record," *Epic Games v. Apple*, 99.

41. Lance Whitney, "Apple, Google, Others Settle Antipoaching Lawsuit for $415 Million," CNET (September 3, 2015), https://www.cnet.com/news/apple-google-others-settle-anti-poaching-lawsuit-for-415-million/.

42. Sarah E. Needleman and Tim Higgins, "Apple Denies Request by Epic to Bring 'Fortnite' Developer Account Back," *Wall Street Journal* (September 22, 2021), https://www.wsj.com/articles/epic-games-says-apple-won-t-reinstate-developer-account-11632331517.

43. Case AT.39740, *Google Search (Shopping)*.

44. Case AT.40099 *Google Android* (Commission received the first complaint on March 2013, opened a formal investigation on April 2015 and reached its decision in July 2018.); Case AT.40411, *Google Search (AdSense)* (Commission formal investigation was initiated in 2016 and resulted in a decision in 2019).

45. See: "Predictions for 2031 | Future Timeline," Quantumrun https://www.quantumrun.com/future-timeline/2031.

46. *In re Facebook, Inc.* (FTC File No. 1823109), Dissenting Statement of Commissioner Rebecca Kelly Slaughter (July 24, 2019) (she could not "view the [FTC] order as adequately deterrent without both meaningful limitations on how Facebook collects, uses, and shares data and public transparency regarding Facebook's data use and order compliance"), https://www.ftc.gov/system/files/documents/public_statements/1536918/182_3109_slaughter_statement_on_facebook_7-24-19.pdf.

47. *In re Facebook, Inc.* (FTC File No. 1823109), Dissenting Statement of Commissioner Rohit Chopra (July 24, 2019), https://www.ftc.gov/system/files/documents/public_statements/1536911/chopra_dissenting_statement_on_facebook_7-24-19.pdf [https://perma.cc/5U9N-SJN7].

48. OECD Background Note: "Start-ups, Killer Acquisitions and Merger Control."

49. Ibid., 3.

50. Malcolm B. Coate, "The Merger Review Process."

51. *Northern Pacific R. Co. v. United States,* 356 U.S. 1 (1958).

52. A Senate report stated that "the purpose of the proposed bill . . . is to limit future increases in the level of economic concentration resulting from corporate mergers and acquisitions." S. Rep. No. 1775, 81st Cong., 2d Sess. 3 (1950). A House report announced a similar purpose: "The bill is intended to permit intervention in such a cumulative process [of acquisitions] when the effect of an acquisition may be a significant reduction in the vigor of competition, even though this effect may not be so far-reaching as to amount to a combination in restraint of trade, create a monopoly or constitute an attempt to monopolize," H.R. Rep No. 1191, 81st Cong., 1st Sess. 8 (1949).

53. Robert H. Lande, "Wealth Transfers as the Original and Primary Concern of Antitrust: The Efficiency Interpretation Challenged," 34 *Hastings Law Journal* (1982): 65, 135–36, https://repository.uchastings.edu/hastings_law_journal/vol50/iss4/11/; Wesley A. Cann, "Section 7 of the Clayton Act and the Pursuit of Economic 'Objectivity': Is There Any Role for Social and Political Values in Merger Policy?," 60 *Notre Dame Law Review* (1985): 273, 278.

54. *United States v. Anthem, Inc.,* 236 F. Supp. 3d 171, 231 (D.D.C. 2017) (finding that the merger is likely to slow innovation in the market), affirmed, *United States v. Anthem, Inc.,* 855 F.3d 345 (D.C. Cir. 2017).

55. See for example concerns over horizontal overlaps between close innovators in Case M.7932 *Dow/DuPont*, European Commission, [2017] OJ C353/9.

56. Video: "Declining Competition: A Transatlantic Challenge," 1:47.

57. *United States v. Sabre Corp.,* 452 F. Supp. 3d 97, 148 (D. Del. 2020), vacated, No. 20-1767, 2020 WL 4915824 (3d Cir. July 20, 2020) (emphasis added). The parties abandoned the merger after the US appealed to the Third Circuit, which ultimately vacated the court's decision.

58. Ibid.

59. Video: "Declining Competition: A Transatlantic Challenge," 1:34.

60. OECD online event: "Competition Economics of Digital Ecosystems" (December 3, 2020, and February 24, 2021).

61. Press Release (US House of Representatives): "Nadler & Cicilline Statement on Federal Court's Dismissal of FTC Antitrust Suits Against Facebook," House Judiciary Committee (June 28, 2021), https://judiciary.house.gov/news/documentsingle.aspx?DocumentID=4626.

62. Leah Nylen, "Apple Wins Round One. Round Two Will Come from Washington," *Politico* (September 10, 2021), https://www.msn.com/en-us/news/technology/apple-wins-round-one-round-two-will-come-from-washington/ar-AAOjlSd.

63. Anna Edgerton, "Apple Ruling Shows Need for App Store Law, Lawmakers Say," Bloomberg (September 11, 2021), https://www.bloombergquint.com/politics/apple-ruling-underscores-need-for-app-store-bill-lawmakers-say.

Chapter 10: Pyrrhus, Ducks, and Proposed Reforms

1. "Antitrust Division (ATR)—2021 Budget Request," https://www.justice.gov/doj/page /file/1246781/download.
2. "America's 350 Largest Law Firms," Public Legal, https://www.ilrg.com/nlj250?page=3.
3. "Federal Trade Commission Congressional Budget Justification—Fiscal Year 2022," 4, https://www.ftc.gov/system/files/documents/reports/fy-2022-congressional-budget -justification/fy22cbj.pdf.
4. Video: Subcommittee on Competition Policy, Antitrust, and Consumer Rights, "Big Data, Big Questions: Implications for Competition and Consumers" (September 21, 2021): 2:05, https://www.judiciary.senate.gov/meetings/big-data-big-questions -implications-for-competition-and-consumers.
5. House Report, 7; see also ibid., 387. ("It is unclear whether the antitrust agencies are presently equipped to block anticompetitive mergers in digital markets. The record of the Federal Trade Commission and the Justice Department in this area shows significant missteps and repeat enforcement failures.")
6. Press Release (US FTC): "Nadler & Cicilline Statement on Federal Court's Dismissal of FTC Antitrust Suits Against Facebook."
7. Press Release (U.S. House of Representatives): "Chairman Nadler Applauds Committee Passage of Bipartisan Tech Antitrust Legislation" (June 24, 2021), https://judiciary .house.gov/news/documentsingle.aspx?DocumentID=4622.
8. Ibid.
9. Ibid.
10. Ibid.
11. Ibid.
12. Once an online platform is designated as a covered platform under the Act, it cannot own or control in a line of business other than the covered platform that (1) utilizes the covered platform for the sale or provision of products or services; (2) offers a product or service that the covered platform requires a business user to purchase or utilize as a condition for access to the covered platform, or as a condition for preferred status or placement of a business user's products or services on the covered platform; or (3) gives rise to a conflict of interest. A conflict of interest under the Act would include the conflict of interest that arises when (1) a covered platform operator owns or controls a line of business, other than the covered platform; and (2) the covered platform operator's ownership or control of that line of business creates the incentive and ability for the covered platform operator to (a) advantage the covered platform operator's own products, services, or lines of business on the covered platform over those of a competing business or a business that constitutes nascent or potential competition to the covered platform operator; or (b) exclude from, or disadvantage, the products, services, or lines of business on the covered platform of a competing business or a business that constitutes nascent or potential competition to the covered platform operator.
13. European Commission, "Proposal for a Regulation of the European Parliament and of

the Council on Contestable and Fair Markets in the Digital Sector (Digital Markets Act)," SEC(2020) 437 final (December 15, 2020), 2 (hereinafter Digital Markets Act).

14. Digital Markets Act, 33.

15. Press Release (Apple): "Japan Fair Trade Commission Closes App Store Investigation" (September 1, 2021), https://www.apple.com/newsroom/2021/09/japan-fair-trade -commission-closes-app-store-investigation/.

16. Ibid., 1.

17. Ibid., 10.

18. Ibid., 10.

19. Ibid., 5 (the Digital Markets Act would prohibit the gatekeepers "from using, in competition with business users, any data not publicly available, which is generated through activities by those business users, including by the end users of these business users, of its core platform services or provided by those business users of its core plat-form services or by the end users of these business users").

20. House Report, 392.

21. House Report, 399 (noting also that generally "false positives" are not more costly than "false negatives" for antitrust enforcement). See also: Jacques Crémer, Yves-Alexandre de Montjoye, and Heike Schweitzer, "Competition Policy for the Digital Era," 4, https://www.bibsonomy.org/bibtex/2f87b8251c8f49b69fd7bddedec8a7a49 /meneteqel: "The specific characteristics of many digital markets have arguably changed the balance of error cost and implementation costs, such that some modifica-tions of the established tests, including allocation of the burden of proof and definition of the standard of proof, may be called for. In particular, in the context of highly con-centrated markets characterized by strong network effects and high barriers to entry (i.e., not easily corrected by markets themselves), one may want to err on the side of disallowing potentially anti-competitive conducts, and impose on the incumbent the burden of proof for showing the pro-competitiveness of its conduct."

22. Jason Furman et al., "Unlocking Digital Competition—Independent Report of the UK Digital Competition Expert Panel" (March 13, 2019), https://www.gov.uk /government/publications/unlocking-digital-competition-report-of-the-digital -competition-expert-panel; ACCC "Digital Platforms Inquiry—Final Report," 30, 105 (recommending amending merger law to incorporate in the agency's assessment "(i) the likelihood that the acquisition would result in the removal from the market of a potential competitor; and (ii) the nature and significance of assets, including data and technology, being acquired directly or through the body corporate"); "Competi-tion and Antitrust Law Enforcement Reform Act of 2021," 117th Congress, https:// www.klobuchar.senate.gov/public/_cache/files/e/1/e171ac94-edaf-42bc-95ba -85c985a89200/375AF2AEA4F2AF97FB96DBC6A2A839F9.sil21191.pdf; Jacques Crémer, Yves-Alexandre de Montjoye, and Heike Schweitzer, "Competition Policy for the Digital Era."

23. "Competition and Antitrust Law Enforcement Reform Act of 2021," 117th Congress,

S. 225; House Report, 387–88, 394–95 (recommending clarifying that the agency would not have to prove that the nascent competitor would have been a successful entrant, but for the transaction; proposing "a presumption against acquisitions of startups by dominant firms, particularly those that serve as direct competitors, as well as those operating in adjacent or related markets" and shifting the burden to the dominant platform for other acquisitions, so that "any acquisition by a dominant platform would be presumed anticompetitive unless the merging parties could show that the transaction was necessary for serving the public interest and that similar benefits could not be achieved through internal growth and expansion"); Video: "Declining Competition: A Transatlantic Challenge," 1:40–1:45, (former top economist of the European Commission, Professor Tommaso Valletti, opining that as markets have become concentrated, there is an argument in favor of changing the benchmark and possibly introducing a structural presumption that is rebuttable).

24. House Report, 395–96 (recommending that "Congress explore presumptions involving vertical mergers, such as a presumption that vertical mergers are anticompetitive when either of the merging parties is a dominant firm operating in a concentrated market, or presumptions relating to input foreclosure and customer foreclosure").

25. Digital Markets Act, Article 12; ACCC "Digital Platforms Inquiry—Final Report," 10 (recommending that "the large digital platforms should each agree to a protocol to notify the ACCC of proposed acquisitions that may impact competition in Australia") and 109; House Report, 388 (recommending that the dominant platforms "be required to report all transactions and no HSR deadlines would be triggered").

26. Press Release (German Bundeskartellamt): "Amendment of the German Act against Restraints of Competition" (January 19, 2021), https://www.bundeskartellamt.de /SharedDocs/Meldung/EN/Pressemitteilungen/2021/19_01_2021_GWB%20 Novelle.html.

27. Ibid.

28. Digital Markets Act, Article 22 (proposing that the Commission in case of urgency due to the risk of serious and irreparable damage for business users or end users of gatekeepers, to order interim measures against a gatekeeper on the basis of a prima facie finding of an infringement of the DMA); for an example under current EU competition law, see Press Release: EU Commission "Antitrust: Commission Imposes Interim Measures on Broadcom in TV and Modem Chipset Markets" (October 16, 2019), and Bundeskartellamt.

29. When it has reasonable grounds for believing that competition is not working effectively in a market, the UK competition authority can use powers under its antitrust laws to obtain information and conduct research for "a wide consideration of issues affecting the market," including a range of outcomes, such as imposing orders to remedy anticompetitive effects, and issuing "recommendations to government, enforcement action and referral for market investigation." Press Release: UK Competition and Markets Authority, "CMA Launches Immediate Review of Audit Sector" (October 9, 2018).

30. "EU Proposal for New Competition Tool" (June 2, 2020), https://ec.europa.eu

/info/law/better-regulation/have-your-say/initiatives/12416-Single-Market-new
-complementary-tool-to-strengthen-competition-enforcement_en. Also note the Digital
Markets Act, Articles 15–17.

31. Digital Markets Act, 40; American Choice and Innovation Online Act, H.R. 3816
(subject to certain affirmative defenses, the Act prohibits the covered platforms from
using non-public data to offer, or support the offering of, the covered platform operator's own products, services, or lines of business that are obtained from or generated
on the covered platform (a) by the activities of a business user; or (b) through an interaction of a covered platform user with the products or services of a business user).

32. Digital Markets Act, Article 6(b) (allowing end users to uninstall any preinstalled software applications on its core platform service without prejudice to the possibility for
a gatekeeper to restrict such uninstallation in relation to software applications that are
essential for the functioning of the operating system or of the device and which cannot technically be offered on a standalone basis by third-parties); American Choice
and Innovation Online Act, H.R. 3816 (subject to certain affirmative defenses, the
Act prohibits the covered platforms from restricting or impeding their users from uninstalling software applications that have been preinstalled on the covered platform
or changing default settings that direct or steer covered platform users to products or
services offered by the covered platform operator; Digital Services Act (proposal, as
modified by the European Parliament) (Jan. 20, 2022)

33. American Choice and Innovation Online Act, H.R. 3816 (subject to certain affirmative defenses, the Act prohibits the covered platforms from conditioning access to the
covered platform or preferred status or placement on the covered platform on the purchase or use of other products or services offered by the covered platform operator).

34. Digital Markets Act, Article 6(d) (refraining the Tech Barons "from treating more fa-
vourably in ranking services and products offered by the gatekeeper itself or by any
third party belonging to the same undertaking compared to similar services or products of third party and apply fair and non-discriminatory conditions to such ranking"); American Choice and Innovation Online Act, H.R. 3816 (subject to certain
affirmative defenses, the Act prohibits powerful platforms "to engage in any conduct in
connection with the operation of the covered platform that (1) advantages the covered
platform operator's own products, services, or lines of business over those of another
business user; (2) excludes or disadvantages the products, services, or lines of business
of another business user relative to the covered platform operator's own products, services, or lines of business; or (3) discriminates among similarly situated business users"
and in connection with any user interface, including search or ranking functionality
offered by the covered platform, treat the covered platform operator's own products,
services, or lines of business more favorably than those of another business user; and
restricting or impeding a business user, or a business user's customers or users, from
interoperating or connecting to any product or service).

35. Digital Markets Act, Article 6(c) (allowing the installation and effective use of third
party software applications or software application stores using, or interoperating with,

operating systems of that gatekeeper and allow these software applications or software application stores to be accessed by means other than the core platform services of that gatekeeper. The gatekeeper shall not be prevented from taking proportionate measures to ensure that third party software applications or software application stores do not endanger the integrity of the hardware or operating system provided by the gatekeeper), and 6(f) (allowing business users and providers of ancillary services access to and interoperability with the same operating system, hardware or software features that are available or used in the provision by the gatekeeper of any ancillary services); American Choice and Innovation Online Act, H.R. 3816 (preventing covered platforms from restricting or impeding covered platform users from uninstalling software applications that have been preinstalled on the covered platform or changing default settings that direct or steer covered platform users to products or services offered by the covered platform operator).

36. Digital Markets Act, Article 6(e) (refraining the Tech Barons "from technically restricting the ability of end users to switch between and subscribe to different software applications and services to be accessed using the operating system of the gatekeeper, including as regards the choice of Internet access provider for end users"); Augmenting Compatibility and Competition by Enabling Service Switching (ACCESS) Act of 2021, H.R. 3849 (requiring a covered platform to maintain "a set of transparent, third-party-accessible interfaces [including application programming interfaces] to facilitate and maintain interoperability with a business user that complies with the standards issued" by the FTC under section 6(c) of the Act. The FTC must issue standards of interoperability specific to each covered platform that "seek to encourage entry by reducing or eliminating the network effects that limit competition with the covered platform, ensure that business users interconnect with the covered platform on fair and nondiscriminatory terms, and protect data security and privacy.").

37. Keith Sutton, "Break Bad Shooting Habits, Bag More Ducks," Ducks Unlimited, https://www.ducks.org/hunting/shooting-tips/break-bad-shooting-habits-bag-more-ducks.

38. Michael G. Jacobides, "Designing Digital Ecosystems," in Michael G. Jacobides, Arun Sundararajan, and Marshall Van Alstyne, "Platforms and Ecosystems: Enabling the Digital Economy," World Economic Forum, Briefing Paper (2019): 13–18, https://www3.weforum.org/docs/WEF_Digital_Platforms_and_Ecosystems_2019.pdf (noting "Ecosystems can be the tool to dislodge established incumbents and change the very definition of a sector, but they can also offer the means to reorganize, and to protect incumbent firms that find themselves under immense pressure to offer far-reaching solutions that encompass an ever-growing gamut of potential complementors. Younger and more established participants alike are keenly aware of the desirability to offer a 'one-stop shop' solution to cover all customers' needs.").

39. Terrence J. Sejnowski, *The Deep Learning Revolution*, 10.

40. As recalled by Eric Schmidt in an interview in 2011: Lillian Cunningham, "Google's Eric Schmidt Expounds on His Senate Testimony," *Washington Post* (October 1, 2011), https://www.washingtonpost.com/national/on-leadership/googles-eric-schmidt-expounds-on-his-senate-testimony/2011/09/30/gIQAPyVgCL_story.html.

41. Building upon Europe's extensive privacy framework, the proposed Digital Markets Act would allow Europeans to opt out of the gatekeepers' combining their personal data across their services and the data collected from third parties and require the powerful platforms to provide the Commission more information on how they are profiling individuals. Digital Markets Act Articles 5(a) (gatekeeper must refrain "from combining personal data sourced from these core platform services with personal data from any other services offered by the gatekeeper or with personal data from third-party services, and from signing in end users to other services of the gatekeeper in order to combine personal data, unless the end user has been presented with the specific choice and provided consent in the sense of Regulation (EU) 2016/679") and 13 (requiring gatekeeper to annually "submit to the Commission an independently audited description of any techniques for profiling of consumers that the gatekeeper applies to or across its core platform services identified pursuant to Article 3").

42. Interview with Cecilia Rikap.

43. Press Release (UK CMA): "UK's New Pro-Competition Regime for Digital Markets" (December 8, 2020), https://www.gov.uk/government/news/cma-advises-government-on-new-regulatory-regime-for-tech-giants.; "A New Pro-Competition Regime for Digital Markets" (July 20, 2021), https://www.gov.uk/government/consultations/a-new-pro-competition-regime-for-digital-markets.

44. Rani Molla, "Poll: Most Americans Want to Break Up Big Tech," *Vox* (January 26, 2021), https://www.vox.com/2021/1/26/22241053/antitrust-google-facebook-break-up-big-tech-monopoly.

45. Maurice E. Stucke and Ariel Ezrachi, *Competition Overdose*.

46. Brian Schwartz, "Big Tech Spends Over $20 Million on Lobbying in First Half of 2020, Including on Coronavirus Legislation," CNBC (July 31, 2020), https://www.cnbc.com/2020/07/31/big-tech-spends-20-million-on-lobbying-including-on-coronavirus-bills.html.

47. Anna Edgerton and Bill Allison, "Big Tech Spent Millions on Lobbying amid Antitrust Scrutiny," Bloomberg (July 21, 2021), https://www.bloomberg.com/news/articles/2021-07-21/big-tech-spent-millions-on-lobbying-amid-antitrust-scrutiny.

48. UNCTAD, "Digital Economy Report 2019: Value Creation and Capture–Implications for Developing Countries" (2019): 88, https://unctad.org/system/files/official-document/der2019_en.pdf.

49. Ben Brody, "Washington's Tech Issues Provide Lobbyists an Opening," *Protocol* (May 4, 2021), https://www.protocol.com/policy/washingtons-tech-issues-lobbyists.

50. "Pyrrhus, The Great King of Epirus," Greece High Definition (December 1, 2020), https://www.greecehighdefinition.com/blog/pyrrhus-king-of-epirus.

Chapter 11: The Way Forward

1. For more on recalibrating the privacy, consumer protection, and competition policies, see Maurice E. Stucke, *Breaking Away: How to Regain Control over Our Data, Privacy, and Autonomy* (Oxford: Oxford University Press, 2022).

2. Christian Hopp et al., "Disruptive Innovation," 446–57 (after surveying the literature on disruptive innovations noting many unanswered questions, including: How can potentially disruptive innovation be spotted? And how early can it be anticipated? Can disruptive innovations be separated from technological advancements that enable disruptive innovations? Will there be one candidate or multiple candidates of innovations than can be potentially disruptive? How can we predict the impact of multiple potentially disruptive innovations relative to each other, and in comparison to the prevailing business model an incumbent employs?).

3. The most creative individuals, according to one study, were those with broad, diverse social networks: those with diverse, horizontal networks were "three times more innovative than uniform, vertical networks." Steven Johnson, *Where Good Ideas Come From*, 166 (discussing Martin Ruef's studies).

4. OECD, "Science, Technology and Innovation Outlook 2021" (January 12, 2021), https://www.oecd-ilibrary.org/science-and-technology/oecd-science-technology-and-innovation-outlook-2021_75f79015-en.

5. Speech: Margrethe Vestager, "Technology with Purpose" (March 5, 2020), https://ec.europa.eu/commission/commissioners/2019-2024/vestager/announcements/technology-purpose_en.

6. Mariana Mazzucato, *The Value of Everything*, 206.

7. *Sears, Roebuck & Co. v. Stiffel Co.*, 376 U.S. 225, 84 S.Ct. 784, 11 L.Ed.2d 661 (1964).

8. John Van Reenen, "Can Innovation Policy Restore Inclusive Prosperity in America?"

9. However, note that in themselves tax incentives will often form an insufficient instrument to guide innovation. See: OECD, "Science, Technology and Innovation Outlook 2021."

10. John Van Reenen, "Can Innovation Policy Restore Inclusive Prosperity in America?"; Delio Ignacio Castaneda and Sergio Cuellar, "Knowledge Sharing and Innovation: A Systematic Review," 159–73 (noting the research on the role of universities in knowledge transfer for the generation of technological innovation and patent licenses, the importance of knowledge exchange between government and academy, and the relevance of networks in innovation dissemination).

11. Interview with Romain Duval, assistant director at the International Monetary Fund.

12. Geoffrey West, *Scale*, 29.

13. The larger city requires a bit less infrastructure per capita (by about .85), which means when a city doubles in population, it will need only 85 percent more gas stations and is thus a bit more productive (around 15 percent). Ibid., 29, 272 (noting that cities scale sublinearly with size, indicating a systematic economy of scale, but with an exponent of about 0.85 rather than 0.75 for living organisms).

14. "The Hidden Maths of Organisms, Cities, and Companies," *Economist* (May 13, 2017), https://www.economist.com/books-and-arts/2017/05/11/the-hidden-maths-of-organisms-cities-and-companies.

15. Geoffrey West, *Scale*, 322. Another contributing factor might be greater diversity. As a city's population doubles, it will not necessarily require double the population of

engineers. As their population grows, cities scale *sub*linearly for infrastructure and energy use (mean they require relatively less—about 15 percent—when their population increases), but scale *super*linearly for socioeconomic activity (so they become more creative, innovate more, and make more by about 15 percent). That potentially means greater diversity in professions and artisans, and greater opportunities for collisions of diverse ideas and fields.

16. Ekaterina Turkina, Boris Oreshkin, and Raja Kali, "Regional Innovation Clusters and Firm Innovation Performance" (citing Rafael Boix and Vittorio Galletto, "Innovation and Industrial Districts: A First Approach to the Measurement and Determinants of the I-District Effect," 43(9) *Regional Studies* (2009): 1117–33; Steven Johnson, *Where Good Ideas Come From*, 163.

17. Michael B. Sauter, "5 Cities Have Lost Half or More of Their Populations Since 1950," 24/7 Wall St (June 7, 2019), https://247wallst.com/special-report/2019/06/07/5-cities-have-lost-half-or-more-of-their-populations-since-1950/2/.

18. Geoffrey West, *Scale*, 32.

19. Ekaterina Turkina, Boris Oreshkin, and Raja Kali, "Regional Innovation Clusters and Firm Innovation Performance" (citing the business literature of the industry life cycle and a firm's organization and innovative activity change during the cycle).

20. Arthur Fishman, Hadas Don-Yehiya, and Amnon Schreiber, "Too Big to Succeed or Too Big to Fail?," 811–22 (noting that "empirically, the consensus is that R&D activity does indeed increase with firm size, but only proportionately (Cohen, 2010). This finding suggests that, contrary to Schumpeter (1942), large size offers no advantage in the conduct of R&D since, holding industry sales constant, the same amount of R&D will be conducted whether an industry is composed of large firms or a greater number of smaller firms.").

21. Geoffrey West, *Scale*, at 33.

22. Interview with Professor Richard Florida.

23. Sarah Jacobs, "10 American Cities That Have Fallen into Decline," *Business Insider* (January 14, 2018), https://www.businessinsider.com/us-census-data-population-decrease-shows-american-cities-in-decline-2018-1#9-scranton-pennsylvanias-population-has-declined-from-its-peak-by-469-2.

24. Ekaterina Turkina, Boris Oreshkin, and Raja Kali, "Regional Innovation Clusters and Firm Innovation Performance," 1193–1206 (noting the consensus "that a high degree of similarity among firms located in the region is not a good thing either since it decreases the probability of more radical innovations that strengthen the cluster's ability to adapt to changing external conditions").

25. Ekaterina Turkina, Boris Oreshkin, and Raja Kali, "Regional Innovation Clusters and Firm Innovation Performance" (citing studies that "emphasize socially driven mechanisms in clusters such as networking among firms, universities, regional authorities and research institutions that ensure collaboration and enable the sharing of resources and knowledge on specific projects").

26. Grant Miles, Charles C. Snow, and Mark P. Sharfman, "Industry Variety and Performance,"

14(3) *Strategic Management Journal* (1993): 163, 166–72, https://onlinelibrary.wiley
.com/doi/abs/10.1002/smj.4250140302. The study also found that such variety decreased
as the industry matured and declined. Ibid., 172.

27. Ekaterina Turkina, Boris Oreshkin, and Raja Kali, "Regional Innovation Clusters and
Firm Innovation Performance."

28. Leyland Cecco, "Toronto Swaps Google-Backed, Not-So-Smart City Plans for
People-Centred Vision," *Guardian* (March 12, 2021), https://www.theguardian.com
/world/2021/mar/12/toronto-canada-quayside-urban-centre.

29. For example, one VC firm from its 2021 survey of companies in its fund identified
this shift. Whereas pre-pandemic, "slightly less than 20 percent of the companies" were
decentralized or remote, by early 2021, over 40 percent of founders said that the best
place to start a company will be in the cloud. See: Kim-Mai Cutler, "DATA: Post-
Pandemic Silicon Valley Isn't a Place," *Initialized* (January 21, 2021), https://blog
.initialized.com/2021/01/data-post-pandemic-silicon-valley-isnt-a-place/.

30. Before the pandemic, a few cities captured most of the innovation gains. Between
1971 and 2007, ten US cities, according to one study, were home to "70% of the inventors of all U.S. patents for computers, 79% of inventors in semiconductors and 59%
of the inventors in biology and chemistry." See: Jon Hilsenrath, "Winning Streak of
Big Cities Fades with 2020 Crises," *Wall Street Journal* (July 19, 2020), https://www
.wsj.com/articles/american-cities-covid-coronavirus-reopen-lockdown-housing-new
-york-boston-los-angeles-11595182903 (discussing work of Enrico Moretti). Another
study found that five metropolitan areas—Boston; San Diego; San Francisco; Seattle;
and San Jose, California—accounted for 90 percent of all US high-tech job growth
between 2005 to 2017, whereas the 377 other metro areas in the US accounted for
only 10 percent of the 256,063 jobs created during that period. Jon Hilsenrath, "Five
Cities Account for Vast Majority of Growth in Tech Jobs, Study Finds," *Wall Street
Journal* (December 9, 2019), https://www.wsj.com/articles/five-cities-account-for
-vast-majority-of-growth-in-tech-jobs-study-finds-11575867660.

31. Note for example the rise of Islamic science in the ninth century in Baghdad and its
subsequent fall. For a short review, see: Jim Al-Khalili, "When Baghdad Was Centre
of the Scientific World," *Guardian* (September 26, 2010), https://www.theguardian
.com/books/2010/sep/26/baghdad-centre-of-scientific-world. For a detailed overview
see: Ehsan Masood, *Science and Islam: A History* (London: Icon Books, second edition, 2017).

Index

Uber, 3, 10–11, 13
unilateral effects theory, 166–167, 257n21
Union Square Ventures, 84
United Kingdom, 61–62, 130–131, 188, 193, 262n29
United Nations, 195–196
University of California San Francisco, 112–113
U.S. Capitol attack (2021), 128
user data. *See* personal data use

Valletti, Tommaso, 178, 262n23
van Hooijdonk, Richard, 112
Vestager, Margrethe, 145, 151, 202–203
Vine, 53
Virtual Competition (Ezrachi & Stucke), 2

Waze, 66–67, 89
Wenger, Albert, 84
WhatsApp
  as disruptive innovation, 38–39, 43, 227n4
  Facebook's acquisition of, 39–40
  in Facebook's ecosystem, 13–14

as toxic innovation, 110, 127
user statistics, 55
white bread industry, 165–166
whitelists, 53
Wu, Tim, 144–145

YouTube, 72, 126–127, 130

Zoom, 76–77
Zuboff, Shoshana, 79
Zucked: Waking Up to the Facebook Catastrophe (McNamee), 84
Zuckerberg, Mark. *See also* Facebook
  on disruption of innovation strategies, 43, 52, 54–55
  mentor of, 84
  on the metaverse, 114, 121
  narrative of innovation by, 15, 18
  on privacy policies, 105
  on ripple effects, 129, 246n20
  on Tech Pirates, 39, 87–88
  on toxic innovation, 120

About the Authors

ARIEL EZRACHI is the Slaughter and May Professor of Competition Law at the University of Oxford, a fellow of Pembroke College, and the director of the Oxford Centre for Competition Law and Policy.

MAURICE E. STUCKE is the Douglas A. Blaze Distinguished Professor of Law at the University of Tennessee College of Law and the cofounder of the law firm Konkurrenz, and has over twenty-five years of experience handling competition and privacy issues in private practice and as a prosecutor at the U.S. Department of Justice.

Their joint research, including their books *Competition Overdose* and *Virtual Competition*, has been central to the policy debate in international organizations and competition agencies. Their work and opinions have been featured in numerous media outlets, including the *Atlantic*, the BBC, Bloomberg, CNBC, CNNMoney, the *Economist, Financial Times, Forbes, Fortune*, Fox News, the *Guardian, Harvard Business Review*, HK Radio, *MIT Technology Review*, the *New York Times, The New Yorker, Nikkei, Politico, Science, Sunday Times, Times, Times Higher Education, USA Today*, the *Wall Street Journal*, and *Wired*.

They were hired in 2017 by the European Commission to research innovation in the digital economy and their counterintuitive findings led to further research and studies, and ultimately to this book.